PILGRIMAGE AND PURI

PILGRIMAGE AND PURI

Nityananda Patnaik

GYAN PUBLISHING HOUSE
NEW DELHI - 110 002

Pilgrimage and Puri
(Religion Philosophy)

Rs. 750
ISBN : 81-212-0865-3

Published in 2005 in India by
Gyan Publishing House
5, Ansari Road, Darya Ganj
New Delhi - 110002
Phone : 011 - 23261060, 23282060, Fax : (011) 23285914
E-mail : gyanbook@vsnl.com
Visit our Web Site At http://www.gyanbooks.com

Lasertypesetting: Tact Computer Graphics, Delhi.
Printed at : Mehra Offset Press, Delhi.

Contents

List of Photographs

Preface

The study of Pilgrimage is a matter of great socio-cultural importance. David B. Smith, Sanitary Commissioner for Bengal has mentioned in his report on Pilgrimage to Juggernauth in 1868, "There is perhaps no country in the world in which devotees have not, at one time or another wandered to and fro. Indeed the desire for pilgrimage may fairly be said to be common to humanity". The pilgrimage covers not only the temples and the famous deities installed in these temples, it also covers many other sacred sites and sacred places which are connected with natural features of the landscape such as mountain, peaks, springs, rivers, woods and caves. Sacred places, in almost every case, demand offerings and these are similar not only in terms of their functions - mainly appeasement, supplication and thanks giving - but also in the nature of the materials and objects that are used.

For Orissa particularly the matter of pilgrimage is of great significance. What W.W. Hunter has mentioned in the Chapter 1 dealing with Jagannath in the history of Orissa is reproduced below.

"For two thousand years Orissa has been the holy land of the Hindus. The ancient texts love to dwell on its sanctity. It is the land that taketh away sin. It is the realm established by the God and its Sanskrit name, Utkala-desa, literally the Glorious Country has crystallized the devotional regard of forty generations of all the regions of the earth, says an inspired sage in explaining the various places of pilgrimage to his pupils, India is the noblest, and of all the countries of India, Utkala boasts the highest renown. From end to end it is one vast region of pilgrimage.

What further he has mentioned in the History of Orissa are quoted below.

"Orissa is divided into four great regions of pilgrimage. From the moment the pilgrim passes the Baitarani river, on the high road forty miles north-east of Cuttack, he treads on holy ground. Behind him lies the secular world, with its cares for the things of this life; before him is the promised land, which he has been taught to regard as a place of preparation for heaven. On the southern side of the river rises shrine after shrine to Siva, the All Destroyer. On its very bank he beholds the house of Yama, the king of the dead; and as he crosses over, the priest whispers into his car the last text which is breathed over the dying Hindu at the moment the spirit takes its flight. In the dread gloom of Yama's halls is the tepid Baitarani River. On leaving the stream he enters Jajpur, literally the City of sacrifice, the headquarters of the region of pilgrimage, sacred to Parvati, the wife of the All-Destroyer. To the south-east is the region of pilgrimage sacred to the sun, now scarcely visited, with its matchless ruins looking down in desolate beauty across the Bay of Bengal. To the south-west is the region of pilgrimage dedicated to Siva with its city of temples, which once clustered, according to native tradition, to the number of seven thousand, around the sacred lake. Beyond this, nearly due south, is the region of pilgrimage beloved of Vishnu, known to every hamlet throughout India, and to every civilised nation on earth, as the abode of Jagannath, the Lord of the World.

This national reverence for holy places has been for ages concentrated in the city of Puri, abode of Vishnu under its title of Jagannath, the Lord of the World. Every year thousands of pilgrims come on pilgrimage to Puri from every part of the country and some come from abroad to fulfill their great yearning after Jagannath.

Sutton's "Orissa and its Evangelization" gives a description of Catholicity of Orissa. The general allusions to Orissa are quoted below.

"It is to India what Jerusalem was to the whole land of Israel. It is the holy land of the Hindoos. As the Israelites went up to worship at Mount Zion, so do the inhabitants of the various provinces of India go on pilgrimage to the great temple of Juggernauth."

William F.B. Laurie has also mentioned about Puri as the most sacred place. What he has said is quoted below.

"Laurie alludes to Jaggernauth as "a venerable fan of Hindoo reverence". He states that pilgrimage thither "is one of the most important acts of observance enjoined to a Hindoo in the ritual of his religion".

By giving the characteristics of Puri as believed in by pilgrims Sutton has described the Puri town in the following words.

Sutton alludes to the Car Festival of Juggernauth as "the general meeting of the Hindoos of all India".

The very ground around Pooree for ten miles, is to the Hindoo mind, of such sanctity as to absolve from the deepest sin all who proceed thither. The priests of Juggernauth speak of it as "the city of heaven upon earth". They say that "the fruit of the trees there is as the fruit of the tree of life; that the tanks contain the waters of immortality that to bathe in them is far more meritorious than to bathe in all the sacred rivers of India that "the people are all holy".

These allusions have proved that Puri has been a famous pilgrim centre and it is necessary to give a detailed account of the town and its sacred characteristics. This is the objective which has compelled one to take up a detailed study of Puri as one of the famous pilgrim centres. The text is the outcome of this compulsion.

Nityananda Patnaik

Acknowledgements

I want to express my deep sense of gratitude to the ICSSR for sanction of a research grant to undertake the study on Pilgrimage and Puri Pilgrim Centre. It is one of the interlocking aspects of the major study on the Sacred Complex in Orissa and it is this organization which provided funds earlier to undertake studies on four other aspects of this complex. I owe the Director and other officers of this organization for their cooperation and assistance in taking up these interrelated aspects of the complex.

I am under obligation to Pandit Shri R.K. Brahma, a Sanskrit scholar and teacher under whose guidance the field investigation was conducted by the Research Assistants such as B.B. Brahma and Dilip Kumar Mahapatra for collection of data from various sources such as the pilgrims who came on pilgrimage to Puri during various festivals which were observed at Puri including the famous car festival (Rath Jatra) of the Lord Jagannath. I cannot forget the hospitality that was extended to me by Mrs. Brahma during my visit to Puri. Pandit Brahma took lot of pain and spent hours in his interviews with the Pandas, Jatri Pandas, and their Gumasthas, concerned officials, the general public including various Silpis (artists such as Chitrakara, Stone carver, Carpenter, Kumbhakar etc.) and Mahantas of different Maths.

My grateful thanks are due to the Administrative Officer and other staff of the SSADRI such as Shri Pradeep Satapathy, Computer Programmer who computerised the report, Shri S. Patra for typing out the drafts of the report and Ms. Nilanjana Patnaik who took pains in editing and proof reading of the report.

I have also the pleasure of expressing my special thanks to Dr. S.S. Rath for extracting the relevant portions from various literatures and books available in different libraries. I am indebted to him for his help in compiling relevant data from various sources and libraries.

I am also thankful to the Mama Studio, Puri for supplying the photographs which are incorporated in the report.

Lastly I also wish to record my indebtedness to one and all with whom I discussed matters concerning my research on pilgrimage and pilgrim centres with them. Their cooperation and encouragement will be remembered for all time to come.

Nityananda Patnaik

1
Pilgrim Centres, Sacred Sites and Sacred Places

Structure and function of holy places

The study of pilgrimage is an integral part of the sacred sites and sacred places which in turn represent the cultural heritage of people. Different peoples have different cultures and it is important to know what kinds of sites and places are important to them and why ? Various cultural studies show that there are broad similarities between peoples from various parts of the world both in the nature of their sacred sites and in their heritage concerns. The people of different parts of the globe show that they share similar relationships with the land as a whole, and with certain parts of the land in particular, such as mountain peaks, springs, rivers, woods, caves etc. which form the natural features of the landscape. It may be mentioned that despite the similarities within a single group and certainly between groups, there are often considerable differences of attitude and opinion regarding the importance and appropriate treatment of specific sites.

The nature of pilgrim places vis-a-vis sacred places

To say that a specific place is a sacred place or a pilgrim place is not to simply describe a piece of land, or just locate it in a certain position in the landscape. What is known as a sacred place or a pilgrim centre carries with it a whole range of people's belief system and behaviour in relation to it, and also implies a set of beliefs to do with the non-imperial world often in relation to the supernatural beings and heavenly elements. The places of pilgrim importance and sacred places demand offerings, and these are similar not only in terms of their functions - mainly appeasement, supplication and thanks giving but also in the nature of the materials and objects that are used.

The sacred places and sites are widely spread all over the world, and by nature are different from one another. Not all sacred places are of pilgrim importance. There may be a few which are sacred for certain characteristic importance being the seat of some important gods and goddesses.

Sumon school atlas has a map of Tourism in India. The places which are important from tourism point of view have been shown in the map of India. These places are included in the list of the places which are important from the point of the tourism. The classified list with names of places are given in the Annexure 1.

Some important Pilgrim Centres

For Hindus a place of pilgrimage is a *Tirtha* or *Tirthasthana*. A pilgrimage is also a *Tirtha* or *Tirthayatra* and a pilgrim is a *Tirthayatri*. Hindu tradition states that a *Tirtha* is a place where one can gain *nirvana*, true enlightenment and also achieve *moksha*, a liberation from the endless cycle of life and death. From the time of the Vedas there has been a tradition of the veneration of rivers and many *tirthas* came up beside them. However, for Hindus the landscape itself-hills, rivers, trees, rocks, pools, and the sea are all holy. Rivers like the Ganga and the Godavari, are all sacred, so are hills like Kailash and Arunachal. Likewise the islands of Rameswaram and Kanyakumari on the sea are all *tirthas*.

The veneration of nature has led to the construction of temples in especially picturesque places. One can discover the ruins of long forgotten temples in the most remote places of the country. The presence of flowing water and the confluence of streams makes the spots even more auspicious. The temples like Kedarnath and Badrinath have come up on high hills in the lap of sacred Himalayas. When an aspect of nature is combined with other spiritual elements a great *tirtha* is created. For instance, Varanasi is considered a famous *tirthasthan*. It offers, the pilgrims the combination of a great river, a powerful god and a venerable temple. Similarly Puri has been considered supreme among the *tirthas* because it has the Jagannath temple, the temple of Purusottam, supreme lord of Vishnu located on the seashore amidst many minor *tirthasthans* like *Markanda*, *Swetaganga*, *Mahodadhi*, *Chakratirtha*, and many monasteries of different sects. Added to these sacred places is the famous car festival which is witnessed by millions of pilgrims coming from different parts of the country. The Jagannath temple which was first built in a small form on a hillock called *Nilakandar*, was sanctified by *Brahma* who came down on earth at Purusottam (Puri) on invitation of the then mythic king Indradyumna.

The tirthas of the seven *Saptapuris* and *Char Dhams* are called *Mokshadayika*. Going to these *tirthas*, worshipping in their temples, bathing in their rivers or tanks makes us free from the burden of sins and also liberates us from the endless cycle of births and deaths. A *tirthajatra* makes it possible for our souls to merge with the supreme oneness of brahman. As the *tirtha* is connected with heaven it is also a place where the devout comes to die. For instance, many Hindus have a passionate desire to die either in Puri or in Varanasi because these *tirthas* are also resonant with the power of purity and goodness that makes the passing away easier. He does not have to pass through the painful taste and punishments in the hands of *Jama's* companions and the soul merges straight with the gods of the heaven. That is why a place has been allotted on the seashore at Puri called *Swargadwara*" where the dead bodies are cremated.

References regarding *tirthas* are available in many books and *Puranas* and *Dharmasastras*. Among all the lists of *tirthas* available in the *Puranas* there are ten *tirthas* which are considered most sacred and the pilgrims recite the hymns relating to these tirthas during their journey of pilgrimage. The simple verse containing seven greatest *tirthas* which is called

Saptapuris is quoted below.

> *"Kashi, Kanchi, Maya Ayodhya Avantika,*
> *Mathura, Dwaravati, Chaiva, Saptaita Mokshadayika"*

Next to *Saptapuris* are the four *tirthas* or *Chaar Dhamas.* These tirthas are called *Dhama* as they are believed to be the abode of *Vishnu* and His *Avatars.* The *Chaar Dhams* are Badrinath, Puri, Dwaraka and Rameswaram. Visiting all these 11 places of pilgrimage is not an easy task. They are spread wide throughout the whole of the Indian subcontinent. Because of this arduous nature of the journey the *tirthayatra* is called the *Mahaparikrama* - the great circuit of the land. The pilgrims long to visit these *Saptapuris* and *Tirthas* even once in life time so that they gain the *Darshan* of their beloved deities for their *Mokshya* in the life and become free from the cycle of birth and death.

The Puranas classify four kinds of *tirthas.* The first category comes under *Daiva tirthas*, the second category comprises places which have been touched by the Holy Trinity of Brahma, Vishnu, Maheswar and the *Devi* (goddess). The third category of *tirthas* is called *Asura Tirthas* meaning that these are the places where the gods defeated demons. Gaya is one of such category where Lord Shiva defeated a demon called Gaya. The *Arsa tirthas* have been created through the great penance and austerities of sages. Finally there are *Manusa tirthas* which have been sanctified by the presence of great solar and lunar dynasties.

What are the important reasons for a *tirthayatra ?* Some of the reasons are mentioned below.

1. The most important reason for a *tirthayatra* is the *darshan* of a deity. The *darshan* in the deepest meaning of the term is being in the presence of a god or even a great being and absorbing some of the aura of sanctity and goodness through this encounter.

2. The religious rituals connected with offering food stuff or any other object remains unaltered for centuries. Taking

bath or washing feet, buying flowers, garlands, incense burning, lighting lamps, offerings offered by the priest with recitation of *slokes,* etc are the same in all cases of *Darshan* of the deity by the pilgrims.

3. Pilgrims pay their visit to the deity during certain rituals like *Homa*, *Yagnya*, etc or some festivals like Car festival or *Dola* festival, etc. It is very common that the pilgrims wait for the occasion when *Mongal Arati* and *Sandhya Arati* (morning time arati or waving of lamps in the evening). These two *Arati* events in the temple are most auspicious which every pilgrim wants to witness.

4. Pilgrims also have some personal reasons for their pilgrimage and therefore they go on a pilgrimage to pray the deities to fulfill their desires and seek through prayers, supplications their blessings which help the pilgrims to fulfill their wishes.

5. People no matter what status they enjoy in the society, whether, rich or poor, king or a common man go on a pilgrimage for the atonement of their sins. *Rama* went to perform a *yajnya* sacrifice at Haridwara as a penance for killing *Ravana* who was a brahmin.

6. Every landmark or any event in a person's life is celebrated at a *tirtha*. Parents bring their newborn child to seek the blessings of the deity and perform hair cutting ceremony or *naamakaran* ceremony.

It was a common phenomenon that when there was no road communication to Puri the pilgrims used to walk miles covering months together through hills forests, rivers and much arduous terrain to reach Puri in time to witness the Car festival of the Lord Jagannath.

Some fairs are considered sacred and during this time pilgrims flock together in such places to take part in such auspicious occasions. Once in every 12 years, the four *tirthas* of Prayag (Allahabad), Haridwar, Ujjain and Nasik come alive during Kumbhamela. Thousands and thousands of saffron clad, ash smeared *Sadhus* and villagers, city people carrying with them their belongings gather together recalling the ancient myth of a pot of ambrosia being carried by Vishnu. The poor people arriving with nothing are provided with clothes, food and shelter in an unprecedented charity which is noticed no where in the world.

One can see even in the most inaccessible places in the hills and mountains *Sadhus* of matted hair, with ash smeared bodies living in remote caves perched precariously by the edge of the cliffs spend all-time in meditation and in search of Almighty. No one knows how they survive or what they are seeking. These enigmas of the spiritual world remain mystery in their psychic pilgrimage within their minds. Shankaracharya's pilgrimage who established *Mathas* at the *Char Dhamas* (four *tirthas*) is well known to all the Hindus. Even today these Shankaracharya *peethas* (seats) continue to be centres of Sanskrit scholarship and Hindu philosophy. Shankaracharya's debating skills are legendary. At the Jagannath temple Guru Nanak composed an exquisite hymn in which he offered the world to God. His *Arati Thali* was the sky itself and on it he placed the sun and stars as lamps.

Objective of Pilgrimage

Adding more to the objectives of Pilgrimage it may be found that under what circumstances do people undertake arduous and deleterious journey to far off places on pilgrimage and what feelings and inducements compel a person to go on a pilgrimage. In this context Shakespear's words are recalled to my mind "A true-hearted pilgrim does not fear to measure kingdoms with his feeble steps". The journey of pilgrimage begins with many hopes and aspirations. This is not a peculiar phenomenon for India. There is perhaps no country in the world where it is conspicuous by its absence. It is a global phenomenon and common to humanity. Writers like Cicero, Gibbon, Chatteabriand and Tasso have left written records giving vivid discussions about this phenomena.

The excited feelings and the spirit of mysterious delight which are observed among the Indian pilgrims are almost the same as those of the devotees of the Greek, Roman, American religious order. The sojourn of the devoted pilgrims coming from every corner of our country on pilgrimage to holy places is an universal phenomenon. The same belief in the virtue of pilgrimage and the same passionate desire to have a *darshan* of the deities in view and to offer prayer for a trouble free journey to the other world without any prolonged sufferings pervade every where in the mind of the pilgrims of any part of the world.

The readiness with which to undertake a journey on pilgrimage which is full of danger, difficulties and hardships even meeting death on the way an event that is cherished and not feared, warms up the heart of a pilgrim. The holy shrines, temples, tanks, rivers and many such other sacred spots beckon a true hearted pilgrim to achieve liberation from worldly ties and salvation in life.

From the History of Orissa by W.W. Hunter the following paragraphs are extracted to throw more light on the pilgrimage.

"The yearning after holy places seems indeed, to form part of the universal religion of mankind. To gaze upon the scenes amid which the deity has dwelt, to bathe in the rivers that once lived his mystical incarnate frame, to halt sometime midday under hoary trees beneath which the divine presence has reposed, to pray upon the mountain hallowed by his lonely communings, and to behold in the ever lasting rock the footprints of the god, are longings which have, at one period or another, filled the imagination, and stirred the innermost heart of all noble races".

"From that ancient night on which the ladder was let down from heaven, and the angles ascended and descended before the sleeper on the pillow of stones at Bethel, till the time when the true cross began to give off its enexhaustible splinters to the Christian world, and thence down to the present hour, a strip of sand and rock has been regarded with passionate tenderness by the august dynasty of religions to which our own belongs".

"In the wildest period of mediaeval history savage nations forgot their feuds and rushed hand in hand to the rescue of those distant shrines. In their defense army after army reddened the Syrian sands with their blood. Even in this unemotional age, a ceaseless stream of pilgrims from Asia, from Europe, from America, from the infidel parts of the Turk, and from the torrid mountains of Abyssinia, still pours into the Terra Sancta at the great festival of the Christian year. Its most solemn shrine is parcelled out in jealously guarded inches to the long separated sections of the primitive church. The coldest of the Teutonic creeds cannot contemplate those scenes untouched, while the Southern forms of Christianity abandon themselves to paroxysms of emotion".

This is a beautiful narration of the world wide practice of pilgrimage in the report on Pilgrimage to Juggernauth in 1868 by, David B. Smith, M.D. Sanitary Commissioner for Bengal. These narrations show that the pilgrimage is a worldwide phenomena and the Hindus in India go out on pilgrimage to pilgrim centres in spite of hardship which they undergo in their journey mostly on foot and there to stay at Puri and other pilgrim centres under the most unhygienic conditions.

2
Overview Of Literature And Conceptual Framework

Overview of Literature

There are large number of anthropological and historical literatures on the Sacred Complex. Robert Redfield's concepts of Great and Little traditions and Milton Singer's study of the city of Madras followed by Mc Kim Marriott's and Cohn's concepts of 'Networks' and 'Centres', inspired Indian Anthropologists to take up studies of Pilgrim centres and sacred complexes in India. Gaya was perhaps the first to be studied by L.P. Vidyarthi (1953-54) and Bhubaneswar was the next to be taken up for the study of Organization of Lingaraj Temple by N. Patnaik.

L.P. Vidyarthi's interest in the study of Gaya and later of Kashi was confined to such concepts as sacred centres, life style of sacred specialists, pilgrimage and processes of transformation in the Sacred Complex. He has shown the trichotomic inter relation of the phenomena described as sacred geography, sacred performances, and sacred specialists. Thus he discussed in the broader perspective covering Hindu Gaya as related to other centres and regions of India.

There after many studies of sacred centres were taken up by the Department of Anthropology, Ranchi University and Anthropological survey of India and by many independent scholars. To mention only a few of such studies are the study of pilgrimage in Nimsar, Temple organization in Goa, studies of Kamakhya, Kalighat, and Chamundeswar temple, and Ascetics of Kashi, Study of Janakpur, Deoghar, Rajgir, Ayodhya, Pasupatinath, Ratnapur, and many other sacred centres. In most cases the Gaya model was followed and in general all these studies were primarily connected with the description and analysis of certain specific religious institutions and certain specific topics. But none of these studies has attempted a holistic view of the sacred complex on a broader perspective in terms of multithematic and inter regional interrelationship as Puri study envisages to achieve.

Besides these works there are many other publications on the same theme of sacred complex which are mentioned below. Symposium on sacred complexes in India (1974) Rising India : An urban Anthropological approach to Puri (1978). The Beggars of a pilgrim city, Puri (1979), Kashi (Myth and Reality of classical cultural tradition (1975), Dimensions of Pilgrimage (1985), Puri Pilgrim study, India Statistical Institute (1976), The Sacred Complex of Badrinath (1990). The title of these works show that attention has been given to specific subject matters and not to a holistic view of the complex.

The Puri Sacred Complex which was first taken up by me in 1962 has certain similarities with the works which are referred to above. But in many respects it is different from these studies both structurally and organisationally. It is not exactly a follow-up work of the research initiated by other scholars who are concerned with the study of sacred complex. In fact, the only published work which suggests a study to be undertaken to get an inter regional and holistic view of a sacred complex is the Cultural Tradition in Puri (1977) by N. Patnaik.

Reference Literature :

Bali, Arun P. — Pilgrimage in Veerashaivism.

Bharadwaj, S.M. 1973 — Hindu places of pilgrimage in India: A Study in Cultural Geography. London, University of California Press.

Bharati, A.N. 1963 "Pilgrimage in the Indian Tradition", History of Religion, 3 (1), pp. 135-67.

1970 "Pilgrimage Sites and Indian Civilisation", in : Elder, J.W. (ed.). Indian Civilisation. 1, pp. 85-126.

Bhowmick, P.K. 1960 "Four Temples in Midnapur", Man in India, 40 (2), pp. 81-108.

Chakrabarti, P. 1976 "A Study of some characteristics and behaviour patterns of the Dharma Yatris of Tarakeswar temple in West Bengal", Folklore, 17 (5), pp. 157-67.

Chowdhury, B. 1976 "The Bakreswar Temple : A Study of Sacred Complex. (unpub. PRS thesis, Dept. of Anthropology, Calcutta University), Calcutta.

Cohn, B.S. and Marritott, M. 1958 "Networks and centers in the integration of Indian civilization", Journal of Social Research, 1(1), p. 1-9.

Diehl 1956 Instrument and Purpose : Studies on rites and rituals in South India. Lund : C.W.K. Gleerup.

Jha, M. 1974 "Pilgrimage and their centres of Pilgrimage in Chatishgarh", in : Vidyarthi, L.P. and Jha, M. (eds.) Symposium on sacred complex in India. Ranchi, University of Ranchi.

Kolenda, Pauline M. 1968 "Region, caste and family structure : A comparative study of the Indian 'joint family' in : Singer, M. & Cohn, B.S. (eds.). Structure and change in

		Indian Society. Chicago, Aldine Publishing Co.
Mukherjee, Ramkrishna	1971	"Family in India : A perspective", Perspective (Indian Journal of Public Administration), 17 (4), pp. 41-106.
	1977	West Bengal Family Structures : 1946-1966. New Delhi.
Patnaik, N.	1977	Cultural Tradition in Puri : Indian Institute of Advanced Study, Simla.
J. McKim Malville & Baidyanath Saraswati	2004	Complexity and Cosmos
Sinha, S.	1972	"Kali Temple at Kalighat and the City of Calcutta", in : Sinha, S. (ed.). Cultural Profile of Calcutta. Calcutta, The Indian Anthropological Society.
Sopher, D.E.	1968	"Pilgrim circulation in Gujarat", Geographical Review, 58 (3), pp. 392-425.

The Conceptual Framework :

1. Puri has been a famous pilgrim centre since time beyond memory. Apart from the myth which tells Brahma coming to Puri on invitation by Indradyumna to consecrate Nilamadhava and instal Him in Nilakandar on the seashore the Mahabharata which, in its Tirthajatra section of the Vanaparva, mentions Svayambhu Lokesvara, a famous Shiva temple located in Puri, frequented by pilgrims testifies to the antiquity of Puri as a place on the pilgrims route. It shows that pilgrimage to Puri was in existence even when no Vaisnava deity was in existence there in the early period of 600 years upto the beginning of the 10th Century.

2. The inscriptions and certain archaeological evidences show that prior to 1135 A.D. Puri was a flourishing Saiva Kshetra. Is it due to this fact that Adi Sankaracharya established a math (Gobardhan math) at Puri in 9th A.D or was there a plan by the followers of Sankaracharya of Puri to exercise supervision and control over any great Vishnu temple that would come up later ?

3. The picture of pilgrimage from the earliest time to the present time becomes clear if a road communication or a route network is drawn up showing places of pilgrimage, sect affiliation and types of pilgrims visiting these places. A map of this type may throw light on inter regional integrational network.

4. The Puri temple records give earliest accounts of pilgrimage to Puri. It would be interesting to find out how was the process of pilgrimage started. Whatever materials are available from the study of Sasan villages they indicate that the *Sasan/Karabada* brahmins who came from outside Orissa encouraged pilgrims to visit Puri. That the brahmins of *Karabadas* served as *Tirthagurus* was an unusual phenomenon.

5. Territorial division of the country among the Pandas or *Tirthagurus* is a special feature of "pilgrim hunting". It is a kind of caste guild system exercising rigid monopoly over the territory with no question of trespassing. Is there no change in this system ? If so what factors are responsible for change (Irregularity in visit, profession not paying, pilgrims choice for a change, economic diversification, care taken deteriorated, Panda-Pilgrim relation weakened, etc.).

6. With the development of road communication and transport facilities the categories of pilgrim Pandas like *Batua* (going out to escort pilgrims), *Ghatua* (waiting at different entry points to contact pilgrims) may not be existing any longer. What changes have taken place in this system and with what effect ?

7. The narrations of previous writers give a vivid picture of hardship and strain the pilgrims endured in their journey. There were pilgrims who came walking thousands of miles covering in four to five months and stayed at Puri only for two to three days.

   Are Shakespeare's words valid now ?

   "A true hearted pilgrim does not fear to measure kingdoms with his feeble steps."

   Some Sadhus used to come on pilgrimage to Puri by measuring their length prostrate along the road all the way from their place of abode for scores of miles. It would be interesting to explore if such feats are resorted to by any pilgrims and motivating factors and mental condition of such cases.

8. While at Puri the pilgrim Pandas or the guides make all arrangements for the pilgrims regarding their stay, their food, their visit to different sacred places and minor pilgrim centres, etc. All expenses incurred under lodging, boarding and travelling are reimbursed by the pilgrims. Since it is a source of income the Pandas make exorbitant charges and squeeze out to the point of snatching the last pie from them. All types of techniques are applied to extract as much money as possible. It would be interesting to find out to what extent are the pilgrims subjected to these heartless harassments now a days. If any change is noticed in this behaviour what is it due to and is it towards better or worse or as usual ?

9. During the British period a pilgrim tax was levied under the Regulation IV of 1806 A.D. Regulation V of 1806 A.D. was passed for preventing persons from evading payment of the tax. The entry points were Attaranallah Ghat on the north and Lokanath Ghat on the south-east of Puri town. It is to be found out which are the present avenues through which the pilgrims enter the Puri town and which avenues are most frequently used and which

least as compared with the past and what possible reasons there may be for such changes.

10. In the earlier dispensation the pilgrims were classified into four categories : (1) Laul Jatris, 2) Nim Lauls, 3) Bhurrungs, and 4) Punj Tirthees (low castes not permitted to enter the temple). This classification is meant for fixing the amount of tax to be paid by the pilgrims, number of days allowed to stay at Puri, restriction or otherwise regarding entry into the temple and some other purposes. The Regulation IV, 1809 was passed for rescinding the Regulations IV and V 1806 as per the orders of the Governor General in Council. It would be interesting to find out under what circumstances it was necessary not to levy tax from the pilgrims and with what effect as a result to the management of the temple affairs ?

11. The pilgrims poured into Puri in thousands particularly during car festival. They used to stay in lodging houses and Dharmasalas under most unhyginic and insanitary conditions. The manner in which they were crammed and crowded in these places that it was simply a story of disease and death at Puri at that time. Various observers of national and international origin have left on record pathetic scene full of incalculable misery, suffering and loss of life in the holy city. Has there been any improvement in lodging in the present time under the present administrative set up ? What do the pilgrims feel about it ?

12. It is the belief in the general public that Puri is a heaven upon earth. But what one observes in reality is all of dirty earthly characters and nothing of heavenly characters. N. Patnaik has given a detailed account of the characters that pervaded throughout the length and breadth of Puri town. The dirty roads and lanes, the filthy open drains, congested houses, heaps of garbage emitting noxious gases, mosquitoes carrying fileria germs, poor conservancy, sacred tanks containing polluted water, the

line of lepers sitting by the side of the streets with their begging bowls make the *Puridhama* unholy and risky to live in.

13. In the midst of such an atmosphere of unhealthy character there pervades a spirit of religious fervour. Here most of the time the devotional songs and the sounds from conches, bugles, cymbals and gongs played in the temples and the monasteries at the time of worship do not suggest any diminution of its importance on the sacred map of India. It is interesting to find out from which sources do the devotees get inspiration and religious fervour. According to the votaries of Vaishnvism and the Apostles of other Hindu religious sects. Puri must continue ever to be a paramount centre of Sanskritic traditions and sacred culture.

14. The organizational network of the Sacred Complex which shows a linkage of the Sacred institutions like temples, monasteries and places, tanks, and kings as guardians of sacred traditions, peasants, Brahmin Sasan Villages, etc. is sustained and stabilized by the pilgrims who function as integrators of the Indian civilization. Pilgrimage is one of the main unifying forces in Hinduism and strengthens the religious fervour. With the weakening of the pilgrimage the constituent elements of the sacred complex is weakened and the inter-regional interlinkage is disintegrated.

Conceptually pilgrimage is something which is to be accomplished even once in the life time of a Hindu on this world. This is an inner yearning which compels one to visit certain holy places for salvation. It is a story of hardship, endurance and fulfilment of certain compulsions like performance of *Shradha* ceremonies at sacred places like Buddhagaya, Tribeni and such other holy places. Certain special occasions like *Gobinda dwadashi* and *Nabakalebara* witness large influx of pilgrims to Puri from near and far off places. The longing after pilgrimage which forms a very important feature in the national character of the Hindu and the journey covering thousands of miles along burning roads, across unbridged rivers and through pestilent forest regions and the joy that over takes the great spiritual yearning at the sight of the blue wheel fixed at the top of the temple of Lòrd Jagannath and the first darshan of the Lord of the Universe without rest (Dhula pae darshan-paying homage on immediate entry into Puri without washing bleeding feet covered with red earth of the road) speak of what pilgrimage means to a pilgrim.

Research Questions and Hypothesis :

Research questions as mentioned in conceptual framework are as follows :

1. To find out how was the process of pilgrimage started ?
2. It is a kind of caste guild system exercising rigid monopoly over the territory with no question of tresspassing. Is there no change in this system ? If so what factors are responsible for change.
3. What changes have taken place in this system and with what effect ?
4. To explore if such feats are resorted to by any pilgrims and motivating factors and mental condition of such cases.
5. To find out to what extent the pilgrims are subjected to harassments by the *Pandas* now a days ? If any change is noticed in this behaviour what is it due to and is it towards better or worse or as usual ?
6. To find out the present avenues through which the pilgrims enter the Puri town and which avenues are most frequently used and which least as compared with the past and what possible reasons there may be for such changes.

7. To find out under what circumstances was it necessary not to collect duties from the pilgrims and with what consequences to the management of the temple affairs ?

8. Has there been any improvement in lodging in the present time under the present administrative set up ? What do the pilgrims feel about it ?

9. Pilgrimage is one of the main unifying forces and great integrators. What evidences and actions prove this role of pilgrimage in the context of the present time as compared with the past ?

Research Methodology

Data Collection :

1. Data collection was done from various sources such as past records preserved in the Puri temple office.

2. Documents maintained by the temple scribe.

3. Panda books.

4. Puri Railway Station for information regarding out flow of pilgrim from Puri town after pilgrimage.

5. Interviewing cultural specialists like Pandits, Silpis, and ritual functionaries, Sadhus and Mahantas of Monasteries, Priests, Pauranic recitors.

6. Records maintained at different lodging houses, Dharmasalas and Panda residential quarters.

7. Government departments, Voluntary agencies.

8. Presentation of sacred spots and route chart by the help of cartographic maps. Also a map showing origin of pilgrims by States with lines of different thickness.

3
Puri Pilgrim Centre

Puri and its environs : its origin and Lord Jagannath

Puri is known variously as Jagannath Puri, Puri Jagannath, Purushothama, Juganat and currently as *Shri Kshetra*, and *Sankha Kshetra*. Some scholars assert that it is identical with *Dantapura*, the resting place for centuries of the sacred tooth of Buddha. The most ancient name of the place was *Nilachala*, or Blue Hill. An Indian authority says that for centuries past the city has been looked upon as the holiest on the face of the earth and the most appropriate name has been prominently and par excellence, Puri. There is a legend which says that those who were earnest about salvation could easily obtain it by dwelling in the secret of the divinity on the sea-shore. In praise there of the Lord said, "On the northern shore of the sea, to the south of the Mahanadi river there is my favourite abode, Alone it can confer all the blessings which are derivable from all the other sacred places on the earth put together.

Brahma appears to have profited by this advice for we find him next standing by the fountain near Nilachala and while there he beheld a crow taking a sip of its crystal treasure and then plunging into it. Instantly its form changed into the counterpart of Vishnu with four arms carrying the four fold emblems of the conch shell, the discus, the mace, and the lotus. Being impressed with the divine merits of the place resolved to extend its glory. Having already referred to the Blue Hill, the

Kalpa tree, and the magical fountain it remains to be added that Puri was at one time a forest and in addition to the landmarks above mentioned had on its side an immitable image of Vishnu in Sapphire and that this stone gave its name to the image whence it was called *Nilamani*, or *Nilamadhaba*. This is in short the background of the origin of Puri.

The legend of the Blue God

Abstracts of it occur in Ain-i-Akbary, Stirling's Cuttack, Hunter's Orissa and other books. The author of the Antiquities of Orissa tells us that a pilgrim of great sanctity having seen Puri in the golden age reported its existence to Indradyumna, a prince of solar Dynasty then reigning at Avanti in the country of Ojein in Malwa. Indradyumna was interested in the pilgrim's story and expressed his desire to proceed to the spot to attain the highest blessings of human existence by beholding the image.

To fulfil his desire *Indradyumna* caused the brother of his high priest, *Vidyapati*, to ascertain the truth of the pilgrim's story. *Vidyapati* accomplished the journey in 3 months and beheld at the foot of the great *Kalpa* tree a number of *Brahmans* each having four hands and bearing the emblems of Vishnu. The chief of this congregation was *Vishwavasu*, a fowler. He alone knew the sacred bower of the Blue God and daily worshipped the image with such simple offerings as he could command. *Vidyapati* asked the fowler to show him the image and after a great deal of hesitation caused no doubt by a tradition to the effect that when *Indradyumna* came, the image would disappear. *Vishwavasu* agreed and took *Vidyapati* to the secret bower of the divinity and loaded him with rich presents including a flower garland from the neck of the image. In due course the messenger returned to his master and reported what he had seen. The king was overwhelmed with emotion and shed tears of joy and resolved to repair to the secret spot, establish his metropolis there and devote the rest of his days to the adoration of the image.

At this stage the renowned sage *Narada*, the mind born son of *Brahma* paid the king a visit and in the course of conversation strengthened his resolve by an elaborate discourse in praise of the Blue God. Immediate preparations were therefore made for the journey. Finally Indradyumna with Narada and his minister proceeded to the Blue Hill at Puri to gratify his long cherished desire of beholding the Divinity-Unfortunately he could not see the Divinity as he had already left that place and gone to *Patala* (underground).

The king saw a dream and was told to sacrifice 1000 horses and eventually when the last offering was poured on the sacred fire news came that a log of wood with insignia of Vishnu has come floating and reached the shore at Puri. As instructed by *Narada* the log was brought to land and 4 images were carved out of the logs. Due to interruption in the middle of the work of the celestial carpenter the images could not be carved in full. That is why the images are unfinished and look like what they are now. The images were eventually consecrated by *Brahma* whom *Indradyumna* brought down from Heaven specially for this purpose. Thus came the Lord of the world to dwell in the holy city of Puri. The details about the holy and sacred characteristics, catholicity of Orissa and Puri and Hunter's description about the Puri Pilgrim and Vishnuism and construction of Jagannath Temple are given in Annexures - II, III, IV, V.

This Lord of the World has undergone many harassments and torture in the hands of Non Hindu rulers several times. It is known from the Oriya temple records that in the year 323 A.D. an army of *Yavanas* came to Puri by way of the sea under the leadership of *Raktabahu* or Red Arm to loot the property and destroy the images. The then ruler of Orissa Prince Subhana Deva unable to cope with the enemy fled from Puri and taking the four sacred images with him buried them under the earth planting a banyan tree over them. From this time until the third quarter of the 5th century the country remained under the Yavanas and the images lay buried under the earth.

In A.D. 474 Yayati Kesari came to Orissa. The important event of his time was the recovery of the images and restoration of the worship of Jagannath. The image was much decayed and disfigured. The Raja repaired the images with requisite materials and clothed them and brought them to Puri. A new temple was built at the site of the old one and the images were enshrined with great pomp. It is during the reign of Anantavarman Codagangadeva that Vishnuism flourished in Orissa and the great temple of Jagannath was built by him. The details is given in Annexure-V which are extracted from " The cult of Jagannath and the regional tradition of Orissa", p-22.

Robert Dunbar has mentioned in his book on the Temple of Jagannath Puri at page 4 of the book that "the close of the 16th century saw Orissa in the entire possession of the followers of the Prophets and then followed a persecution which has left its mark on the Province to this day. The magic kettle drum of Kalapahar the Afghan conqueror, at the sound of which the ears and feet of the idol would drop off for many miles all round, resounded in the sacred *mandaps* of Jagannath and penetrated his holy of holies. It was at this time that the high priest of Jagannath with other assistants, stole away in a covered cart with three carefully wrapped up images to conceal their hideous treasures in the hills adjacent to the Chilika lake, until a favourable opportunity came for again setting them upon their throne in the temple".

Kalapahar having come to know the hiding place of Jagannath dug him up and carried him off on an elephant to the Ganges. He then collected a large pile of wood and setting fire to it threw the idol on the burning heap, but immediately all his limbs dropped off and he perished miserably. A bysatander observed, this indignity offered to the Lord Jagannath of Orissa. He snatched the image from the flames and threw it into the river. A votary of Jagannath managed to extract the sacred part from the half burnt images and handed it over to the Khandayat of Kujang. The sacred part (Brahma) was subsequently recovered by Ramchandra Dev who assumed the title of Maharaja and in 1580 AD set up in the temple the image with great pomp and solemnity.

After the Muslims were defeated the Marathas ruled Orissa till 1803 and thereafter the British Raj came up and continued their administration until the country won independence in 1947.

A brief account of the management of the Jagannath temple during Mughol rule, followed by Maratha rule and thereafter British rule is given in some detail in the following section.

Puri During Various Rulers

The Jagannath Temple during Mughol Period

The history of the Mughol rule was the history of destruction of Hindu gods and goddesses, repeated removal of Jagannath to places of safety and plunder of Jagannath temple and property. These destructions started with Kala Pahad who reached Puri from Jajpur in the 16th Century A.D. During the period from 1568 to 1589 Raja Mansingh set out for the conquest of Orissa and after departure of Mansingh the Afghans defied Mughal authority and desecrated the Jagannath temple. Mansingh again marched to Orissa in the years 1591-92 AD and the situations were such that he favoured Raja Ramchandra Deva stationed at his capital Khurda and nominated him as the custodian of the Jagannath temple. To make the story short Mansingh made Ramchandra Deva the Raja of the kingdom of Orissa. It was during this time one Gouri Mahadei, a consort of Raja Mansingh, built the hall of the *Mukti Mandap* within the Jagannath temple precincts. The Jagannath temple became the most famous Hindu temple in the Mughal empire. It was unbelievable that those who plundered the temple and carried off the idols to throw them in the river Ganges or burnt them into ashes changed their mind and looked upon them with the greatest reverence and respect.

But this attitude of respect did not last long. During the reign of Jahangir the Jagannath temple was the target of attack by the Mughal Subadars of Orissa. Orissa was made a *Suba* in 1607 when one Hashim Khan was appointed as a *Subadar* of Orissa. Many a time the deities were carried away to places of safety in order to avoid destruction of the temple by the Mughal chiefs. During the time of Murshid Quli II who became the Deputy Subadar of Orissa in 1734 the deities were brought back to the temple by the priests as permitted by Murshid Quli II because the absence of Jagannath from the temple at Puri caused annually a huge loss of Rs. Nine lakhs which the pilgrims were paying as pilgrim tax. The ordeal of Jagannath was at last over when the Marathas took over Orissa by defeating the Mughal rulers. It was Bira Kishore Deva who was then the Gajapati Raja of Orissa stationed at the Khurda capital. During his rule Raghuji Bhonsle marched towards Cuttack and sent his agent named Bahadur Khan with a letter addressed to the priests of Jagannath not to get *panicky* due to the Maratha raid and continue their services in the Jagannath temple as usual. The Muslim rule in Orissa ended in 1759. With the appointment of Sheo Bhat Sathe as the Subardar in 1760, Orissa came directly under the control of the Marathas.

The Jagannath Temple during Maratha Period

After the Mughol rule came the Maratha administration. Being Hindus they had a great honour for the Lord Jagannath. During the Maratha rule there was no need to shift Jagannath from the temple to safer places as was done during the Mughol rule. The Maratha rulers were spending annually 20,000 *Kahanas* of cowries or about Rs. 6000 in those days for the charitable purposes in the Jagannath temple. The Maratha government took keen interest in the management of the temple and performance of the daily *nitis* or *sebapuja* of the deities. The Maratha rulers extended help and support to those who were coming on pilgrimage to Puri.

In those days the pilgrims used to come to Puri by the help of elephants, horses, palanquins, boats and most of them came by walking covering long distance from their native place. While walking they had to face many difficulties such as robbery, illness, attack by wild animals. Generally the pilgrims travelled in a group so that they protected themselves and the robbers could not attack them. In spite of these troubles the pilgrims were encouraged to visit Puri because of the care taken by the Maratha Government. Passports (*Dustak*) were issued to the pilgrims without any cumbersome procedures to enter the Puri town and have *darshan* of the deities. The State governments were intimated to issue similar passports to those who intended to come on pilgrimage to Puri

The Government gave special attention for the safety of the pilgrims coming to visit Puri and made necessary arrangements at Puri for the comfort of the visiting pilgrims. The organization of tourism was well developed and was one of the principal functions of the Maratha Government in Orissa. Prof. Pravat Mukherjee has given many instances of persons to whom passports were issued to come on pilgrimage to Puri individually or in a group or with their family members. Some of these instances are listed in the Annexure-VI.

The letters show that during the Maratha rule, the road to Puri was not safe. Rich persons like Ram Shankar and Bishannath took with them armed retainers, coolies, horses and carried food materials. The Maratha officers were requested to give them facilities during their journey to Puri.

The Maratha Government was also very liberal in issuing passports even to the muslims to visit Lord Jagannath at Puri, particularly during car festival when the deities were brought out of the temple and seated in their respective cars drawn from the temple to *Gundicha ghar* along the grand road. This is the time when the public irrespective of caste, creed, nationality got a chance for *darshan* of the deities. The devotees of Lord Jagannath who were forbidden to enter the temple on the grounds of their birth in low caste communities availed themselves of the opportunities to have *darshan* of Jagannath while in car outside the temple during car festival.

In the 18th century there were no convenient route to Puri. People coming from Banaras used to make boat journey in the river Ganges upto Calcutta from where they came walking to Puri. Generally people walked on the banks of the rivers upto certain distance and cover the rest of the distance by walking. During the period of Raja Ram Pandit who was the governor of Orissa the pilgrims coming from distant places like Bombay, Gujarat, Maharastra, were given maximum assistance in Orissa for their comfortable stay at Puri and have *darshan* peacefully. When Sankar and Visvanath came on pilgrimage to Puri nearly 60 people accompanied them. The Government made all necessary arrangements for their stay at Puri comfortably and also for their return journey after having *darshan* of the Lord Jagannath with least difficulties.

During the Maratha rule the temple of Lord Jagannath was managed under the superintendence of the Raja of Khurda and the sources of income were of the revenue collected from *Sataisa Hazari Mahal*, a vast landed property donated by Raghuji Bhonsla of Nagpur. Other sources were town duties, sales tax from businessmen, sale proceeds of *Mahaprasad* and *Kotha Khanja* or assignment of land revenue. Due to mismanagement the income from these sources was not sufficient to meet the expenses of the temple. In such a situation the Maratha Government had to provide additional funds to meet the deficiency.

During the Maratha rule the management of the temple was vested with the *Parichhas*. There were 3 *Parichhas* and among them the first and the third *Parichhas* were the Marathas and the second one was a man of the soil. He was called Jagannath Rajguru. The third one was called *Satais Hazari Mahal Parichha* because he was collecting revenue from the *Satais*

Hazari Mahal. The revenue collected was of Rs. 27000 *Kahanas* of cowries.

The *Parichhas* became corrupted and as a result the Government had to pay additional amount to meet the deficiency that occurred in the temple treasury.

In addition to this the Government had to meet the expenditure for the construction of the chariots, which was of the order of 30 to 40 thousand rupees per annum. The Raja of Daspalla used to supply logs of wood free of cost and therefore he was exempted from paying tribute unlike the Rajas of Mayurbhanj, Nilgiri, Khurda who were paying tribute to the Maratha Government.

In order to recompensate the loss that occurred due to the heavy expenditure required for the construction of the Cars the Maratha Government continued the practice of collecting pilgrim tax which was levied since the time of Mughol Government. The *Pratiharis* of the temple used to collect at the rate of six annas per rupee from the pilgrims and the Maratha Government imposed a tax on the *Pratiharis* in order to make up the loss to some extent.

The Jagannath Temple during British Period

The British conquered Orissa and took possession of the Jagannath temple administration in the year 1803. Lord Wellesley, Governor General intimated to Lieutenant Colonel Lionel Campbell who was despatched to take possession of the province of Cuttack, that he should take utmost care and precaution so that the inhabitants of Orissa should not rebel against the British authority. He wanted to secure the goodwill of the people of Orissa by appealing to their religious sentiment. He was aware of their deep veneration for Jagannath, the temple of which was most celebrated in India.

Campbell was told : "The question of pilgrims who resort to the Jagannath temple from all parts of the country will require your particular attention. You will be careful to afford the pilgrims ample protection and treat them with every mark of consideration and kindness. On your arrival at Jaggernaut (Jagannath) you will employ every precaution to preserve the respect due to the Pagoda and to the religious prejudices of the Brahmins and pilgrims". Campbell was also warned : "The Brahmins are supposed to derive considerable profit from the duties levied from the pilgrims. It will not be therefore possible at the present moment to interrupt the system which prevails in the collection of those duties".

A Board of Commissioners was constituted on 3rd August 1803 to look into the affairs of Cuttack. The Board appointed James Hunter as Collector of Jaggernaut to collect revenue and to superintend the temple affairs. The Commissioners were anxious for smooth celebration of the Car festival to be held for the first time under the British rule in July 1804. On 29 October 1804 Charles Groomes assumed office as the Judge, Magistrate and Collector of the Southern Division. The Board of Commissioners directed Groome to pay Rs. 10,000 to Dol Govinda, the *Rath Parichha* to enable him to construct the Cars (*raths*). The Commissioners wrote to the Secretary to the Government of Bengal seeking his approval of renewing the Toll which was levied on the pilgrims during the Maratha regime. The Governor General wanted a report on the internal administration of the temple before making any legislation for the removal of the pilgrim tax. Groome was directed by the Board of Commissioners to proceed to Puri and submit a report on the customs regarding levying and collecting taxes from the pilgrims during the Maratha rule. The relevant clauses of Groom's report is given in the Annexure VII.

Grooms in his report recommended imposition of the pilgrim tax after modifying the system of collection that prevailed under the Maratha rule. The Board of Commissioners submitted a draft of a regulation for the management of the temple of

Jagannath to the Board of Revenue. They recommended imposition of the pilgrim tax and appointment of a Collector of Pilgrim tax. The Board of Revenue on 17th June, forwarded the draft to the Bengal Government which received the approval of the Governor General in Council.

In July 1805 Harcourt visited Puri to witness the Car festival. He wrote that the 'pilgrims and the priests appeared to be highly gratified by the attendance of European Gentlemen and received them with shouts and clapping. He also observed that the pilgrims and the priests were highly gratified by the actions taken by the British Government for the feelings of respect and attention to the priests.

On 5 Sept 1805, Regulation XII of 1805 was passed, making provision for the collection of tax from the pilgrims resorting to the temple of Jagannath.

In November 1805, the Board of Revenue prepared the draft of a Regulation in conformity to the provisions contained in section 31 of Regulation XII of 1805, for the collection of a tax on the pilgrims resorting to the temple of Jagannath. One James Hunter was deputed to officiate as the collector of pilgrim tax. He was appointed on 21 November 1805 on a salary of Rs. 500 per month with a commission of 1 percent of the gross collection of the pilgrim tax. The pilgrim tax was collected from January 1806, and was imposed on 22 January 1806. But on the first day, the pilgrims were allowed to enter Puri without making any payment. Next day five *Bhurrung Jatrees* paid Rs. 2/- each. The number of pilgrims considerably increased within a few days. The crowd was so great that it was necessary to station four "*Batpeadas*" (road peons) to control the crowd at *Athuranulla ghat*. Hunter asked the *Pandas* not to take presents from the pilgrims without the knowledge of the Collector of the pilgrim tax. In addition to the pilgrim tax the Pandas were allowed to collect a fee from the pilgrims exclusive of the tax payable to Government.

A Regulation IV (Annexure VIII) was passed on 3rd April 1806 fixing the rate of tax to be paid by the pilgrims. A tax at *Athuranulla ghat* was fixed at 10 rupees and at Lokanath, 6 rupees on each person of the class of pilgrims called '*Laal Jatrees*'. The tax on all other pilgrims was levied at the rate of 2 rupees. The officers attached to the temple were strictly forbidden from making any demands of money exclusive of the tax and the fees specified. The superintendence of the temple of Jagannath and its interior economy, the conduct and management of its officers and the entire control over the priests, officers and servants attached to the idol and to the temple, were vested in an assembly of Pandits or learned Brahmins, who on all occasions, were guided by the recorded rules concerning the institution of the temple and by long established usage.

The government released Mukunda Deva from confinement. He was allowed to stay at Puri and was granted *Malikana* amounting one tenth of the revenue of the Khurda estate from 1808-1809.

George Webb the Collector of Cuttack was asked to bring up the accounts of the receipts and disbursement and to make a full enquiry respecting the lands assigned for the support of the temple. On the 19 December 1807 Webb submitted his repot to the Board of Revenue. The accounts given in his report are as follows.

1.	Average expenses of the Temple of every kind for the last six years (two years of Maratha rule and four years of British rule)	Rs. 65, 999-5
2.	Average receipts during the last six years	Rs. 30, 884-0
3.	Cash advanced	Rs. 29, 335-11
4.	Aggregate amount proposed sicca	Rs. 56, 342-9

According to Groome's Report, the revenue of the Temple at the time of the British conquest was derived from the following sources :

1.	Eleven Mauzas comprising twenty villages in the Satais Hazari Mahals *	Rs. 11,848
2.	Small plots of land	Rs. 157
3.	Khanjahs or fixed moneytary assignments in Mogulbundee or British Orissa	Rs. 17,177
4.	Khanjahs in rent free lands in Mogulbundee	Rs. 7,262
5.	Khanjahs in certain killas	Rs. 778
6.	Resources of the Temple under various heads such as poll tax	Rs. 10,638
	Sicca Rupees	Rs. 47, 877-7-6

The Board of Revenue asked George Webb, the Collector Cuttack, to suggest rules for regulating the Pilgrim tax. Webb suggested that 'Laal Jatrees should be allowed access to the temple for 16 days. He also suggested provision for a second class of pilgrims to be called *'Nim Laal'*. They would be allowed access to the Temple for a week, paying Rs. 5 at Atharanalla and Rs. 3 at Loknath ghat.

The Bhurrangs, paying Rs. 2 at Atharanalla ghat, would have access to the Temple for 4 days, instead of 5 days, as was

* Satais Hazari Mahals : There were originally five villages-Kapileswarpur, Batgaon, Bir Pratappur, Salejoree, Ootarkona, which were given three hundred years ago by the Rajas of Kurda. Subsequently, Swanlo, Pruohitpur, Alsurrang (Astarang) and Mohuree etc., were granted by other persons. Majority of the villagers were situated in pergunah Rahang.

The revenue of the Satais Hazari Mahals was much less than rupees twenty seven thousand. Groome in his report pointed out that taking advantage of the change in the administration the Matdharis "shamelessly practised embezzlement" and appropriated the lands which were given to them as 'Kothkhanjah" or supply of bhog to the temple.

An endowment of the temple of Jagannath known as Math Rajoo was held by Narain Das, who sold a portion of it to a Muhammadan named Latif Khan, for a small sum. The property known as "Latif Jumma' was sold by the owner after four years to a person named Sivaprasad Singh. Scott Warring Offg. Collector, held all these transactions to be illegal in 1811.

hitherto allowed. The fourth class, commonly called the *Kangals*, "being pilgrims in actual state of poverty" would have access to the Temple for one day. Webb insisted that the *Nim Laal*, *Bhurrang* and *Kangal* pilgrims must be attended by the Pandas to guide them through the ceremonies. At this juncture the Board of Revenue seriously felt to entrust the Raja of Khurda with the affairs of the temple as soon as possible.

The Governor General asked Charles Buller, who was stationed at Cuttack as settlement commissioner to submit a scheme for collection of tax. Charles Buller, a member of the Board of Revenue, consistently insisted on the appointment of the Raja of Khurda as the superintendent of the Temple. He wrote to the Governor General suggesting that a regulation be immediately enacted for vesting superintendence of the temple of Jagannath in the Raja of Khurda.

The draft of the proposed Regulation was sent to the Court of Directors for confirmation. After deliberating pros and cons of the matter at various levels of the Government it was decided to vest the affair of the temple with the Raja of Khurda. The decisions taken in this matter are stated below.

A regulation for rescinding regulations IV and V of 1806 and for substitution of rules in lieu of those enacted in the said regulations, for levying duties from the pilgrims resorting to Juggernath, and for superintendence and management of the affairs of the Temple was passed by the Governor General in Council on 28 April 1809, (1224 Higree, 1216 Fassili), Annexure X.

It was stated in preamble : "Whereas it has appeared that the rules at present in force for levying duties from the pilgrims and for the superintendence and management of the affairs of the temple of Jugernath have been in some respects attended with difficulty and inconvenience, the Governor General in Council with a view to afford every facility to the different classes of Hindoos in the performance of their religious ceremonies and with a view to the better management of the internal affairs of the Temple" passed the following regulation.

The clauses were : First "The superintendence of the temple of Juggernath and its internal economy and management of the affairs and control over the priests and servants attached to the temple are hereby vested in the Rajah of Khoordah who on all occasions shall be guided by the recorded rules and institutions of the temple or by established usage".

Second "The Rajah of Khoordah and his successors shall have the charge vested in them so long as they shall continue to conduct themselves with integrity, deligence and propriety; but nothing contained in the Regulation shall be constrained to preclude the Governor General in Council from removing the present Rajah or any of his successors on proof of misconduct in such persons made to the satisfaction of the Governor General".

The Third clause is unimportant.

Fourth : "Three *Dewl Purchas* are to be appointed by the Collector of Cuttack subject to the confirmation by the Governor General and they are not to be removed from the office without the sanction of the Governor General".

"In the event of any orders issued by the Rajah being inconsistent with the recorded rules and institutions of the temple or with its ancient and established usages, the Purchas are to represent to the Governor General in Council, if it should appear that the interposition of Government is necessary for the restoration of good order and the prevention of disputes and irregularity.

"The Third *Dewl Purcha* shall execute the duty of the *Sattais Huzzaree Purcha*, and it shall be his duty to give an account to the Collector of the tax of all offerings and presents made to the idol".

Fifth : "A tax shall be levied on the part of Government (as was heretofore done under the late Marhatta Government and as also been done under the British Government since the conquest of the province of Cuttack) on the pilgrims resorting to the temple of Juggernath".

"The collection of the tax shall be entrusted to an officer with the official designation of the Collector of the tax on pilgrims, subject to the authority of the Collector of Cuttack".*

An intermediate class known as *Nim Laal* was introduced. The Regulation IV of 1809 prescribed a certain number of days to different classes of pilgrims for access to the Temple. The Regulation IV of 1809 ended the direct administration of the Jagannath temple by the East India Company. It was a comprehensive measure, changing the system of the management of the Temple. It took into consideration the problems which arose after the imposition of the Pilgrim tax. It sought to restore the conditions which existed before the Marathas took over the management of the Temple. The Regulation vested the superintendence of the temple; and its internal economy and the control over the temple priests to the Raja of Khurda.

The British Government thus gave up the idea of appointing a committee of *pundits* to supervise the administration of the Temple. At the same time, restrictions were imposed on the authority of the Raja of Khurda. The Raja and

---

* The Regulations and Laws in Bengal, Vol. VI : Regulation IV of 1809 (Annexure-X). "The Regulation prescribes the rules for the management of the internal affairs of the Temple under the superintendence of the Rajah of Khoordah and specifies the Collector of Cuttack and Collector of tax as the European, authorized to interfere in the nomination of officers and to act as a check on the Rajah on the conduct of his duties subject to the orders of the Governor General in Council - the direct interposition of Government when necessary to restore good order appears to be throughout contemplated".

R. Ker, Commissioner, to Government of India, Territorial Department : November 1818, Bengal Revenue Consultations, No. 21 National Library.

his successors were to hold the position so long as they conducted themselves with integrity, diligence and propriety and were liable to removal by the Government on the ground of misconduct. The Raja was to be guided by the recorded rules of the Temple.

It was evident that the Raja of Khurda was mistrusted. It was apprehended that he might abuse the power which would be vested to him. The Government retained the power of appointing and dismissing the chief temple priests - the *Deul Parichhas.* They were given the right of checking any deviation from the customary usages and recorded rules of the temple on the part of the superintendent by making representation to the Collector of Cuttack. The Government also questioned the discretion of the Superintendent to exclude the persons whom he refrained from entering the temple.

Though the Raja of Khurda was given the management of the Temple affairs, the Government did not give up its close association with the Temple. The Government realised money from the pilgrims resorting to the temple of Jagannath, and fees from the "Pilgrim hunters' - *Pundas* and the *Pratiharis.* It paid money for the establishment charges of the Temple and scrutinised the accounts.

Thus the Regulation of 1809 was a compromise between the views of the Board of Revenue supported by the Court of Directors, and of the Board of the Commissioners for the affairs of the temple. It introduced a Dyarchy in the administration of the Jagannath Temple. The superintendence of the temple was vested in the Raja of Khurda. But the Government reserved the right of supervision for the restoration of good order and prevention of irregularity in the Temple administration.

The collection of pilgrim tax in the beginning fell far short of expectation. In order to improve the situation one Mr. Busby was appointed as an assistant Collector on a salary of Rs. 300/- per month with a commission of two per cent on the collection. The collection of pilgrim tax by the queen of Mayurbhanj State was abolished and the native military officers, sepoys, and servants of the European officers and the local pilgrims called Desees were exempted from payment of pilgrim tax.

The Jagannath road was in a deplorable condition and therefore the pilgrims belonging to upcountry and Bengal did not like to undertake the Journey. A good road along the old route was built with donations from Maharaja Sukhamoy Roy a *Zamindar* of Calcutta. Moreover, as recommended by the collector of pilgrim tax the walls of the temple which were in a bad shape were repaired. The expenses of these types of work necessitated imposition of pilgrim tax which was finally done in the interest of the Jagannath temple. Moreover, the British government took charge of the whole expenses of the temple which was of the order of Rs. 72438-6.

The Missionaries blamed the Government for collection of tax from the pilgrims visiting the Jagannath temple. They argued that the idolatrous worship in that temple would lapse without the Government support which implied in the collection of the pilgrim tax. On 6 June 1837 Rickets, commissioner wrote a letter to Wilkinson Collector of Puri regarding the proposal of abolition of the pilgrim tax and withdrawal of the Government interference in the affairs of the temple of Jagannath including the intention of the Government to rescind the Regulation IV of 1809 and XI of 1810. Rickets forwarded the letter of Wilkinson giving his suggestions in respect of future administration of the Jagannath temple. "That the officers shall be relieved from interference in the internal affairs of the Jagannath temple by abolition of the Pilgrim tax. The *Sattais Hazari Mahal* be brought to the rent roll of the district. That an annual donation of Rs. 44776-6-6 shall be paid for the support of the temple. That the Superintendent Rajah Ramchandra Dev be vested by the Government with full powers in everything connected with the temple and its ceremonies and that small increase shall be allowed to the police establishment at Puri. On 20 April 1840 Act X of 1840 (Annexure XI) was passed which abolished the tax and fees upon the pilgrims resorting to Puri. It was provided in the Act that the Superintendence of the temple of Jagannath and its interior economy, the conduct and the management of its affairs and the control over the priests, officers and servants attached to the temple shall continue to be vested in the Raja of Khurda for the time being. The Collector, Puri wrote to Commissioner on 6 May 1840 "acting upon the provision of Act X of 1840 as published in the Gazettee of 29 April I prohibited the collection of any tax from the pilgrims from 3 May. "At Puri on the 3rd May amidst the most tremendous storm in which the sacred wheel on the summit of the Pagoda tower was bent, the gate was thrown open and the pilgrims entered the barrier free".

Raja Birakishore Dev had to sign an agreement which would permanently alienate a portion of the State of Khurda. The Raja however did not like to sign the agreement but finally he had to sign the agreement under the force of the Government. Finally after official pressure put on the Raja he signed the deed before the Collector. The agreement gave legality to transactions by which by transferring land in lieu of money allowances, the Government discontinued payment of Jagannath temple from the treasury retaining only the control over the Jagannath temple Police establishment. By this there ended the rule of East India Company. The end of the East India Company's rule in India synchronised with the end of direct connection of the Christian Government with probably the most celebrated Hindu temple in India.

As pointed out earlier the East-India Company abolished the Pilgrim Tax and bypassing Act-X of the 1840 vested the then Raja of Puri with full authority in regard to the management of the temple and its properties. This Act prohibited the temple authorities to impose any restriction upon the pilgrims for admission into the temple and performing ceremonies free. At the same time the Government scrupulously maintained the pledges on the strength of which the temple continued to be under the protection of the Government. The Government made an annual payment to meet the expenses of the temple which was of the order of about Rs. 53,000 per year. In 1843, the Estate of Satais Hazari Mahal yielding an annual rent of Rs. 17,000 was made over to the Raja. Thereby the annual money payment made by the Government was reduced to Rs. 35,738. In 1845 it was ascertained that out of this sum Rs. 23,000 represented an assignment of revenue granted by the Raja of Berar and therefore the annual payment was further reduced to Rs. 23,321.

The Government found out the neglect by Birakishore Dev the then Raja superintendent of the temple of the management of the temple. In order to provide protection to the pilgrims the Government appointed a police establishment at an annual expense of Rs. 7,000 which was deducted from the Government grants to the temple. In 1858, the Government lands under Ekrajat Mahal were placed with the Raja in lieu of their cash payment to the temple. With the transfer of certain other lands yielding an equivalent grant of the Government, the Government ceased to have any connection with the management of the temple since the year 1863.

After the death of Birakishore Dev his widow Suryamoni Patamahadei took charge of the management of the temple because Divyasingh Dev the adopted son of Birakishore Dev was a minor at the time of the death of his adopted father. The management of the temple went from bad to worse and Divyasingh Dev was sentenced to transportation for life as he was accused of a murder case in 1878. When Divyasingh Dev was sentenced to transportation for life in 1877 his son Mukunda Dev was minor and therefore his grand-mother Suryamoni Patmahadei acted as the guardian of her grand son. The mismanagement in the temple continued and the office of the superintendent of the temple was declared vacant. In such a situation a suit was filed in the court of law by the Government to get a decree for appointment of new trustees and for the settlement of a scheme for the management of the temple. The suit was compromised and the terms and conditions of the compromise are as follows.

1) The management of Sri Jagannath temple which had been entrusted under Regulation IX/1809 and Act-X/1840 to the Raja of Khurda shall continue in hands of Mukunda Dev. But during his minority his grand-mother and guardian Rani Suryamoni Patmahadei was to act for him.

2) During the period of her management Rani Suryamoni Patmahadei was to employ a competent manager and shall transfer to him all her powers over the Sebakas of the temple. But the manager could not remove any Sebaka without the consent of the Rani.

3) If the Rani was to remove the manager she should appoint another manager within reasonable time and on default the civil court shall have power to appoint a competent manager to the said vacancy.

4) This decree was to have no force after the Raja came of age.

This compromise was made in the year 1888, and it ceased to have any force by 1897 when Raja Mukunda Dev attained the age - after he came to age Mukunda Dev was recognized as Superintendent of the temple. Even during his time mismanagement continued in the affairs of the temple. Therefore, Raja Mukunda Dev was forced to take a Government Officer as Manager. Thus the management of the temple continued to be in the hands of Government servants of Gazetted rank. After the death of Raja Mukunda Dev in 1926 his adopted son Raja Ramachandra Dev took charge of the temple. After the death of Raja Ramachandra Dev came other Gajapati Rajas in the succession and acted as Raja superintendent of the temple, even after independence. This is just a brief outline of the history of the great institution which is unique in its nature and run by ancient traditions and visited by thousands of pilgrims almost everyday and even more on special festivals. Puri, the abode of Lord Jagannath, the God of Universe has been a pilgrim centre of national and even international repute.

The Pilgrim Tax in Different Periods

The Maratha Government was collecting pilgrim tax not only from the pilgrims coming to visit Lord Jagannath but also they were collecting the tax from those coming to visit sacred shrines. 12 *Caukis* (stations or centres) were established between Rajghat and Balasore for collection of tax from the pilgrims. This was the centre of Northern entrance through which the pilgrims coming from Bengal, Bihar, Uttarpradesh, Assam and other places were coming to Orissa to visit Lord Jagannath. The tax paid by those passing through northern gate used to pay Rs. 10/- and those coming from South paid Rs. 6/- per head. Those coming from south used to enter Puri town through Lokanath ghat and those coming from north enter via *Atharanalla ghat.* At both these *ghats* pilgrim tax was collected.

In addition to the payments of tax at the *ghats* the pilgrims used to pay tax at different places enroute to Puri. Some of these places are Balasore and Khunta located in Mayurbhanj border and as they approached Puri they had to pay tax at *Atharnalla* and *Lokanath* ghats as stated above. The pilgrims used to pay tax while passing through the territories of zamindars. Although the amount of tax to be paid by the pilgrims was fixed by the Government but it was not adhered to by the Tahsildars who were in charge of collection at different ghats. The amount of tax collected from the pilgrims was of the order of 2 to 5 lakhs of rupees annually.

In addition to the pilgrims tax the pilgrims had to pay a toll tax of 15 *annas* per head while entering the temple. The *Sanyasis*, and *Kangalas* were exempted from paying poll tax. At places the pious people built rest houses for the pilgrims to take rest. They also dug tanks and wells to supply water to the pilgrims. Many people and the chiefs of the States planted trees on the roadside for the pilgrims to take rest under such trees. The places at Balasore and Bhadrak were dangerous because at such places the robbers used to plunder the travellers and made them destitutes (*Kangalas*). The robbers used some intoxicating preparations and applied into the nostrils of tired pilgrims to make them senseless and sleep sound sleep. When they woke up in the morning they woke up stark naked because even the clothes they put on were stripped off from their body by the robbers.

The Jagannath Temple was a great source of income for the Maratha Government. When the British took over the administration of the temple the Maratha Government put up a strong fight against the British interference. But finally the Maratha Government had to quit. However in the interim period certain conditions were provided in the treaty between the British rule and the outgoing Maratha regime.

The conditions are as follows

1. The Jagannath Pagoda and all the duties collected from the pilgrims shall remain to the Marathas.

2. A Maratha governor will be posted in the temple and he will have supreme authority over the functionaries and the pilgrims visiting the temple.

3. The villages and the landed properties which were allocated during Maharaja Janugi's governance for the support of the Brahmins of Brahmin Settlements shall remain under the control of the Marathas.

4. The religious ceremonies which were performed annually by the pilgrims in the Jagannath temple shall be continued and two officials posted in the temple to collect duties or fees which the pilgrims used to pay on these ritual occasions and make payments to the Marathas.

5. All villages and lands formerly donated to the Brahmins should remain in their possession as before.

6. Moral Pandit and Sewaji Pandit who were appointed before as *Parichha* in the Jagannath temple should continue in their posts as usual even after the Maratha were withdrawn when the British took over administration of Orissa in 1803 AD.

From year after year the Anglo-Maratha conflict arose on different fronts and it got intensified as the years passed by and finally it ended in the war which was declared against the Maratha Government on 3rd August 1802 AD. and the British took over the administration of Orissa in 1803 AD including the management and control of the Jagannath temple.

Briefly speaking, during the administration of the Marathas in Orissa, they treated the pilgrims to Jagannath with a degree of attention and consideration. It was of course their interest to do so. To take particular care about the collection of the pilgrim tax - to entice as many pilgrims as possible and to afford them the protection of the State, while they enjoyed their devotion in the holy land. It was a portion of their policy. The pilgrim hunters of the latter half of the 18th century must have found little difficulty in causing multitude to undertake pilgrimage.

. In conclusion, Laurie observed "yet these people in the gradual sunset of their glory, even with their rapacity and violence must have commanded a considerable portion of their veneration. They adhered strictly to the rule of Brahma. This, in the eyes of the people of Orissa, must have covered a multitude of sins".

Jagannath Temple Administration After Independence

The temple of Lord Jagannath at Puri is an Institution well-known throughout India and elsewhere. Its national importance is so great that it needs no mention to the public of India. For better administration of the Temple and its affairs and to prevent mismanagement thereof which unfortunately has appeared since the last few years, the Government of Orissa as a preliminary step towards undertaking a comprehensive legislation about the temple, have passed Act XIV of 1952 providing for appointment of a special officer to consolidate and prepare record-of rights and duties of the various classes of *Sebakas* and other persons connected with the *Seba Puja* of the Temple. The necessity for this legislation can very well be gathered from the statement of objects and reasons given by the Hon'ble Shri D. Sahu, the Minister, Law and Home, while introducing the Bill in the Assembly :

Statement of objects and reasons

"The Puri Temple of Lord Jagannath which occupies an unique position not only in the State of Orissa but also in relation to the whole of the union is in a sad plight.

Abject mismanagement, a standing disgrace to the citizens and their administration, prevails in spite of all efforts to remedy it. There is no escape but that in the interest of the public, State Government must step in and take effective measures in order to save it from ruination.

In the absence of any guidance from the Raja and sufficient contribution from him for the regular expenses of the Temple, the scheduled and disciplined performance of the *Nitis* has suffered beyond imagination and the Raja has practically lost all control over the different *Sebakas* and other temple servants.

Economic rivalry and moral degeneration of the servants and Sebaks has divested them of all sense of duty and cooperation. Specific endowments are regularly misapplied and misappropriated. Strikes amongst various classes are of common occurrence. The non-availability at the appointed hours of the Mahaprasad coveted and adored by millions of pilgrims is always there in these days. The lapses into unorthodoxy has resulted in extremely unhygienic conditions inside the temple and commission of heinous crimes even within the Temple precincts is not rare even the image of the deity has been at times defiled and its precious jewellery removed. Peace and solemnity inside the temple has given way to sheer goondaism and it is mainly the servants of the temple that make up the unruly elements responsible for such lawless state of affairs.

For the purpose of exercising effective supervision over the administration of the Temple and its endowments, a Bill was prepared and introduced in the State Legislature in June 1948. Provisions for constitution of a Committee with the Raja of Puri as Chairman ex officio, was made for an effective administration of all the religious and specific endowments - jewels and the properties vested in the deity subject to the control of the State Government. Provisions for constitution of a council of religious rituals was also made to settle disputes regarding rituals in the temple. This committee was required under the said bill to report upon disputes relating to the rights of Sebaks, etc., and to control the daily time-table relating to the performance of ceremonies in the temple. This bill further provided for giving loans by the State Government to the funds of the temple for proper administration of the same. This bill was not however enacted and reasons are not known. The fact remains that the Bill fell through perhaps due to constitutional difficulties. All efforts from 1937 to 1948 to enact legislations have still failed due to initial difficulties as to the nature of rights and duties of the principal persons interested in the Seba Puja of the deity and other idols.

In the result, the failure of these above attempts has mainly been due to the the fact that no proper efforts have yet been made to have an authenticated record of different individuals and classes of persons on whom the various rights and duties in the complex scheme of Seba Puja has from time immemorial devolved. Even there has never been a proper assessment of the position of the Raja visa-vis the deity. The state legislature do not propose to interfere so as to alter the existing services. But preserving all that in tact, the proper carrying out of the scheme by emphasising the details of the administration of the properties and the income of the deity and enforcing accordingly each and every item of activity enjoined on the respective persons is undoubtedly feasible. The different *Sebakas* may have the full liberty of managing the religious affairs of the institution but it is as pointed out above in the interest of the public that their propensity to mismanage such affairs of the institution should in no manner be tolerated and so far as law allows, the state must intervene.

This obviously can only be effected by a specific legislation directed to meet the peculiar needs of the situation and any half-hearted measures will be of no avail. Such legislation must aim at making all manner of default on the part of the temple servant an offence punishable with fine and every strike illegal, the fines being appropriated towards the funds of the temple. This is the least that can be provided for as a preventive measure.

But before that final stage of legislation can be launched upon and made effective and even be justifiable, it would be absolutely necessary, firstly, to have it determined the nature of all services that are to be rendered; secondly, the individuals on whom the liability of such performance rests; and thirdly, the rights and privileges attached to such services. It is then only that it would be possible to apply with any precision the preventive measures by penalising the defaults.

A legislative process was proposed to provide for the preparation of a record-of-rights and duties by an officer appointed by Government for the purpose. The steps taken in this regard are discussed in the following chapters.

4
Shri Jagannath Temple (Administration) Act, 1952

(Orissa Act XIV of 1852)

Preparation of record of rights

As the time passed by the management of the temple went from bad to worse. Besides many other adverse situations the *Raja* of Puri became very neglectful in giving his attention to the management of the temple. Mismanagement of the temple funds and lack of control over the *Sebakas* degenerated the performance of the *nitis* and *sebapuja* of the temple. Economic rivalry and profit motive divested the *Sebakas* of all sense of their ritual duties and mutual cooperation. Strikes and creation of troubles by the *Sebakas* became of common occurrence. The situation was in such a bad shape and awful plight that it was necessary on the part of the Government to initiate legislative measures for exercising effective supervision and control over the administration of the temple.

A bill was introduced in the State legislature in June, 1948 for achieving this objective, but it failed due to constitutional difficulties. The next step in the legislative process was to pass an act (Act XIV of 1952) providing for appointment of a Special Officer to consolidate and prepare a Record-of-Rights and duties of various classes of Sebakas and other persons connected with the Seba Puja of the temple. In pursuance of the Act rules were framed providing for preparation of a plan of the temple and all other temples within its compound for preparing a record of *nitis*, obligatory to conduct throughout the year, record of all the various classes of Sebakas and other persons connected with the *Seba Puja* giving in detail all their rights and duties and lastly a record of all the properties of the temple, movable and immovable including an inventory of articles which are present in the *Ratnabhandar* of the temple. The report prepared by the special officer appointed under the Puri Shri Jagannath Temple (Administration) Act, 1952 were published part by part in extra ordinary Orissa Gazettee of 1954-55.

A statutory committee with the following members was formed. The members who formed the committee are as follows.

1.	Raja of Puri	Chairman
2.	Sri Srinivas Ramanuj Das, Mahant, Emar Math	Member
3.	Sri Rama Chandra Mohapatra, Secretary, Muktimandap Pandit Sabha, Puri	Member
4.	Swami Bichitrananda Das, Advocate Dagarpara, Cuttack.	Member
5.	Sri Dwarikanath Patjosi Mohapatra, Harachandi Sahi, Puri	Member
6.	Sri Ramesh Chandra Mitra, Retired District Judge, Puri	Member
7.	Dr. Parsuram Mishra Ex-Vice-Chancellor, Utkal University	Member
8.	Sri Jagatbandhu Mohapatra, Grabandu Balisahi, Puri	Member
9.	Commissioner of religious endowments, Orissa, Cuttack	Member
10.	Sri Biswanath Padhi, Swar Nijog, Puri	Member
11.	Administrator	Ex-officio member

By the Shri Jagannath Temple (Amendment) Act 1961, the strength of the statutory committee was raised from 11 to 15 and the Collector of the district of Puri became an ex-officio member and vice-chairman of the Committee. In the beginning the Raja of Puri did not attend the meetings of the committee, but later on he was more or less regular in his attendance. For example, there were 22 meetings during the period from the 27th October, 1960 till the 31st March, 1961. In 18 meetings the Raja who was the statutory Chairman of the Committee did not attend and some other member had to be chosen to be the Chairman in the respective meetings. Similarly, in 1961-62 there were in all 26 meetings of which in 8 meetings the statutory Chairman could not attend.

For attending the meetings the members were allowed each a daily allowance of Rs. 10/- in addition to first class T.A. to outside members for journey undertaken by them. However, two members Sri S.R. Das, Mahant, Emar Math and Sri J.B. Mohapatra did not draw any daily allowance for attending any of the meetings from the inception of the Committee till the 31st March, 1963. Their intention was not to draw the allowance from the Sri Jagannath Temple fund.

Shri Ananda Chandra Mohapatra, O.A.S. was the first Administrator and was in office since the 17th November, 1961. He was drawing a salary of Rs. 712/- a month including Rs. 120/- as dearness allowance, and house rent allowance of Rs. 60/- a month. He was succeeded by Sri Laxman Mishra, I.P.S. (Retd.) who was drawing Rs. 800/- a month. In the beginning the staff of his office comprised one office Superintendent, one Accountant, one Cashier-cum-record keeper, one Diarist and despatching clerk, one *Nazir*, one meeting and correspondence clerk, one steno-typist, one orderly for Chairman and two orderlies for administrator. But subsequently as the work became multifarious the temple establishment had to maintain a large staff.

Since its inception the Committee has been holding its office in the building which was all along occupied by the temple office of the hitherto Superintendent of the temple and also bears the signboard "Office of the Raja Superintendent, Jagannath Temple, Puri".

The Committee had taken charge only of the office with some furniture used by the office staff. But the ex-Raja superintendent did not make over full charge of old records and accounts relating to the property of the temple. Certain rooms in the building were kept under lock and key kept by the Gajapati Raja of Puri up to the year 1969 when Shri Birakishore Dev was pleased to place these rooms in the building with records and furniture therein at the disposal of the administrator. This matter was hanging on since 1960. The records are now being sorted out and indexed by employing necessary staff for the purpose. There was no cash balance or other articles of value in the office on the date of taking over charge. However, the Committee took charge of the temple with all subordinate shrines and other belongings in the temple excepting the Ratnabhandar which has been accorded a special treatment under rule 5 of the Sri Jagannath Temple Rules, 1960.

Out of the three elephants and the establishments connected there with maintained from the temple funds the Ex-superintendent gave to the Committee only one elephant and kept for himself the two other elephants claiming them as his private property. This elephant Jagannath Prashad by name and its Mahunta, are at present being maintained from the Jagannath Temple Fund. During the Committees regime one cow and a calf were received as gifts to Sri Bimala Devi and these were kept in charge of Nati Bhoi (a Rath Bhoi) on specific conditions. These were the only livestock in charge of the Committee.

It may be stated that the elephant which came under the management of the Committee died on the 4th June 1965 and with its death the staff (Mahunt and Mento) attached to it was disbanded. The cow and the calf which were donated to Shri Bimala Thakurani were sold away in 1965-66.

As regards immovable properties of Lord Jagannath the Committee took charge of and received revenue from the lands granted by the Government which are known as the *Sataishazari mahal* and the *Ekharajat mahal* and from the donations to the Lord Jagannath such as Bagha, Bhikaripara and lands in the Cuttack Mahal. As regards the properties which are believed to be in almost all other districts in Orissa and other States of the country the Committee requested the Government to furnish the information as already collected by the special officer appointed under the Sri Jagannath Temple (Administration) Act, 1952, Lacking accurate and definite information about the landed properties great difficulties were being experienced in the collection of revenue and also for the payment of Government dues.

Sources of Income

The various sources of income have been listed in Chapter VI of the report prepared by the Special Officer under the Jagannath Temple (Administration) Act, 1952. The most important sources are the landed properties which may be classified as follows :

(1) The endowments made by various Rajas of Orissa who founded the temple, initiated various *Nities* and appointed *Sevakas.* There is no trace of these lands now except a very few *Jagir* lands enjoyed by a very few classes of *Sevakas* as mentioned in the Special officer's record-of-rights.

(2) Lands granted by ruling chiefs of the country in lieu of cash grants paid by them to meet deficits caused by the expenditure for the temple over and above the income thereof.

These are the *Sataishazari Mahal* located in Sadar sub-division and the *Ekhrajat Mahal* in the Khurda sub-division of Puri district. *Sataishazari Mahal* consists of 59 villages comprising an area of 9,758.19 acres with revenue of about Rs. 55,000 excluding cesses but including paddy, garden crops and other miscellaneous revenues.

The *Ekhrajat Mahal* which was granted in two instalments in 1858 and 1863 consists of 155 villages comprising an area of 67,685 acres. Some lands costing about a lakh of rupees have been acquired by the South Eastern Railway. This Mahal yields a revenue including the value of paddy and other grains together with miscellaneous revenue from forests, fisheries and lastly querries of about Rs. 50,000/-.

Out of the waste lands in *Ekharajat Mahal* in Khurda and Bhubaneswar sub-division an extent of 1,409 acres was placed at the disposal of the soil conservation department, Orissa for cashew nut plantation during 1964-1966. Over and above the said area; a further extent of about 2,000 acres has been requisitioned for cashew nut plantation by the soil conservation department and the forest department.

(3) Properties endowed by various persons for a specific purpose

Such properties as could be traced so far are there which were donated by one late Ganeswar Bharati in Puri and Cuttack districts and the *Athgah Khanja* lands in Bhikaripada village of Puri district. The Bhikaripada lands now yield a revenue of about Rs. 4,000 annually and the expenditure from it for the specific purposes for which the lands have been granted, is Rs. 1,100 p-. This expenditure which was discontinued by the previous management has been revived by the committee since January, 1963 by spending Rs. 3/- daily for *Khiri* and *Amalu Bhog* of Lord Jagannath in the morning and distributing it to Sadhus and Sanyasis under the supervision of the Basudev Trust Board as mentioned in the record-of-rights.

Out of the lands donated by late Bharati and situated in the Puri and Cuttack districts most of the lands have been vested in Government under the Orissa Estates Abolition Act thereby putting the temple to a heavy recurring annual loss in revenue.

The remaining lands in Cuttack district are scattered bits over an extensive area fetching a revenue of about Rs. 2,000/- nearly for the collection of which a machinery costlier than the revenue is required. The collection of revenue is in charge of the law agent Cuttack in addition to his duties of Tahasil work. As a result the collection work suffers and there are large amount of arrears of revenue.

(4) Properties endowed for Amrita Monohi of Lord Jagannath and for various other specific purposes in the marfatdarship of the Mahantas of several maths and sevakas of Lord Jagannath.

Some of the grants coming under this category have become extinct by being vested in Government under Orissa Estate Abolition Act. In many cases the grants are not utilized for the purposes for which such properties were granted. Some such lands have been acquired by the Government in the public interest without payment of any compensation for such acquisition because the *Marfatdars* are not competent to dispose of the lands by sale, or otherwise. The Committee has moved the Government for the payment of perpetual annuities or compensations for Amrit Monohi lands to the temple.

(5) Properties donated by individuals to Lord Jagannath and left in charge of their relatives or appointed persons to pay the net income or portion thereof to the temple for utilization for the purpose intended by the donor. These properties are scattered throughout Orissa and India. But no comprehensive record of these lands is available.

In pursuance of a notice published in this regard by the Administrator in the daily 'Samaj' in 1962 some information about scattered bits of lands donated to Lord Jagannath here and there is being received from time to time and a register has been opened to record them. Correspondence is also going on about the income from the lands and the manner in which the produce is utilized. The correspondence shows that most of the lands of this category have been vested to the Government and the temple is getting only nominal annuity.

The next source of income in importance is that relating to *Bajemahal* such as *Paniki Mahal* (sale of right to dress vegetables for outside bhog offered by pilgrims and visitors) and *Saragharas* and *Chulas* (stores and ovens). It may be noted that these items were at one time substantial sources of income but in the present time the income has considerably declined for lack of proper management. A sub-committee has been appointed to suggest suitable ways and means by which revenue from such sources could be augmented and the management in this regard streamlined.

Other sources of income worth mentioning are (1) *Pindika*, (2) *Parimanika*, (3) Name plates, (4) *Dhwaja*, (5) Donations, (6) *Ghoda Darsan*, (7) *Sadhibandha*, (8) *Chamar seva*, (9) Offering *chapan bhog*, (10) Lighting of *Lakhshabati*, (11) Offering of dresses and jewels.

For the sake of illustrations the collection in respect of a few important items are given below.

Pindika : The offering made by the devotees and pilgrims at the feet of the deities and those made in the name of the deities in other premises of the temple are known as *Pindika* collections. These are in the shape of cash, jewellery and other articles like silk and cotton clothes, etc. The collections from this source for five years in cash, gold and silver are as follows :

Year	Cash (Rs.)	Gold tolas	Silver tolas	Other articles (old silver coins)
1	2	3	4	5
1962-64	18,543	63-11-0	823-15-9	1993
1964-65	20,954	66-7-9	938-0-6	2143
1965-66	20,493	73-7-9	854-4-6	2682
1966-67	15,075	50-7-4	669-24-6	2122
1967-68	27,986	81-7-0	744-1-9	2648

For proper collection of *pindika* a closed box with a silk cover at the top was placed near *Bhitar katha* in March 1963. The *Khuntia Mekapa* took resort to civil suit against this arrangement saying that it was not a precedent and that it went against their interest. As per order of the civil court in this case the box was removed in April 1963. There were appeals and counter appeals from each side as a result of which the right to place the box was allowed at some time and disallowed at other time in obedience to the injunctions issued from time to time. The matter is now settled and three boxes one in front of each deity are placed on the *Sinhasan*.

Parimanik, Dhwaja and other miscellaneous collections : The system of allowing *Darshan* to the devotees beyond *Sahanamela* on ticket basis was continued with a fee of Rs. 1/- per head at the time of *Mangla Arati* and *Abakas* and at Rs. 1.25 per head on the occasion of *Sakal Dhup*, *Madhyanna Dhup*, *Sandhya Dhup* and *Chandanlagi* before *Badasinghara* in the night. The total collections for five years are as follows :

Year	Parimanik fee collected	Sale proceeds of Dhwaja
1	2	3
1963-64	12,278.73	2,418.00
1964-65	12,185.49	4,457.00
1965-66	12,041.56	3,837.00
1966-67	15,075.27	3,498.00
1967-68	19,361.01	5,375.00

Collections of fees were also made in respect of other items, namely (1) putting stone slabs within the temple compound (2) fees on performance of *Sradhas*, (3) fees on performances of *Sankritan*, (4) *Sadhi bandha* done by sebakas, (5) allowing *chamar seva*, (6) burning of *Lakshyabati*, (7) offering of *Chhapan Bhog*, (8) *Dakhina* for offering ornaments, dresses, etc. to the deities, (9) application fees and (10) allowing *Handi Kudia* inside the temple compound. Collection of fees on these miscellaneous items are as follows :

Year	Amount realised (Rs.)
1963-64	3,167.47
1964-65	18,758.00
1965-66	18,602.13
1966-67	18,924.98
1967-68	23,445.48

There are several minor sources from which some collections were made to augment the income of the temple. A list of these sources and the income received there from for 5 years is given below :

Sl.	*Name of Mahals*	*1963-64*	*1964-65*	*1965-66*	*1966-67*	*1967-68*
1	*2*	*3*	*4*	*5*	*6*	*7*
1.	Chhapan Bhog Pasara shop	1,296.00	2,316.00	2,520.00	2,520.00	2,340.00
2.	Deepa shop	1,419.00	2,737.00	3,245.00	3,260.00	3.263.00
3.	Electric charges	1,875.00	2.124.00	2.220.00	2,184.00	2,184.00
4.	Chhapanbhog in Sun Temple	27.00	27.00	27.00	27.00	27.00
5.	Chapan bhog in Burdhaman temple	27.00	27.00	27.00	27.00	27.00
6.	Rent for Sarghar	343.00	343.00	343.00	343.00	343.00
7.	Outside shops near Pejana	1,204.00	204.00	204.00	204.00	204.00
8.	Fees for upadhi curries	105.00	—	—	—	—
9.	Sale of curries	610.00	—	—	—	—

10. Ram Laxman temple	27.00	30.00	30.00	—	—
11. Nirmalya	2,750.00	2,780.00	2,800.00	2,000.00	8,800.00
12. Chitrapati	—	230.00	220.00	300.00	315.00
13. Mali, Patfull & Sindur	--	—	—	50.00	55.00
14. Salt and leaves	110.00	130.00	150.00	175.00	10.00
15. Earthen pots	700.00	800.00	1,800.00	1,100.00	1,150.00
16. Rohinikund and Paduka Kund	850.00	870.00	1,210.00	1,005.00	1,450.00
17. Wheat, flour and spices	1,500.00	1,000.00	1,000.00	1,050.00	1,450.00
18. Fuel	3,500.00	—	—	—	—
19. Sale of ghee to deepa sellers	1,450.00	—	—	—	—
20. Polang oil	160.00	170.00	185.00	—	—
21. Licence to watch shows and umbrella	2,065.00	5,001.00	4,000.00	8,200.00	8,400.00
22. Narendra Sankalp Chandanghar	2,500.00	3,100.00	4,700.00	4,125.00	3,600.00
23. Paisa shop	150.00	155.00	165.00	165.00	170.00
24. Gundicha Madira	15,600.00	18,400.00	26,000.00	20,000.00	20,550.00
25. Sale of three cars	4,000.00	4,101.00	3,200.00	2,500.00	3,500.00
26. Kara Gumuta	2,100.00	1,550.00	2,325.00	2,350.00	3,800.00
27. Chandan Chakada	25.00	50.00	55.00	60.00	
28. Chandan Mandan	255.00	340.00	410.00	380.00	—
29. Chandan Deepa	22.00	25.00	27.00	25.00	—
30. Kitchen during Gundicha	370.00	—	200.00	240.00	—
31. Ghee, Salt & Chillies etc. during Gundicha	30.00	33.00	35.00	35.00	—
32. Making of Chhapan Bhog during Gundicha	30.00	32.00	35.00	36.00	—
33. Ghee Pradeep during Gundicha	85.00	90.00	95.00	235.00	—
34. Bhog Mandap	22.00	15.00	18.00	18.00	—
35. Darshan on Ganesh Puja day	21.00	—	—	—	—
36. Bala Dhupa articles	175.00	175.00	180.00	200.00	—
37. Sale of books under Banian tree inside temple	7.00	12.00	12.00	12.00	—
Total	*44,410.00*	*46,867.00*	*56,490.00*	*53,826.00*	*61.428.50*

Organisational changes

The articles required for the preparation of *Bhog* were at first supplied by tender system. As the things supplied by the contractors were not of good quality there were complaints by the *Sevakas* and the committee members. For sometime in the past articles were purchased weekly under the supervision of the Administrator. But this system also did not work properly because of administrative difficulties. It was decided to set up a co-operative store for the temple, *Sebakas* and *maths* in the temple. In fact, the Puri whosale co-operative store was allowed to open a branch of grocery store in the temple compound with a *Kutcha* shed. But they constructed a pucca building of 3 rooms and started functioning since the 10th June, 1964. It was contemplated that the store should pay *salami* of Rs. 20/-, a monthly rent of Rs. 100/- for the structure and a levy at 2 percent on the sale proceeds of fire wood and one percent of the sales of other articles.

During the year 1964-65, goods worth Rs. 1,27,870/- were purchased for the *Bhog* of the temple from the store. As the prices of the commodities purchased from the store were found to be higher than the market rates, the transactions with the store were stopped with effect from the 6th March, 1965.

As already stated the *nities* are so complicated and involve such a large number of *sebakas* that unless there is cooperation among them in helping one another and performing their duties timely there is bound to happen disorganization in the services. According to previous practice the *sebakas* concerned were to be sent for when their presence was required. There is a staff known as *Charcha* who used to go to them and call them. This calling of the sevakas naturally took time and on many occasions the *nities* were delayed.

Since the committee has taken over, there is regular supply of all articles required for *bhog* and the timings of different *nities* which are performed in a day have been fixed. The *sebakas* are intimated in advance their turns of services as per *Beda patra* and in such a situation the *sebakas* are expected to turn up in time to perform their respective services. To ensure timely performances of ritual services apart from intimating personally to the *sebakas* their turns of service the Committee put up in the notice board the names of the sebakas and time of services everyday so that the concerned sebakas take notice of their duties in advance.

In spite of these measures of informing their duties in advance there were lapses in the Seba puja and *nities* of the temple. The main causes of such irregularities are related to the rights, privileges, duties and obligations of sebakas which concern not only the temple administration but also all classes of *sebakas*. These issues gave rise to disputes among the sebakas who went on strike and created trouble in the organization of services.

A detailed list of the festivals which are observed in the temple is given in the Annexure - XII with temple rituals. The most important and famous is *Rath Jatra* or Car festival. Previously the feudatory states such as Daspalla and Ranpur used to supply required timber for the construction of three cars. Now the Government supplies the timbers from the Daspala and Ranpur forests, 862 logs of wood of prescribed girth and length are collected from Daspalla forest and 174 pieces of green timber from Ranpur forest. The timbers are transported by water ways upto Dandia located in the bank of the river Bhargavi and from there the *maths* located in Puri town used to transport the timbers by means ot bullock carts to the place in grand road in front of the palace of the Raja of Puri where the cars are constructed.

But now-a-days many *maths* fail to perform this customary duty and as a result carts are hired at a higher cost by the temple organization to transport the timber from the side of the river to the grand road. The carpenters used to provide their services for the construction of cars on payment of *Khei* and nominal charges. They have also defaulted in their work in the present time and the work is done by hiring carpenters at a high cost.

Repairing of existing buildings and construction of new structures are being taken up under the management of the committee for improvement of the temple. Some such works are listed below.

1. Construction taken up by the committee administration :

    (a) Reconstruction of R.C. roofed, two roomed house in the garden to the southwest of the temple for preparation of flower garlands for the deities.

    (b) Installation of water pump in the well in the above garden.

    (c) Clearance of vegetation from the above stated garden. For the works against items (a) and (b) Sri J. Dalmia donated one water pump run on motor and gave a cash donation of Rs. 500.00.

    (d) Electrification of the temple and its precincts with underground lines in the temple courtyard and removal of the old wiring which does not work properly due to leakage.

This work was done through Electricity Department of the State Government at a cost of Rs. 98,315.79. A sum of Rs. 65,000 has been deposited so far with the Executive Engineer, Electrical Division, Bhubaneswar and Rs. 33,315.79 is still payable. For this work a sum of Rs. 25,000/- was received from the Puri lodging house fund as matching grant and Rs. 40,000/- was paid from the temple fund during the period under report. Since the electrification of the temple is in the interest of the general Hindu public, the State Government has been moved to meet the entire cost of electrification and its maintenance.

    (e) The Bharat Chaturdham Veda Bhavan Nyas Trust proposed in 1963-64 to open a branch within the temple area, for which purpose the trust deposited a sum of Rs. 50,000 with the temple administration.

The foundation of the Veda Bhavan was laid on the 5th May, 1965. For preparation of the site and for the foundation lying a total sum of Rs. 1,932.39 was spent and with the interest accrued on the balance a total amount of Rs. 50,640/- was kept in the State Bank of India under fixed deposit.

2. Works executed by private voluntary organisations and other private persons.

The following temple improvement works have been done by a private body under the guidance of Pandit Shri Sadashiva Rath Sharma.

(a) Removal of trees, replastering and colouring, etc. of the *Dakhinighar* including the *Beharan Mandap.*

(b) Repairing, replastering and colouring of the Lion's gate.

(c) Improvement to *Beharan dwar* with extension, painting and colouring.

(d) Improvement to the gate to *Gumta* and *Baisi Pahachha* and the gate to *Ananda Bazar* from *Baisipahachha.*

(e) Shri Rama Chandra Mohapatra, one devotee from the Garabadu Sevak class has set up at the outer southern gate statues of two horses with riders there on and has effected decorative painting at his own cost.

In course of time some new avenues have been created as sources of income of the temple. A short account of a few of them is given below.

(i) *Anand Bazar* : The place surrounding the *Snan Vedi* in the North-Eastern corner within the compound of the temple known as *Anand Bazar* was in a very bad shape. It was repaired and cleaned and new shops were put up with electric fitting in a fashion befitting the name *Anand*

Bazar'. These shops were leased out from November, 1968 which fetch a monthly revenue of Rs. 5,148. A supervisor and an Assistant Supervisor were appointed to look after the area of collect the revenue.

(ii) A permanent cultural exhibition called Niladri Bihar in the North-West corner within the compound of the temple has been set up with effect from 22nd January 1969. It throws light on the various *nities* connected with the Jagannath temple. Cultural activities such as *Yogasan* training, instructions in music are also being undertaken in this place, *Satsanga* meetings are also held at this place. A priced bulletin namely 'Mandir Samachar' is being published from 22nd January, 1969.

(iii) *Roshai* : The kitchen area has also been improved and some of the dilapidated sheds have all been removed. Pilgrims are allowed to see the kitchen and its precincts from outside throughout the year on ticket basis.

(iv) *Laksmi Bhandar* : A branch of consumer wholesale co-operative store was catering to the needs of the temple. In its place a wholesale store to meet the requirements of *Kothabhog* (*Bhog* offered to Lord Jagannath by the Administrator) and those of the *Suar ṣebakas* who prepare *bhog* for the pilgrim has been started by the administrator of the temple. It has functioned from 1969 to the benefit of both the temple and the *sebakas* especially *Suar sebakas*.

(v) Transport services : A bus has been purchased and it plies as a public transport service in some sectors in Orissa. A driver and two cleaners have been appointed for this purpose. The income derived from January to March 1969 was Rs. 26,995.

In the *Anand Bazar* a *Mahaprasad sebasadan* has been started to enable those pilgrims who would like to take *Mahaprasad* in *Anand Bazar*. Better lighting has been arranged.

A public relation wing with an assistant has been started to announce nities of the temple to the public. The Mandir Samachar bulletin also publishes the rities in advance and other information regarding the temple for the information of the pilgrims. Certain pamplets and booklets containing information about the temple and other shrines and published by the temple and sold in the public.

Since the beginning of the temple administration by the committee in 1960 no rules or procedures for the temple office and staff in respect of service conditions, office procedures, travelling allowance and maintenance of records, etc were framed. Four regulations were framed by the committee in exercise of the power under section 31 of the Shri Jagannath Temple Act, 1955 are stated below.

(i) The Shri Jagannath Temple (office procedure, financial and misc.) Regulation, 1967.

(ii) The Shri Jagannath Temple (Employees condition of service) Regulation 1967.

(iii) The Shri Jagannath Temple (Employees Travelling Allowance) Regulation 1967.

(iv) The Shri Jagannath Temple (Revenue Estate, Encroachments, etc.) Regulation 1967.

After approval by the Government in the Law Department these regulations came into force with effect from the 17th November, 1967.

5
Ritual Functionaries, Ritual Festivals and Sahi Organisations

Ritual functionaries and their duties as mentioned in the record of Rights

In this section we shall describe the different sebakas and the services they perform in the temple. There is a popular notion among the people that the sebakas of Shri Jagannath temple consist of 36 kinds whose services in combination is called the *Chatisia Nijoga*. But it will be seen from the record of rights that there are more than 140 kinds of sebakas. Besides there are various other institutions and persons connected with the ritual services of the temple. In fact, there is no hierarchical order among the sebakas. Each sebaka has a specific duty to perform and they are all equal in the eyes of the Lord Jagannath, except that by the very nature of the services some sebakas have control over others, and being the founder of the temple and paramount king of Orissa, the Raja of Puri is recognised as the foremost sebaka of the temple. Therefore in the list of sebakas which is given below we have mentioned first the Raja and his services and then other sebakas.

Sl.No.	Sebaka	Function	Status
1.	Raja of Puri	Superintendence of the administrative matters of the temple at the apex level.	
2.	Parichha or *Parikhya*, Supervisior	Management of temple affairs and supervision of ritual services.	
3.	*Chhatisa Nijoga* Naik, Pattajoshi Mahapatra, Chief of 36 Sebaka *Nijogas*	Management and supervision of daily rituals, temple store and food offerings	
4.	*Bhirarachha*	Daily door opening of the temple and inspection of flower arrangements of the deities.	
	Muduli Mahajana	Decoration and adornment of the deities on festive occasions.	
	Amonia Parichha	Arrangement of food offerings and maintenance of its sanctity	
5.	*Talichha*	Light waving at the deities, daily door closing of the temple and inspection of food preparation in the kitchen.	
6.	*Mudrahasta* or *Mudaratha*	Ritual services of the Raja in his absence.	
7.	*Dewl Purohit*	To sanctify services and to preside over special ritual functions.	

8. *Puja Panda*	Worship of the guard-deities of the temple and inspection of food offerings placement.
9. *Badapanda*	Service supervision of the Puja Panda sebakas.
10. *Puspalaka*	Adornment, flower decoration and dressing of the deities.
11. *Mahajan*	Tiffin offerings to the deities
12. *Mudra*	Sandal paste supply for the anointment of the deities
13. *Khuntia*	Flower garlands and *Tulsi* leaves supply to the Puspalaka.
14. *Bhera Khuntia*	Arrangement of flower garlands to be sent to the palace
15. *Bileijaga Khuntia*	Cat-watching during food offerings
16. *Ghoda Barika Khuntia*	Cover fixing on the Lion's platform
17. *Rukunaharana Khuntia*	Story recitation
18. *Bhandara Mekapa*	Store keeping
19. *Palia Mekapa*	Flower decoration of the deities and inspection of door opening in the temple
20. *Akhanda Mekapa*	Lighting and arrangement of lamps
21. *Changada Mekapa*	Cloth arrangement of the deities

22. *Khataseja Mekapa*	Bed arrangement for the deities
Dambaru	Dambaru related works
Dandapahada	Carpet spreading
23. *Pratihari*	Name calling and door related rituals
24. *Daita*	All ritual services during car festival, *Nabakalebar* and *Anabasar*
25. *Pati Mahapatra*	Work of a Daita in his absence
26. *Patri Badu*	Ritual ingredients supply
27. *Garabadu*	Supply, storage and water pouring during ritual performances
28. *Saurbadu*	Floor clearing
29. *Bhogasaita Suarbadu*	Food collection after offerings
30. *Jyotisha*	Astrological calculations and forecasting
31. *Mukhapakhala Sebaka*	Supply of tooth sticks and tongue cleaners and flower in the morning.
32. *Ghatuai*	Amala, camphor and sandal paste supply
33. *Baitti* Sebaka	Road lighting between the kitchen and the offering place.
34. *Ghochhikar*	Entry control and regulation of the Pilgrims.

35. *Sunagoswami*	Lion's platform, cleaning and water collection for bathing ritual
36. *Muduli*	Store keeper of various articles such as cups, plates, whisk and camphor etc.
37. *Arati Balita*	Wicks supply
38. *Purana Panda*	Purana recitation during food offering
39. *Data Mahapatra*	Face cleaning of the deities
40. *Lugadhua Panikunda*	Water supply to the sebakas
41. *Lugadhua*	Cloth washing of the deities
42. *Ballava Jogania*	Sweets supply to the sebaks from the store
43. *Bimanabadu*	Palanquin/carriage lifting
44. *Anasara Sudha Suar*	Sweet water supply to the deities during Anabasar days.
45. *Sudhasuar*	Floor washing for food offering
46. *Hadapanaik*	Betel supply
47. *Bidia Jogania*	Betel preparation
48. *Asthana Pratihari*	Water sprinkling after food offering, distribution of food gift among sebakas

49. *Kothabhog Jogania*	Food ingredients and fuel supply to the kitchen from the temple store.
50. *Pradhani*	House calling of the Panda sebakas
51. *Paik*	Responsibility of engaging the sebakas other than the Pandas in their work
52. *Lenka Sebaka*	House calling of the sebakas and kitchen work
53. *Jagia Mahasuara* or *Rosa Amina*	Inspection of consecrated food preparation
54. *Badusuar*	Cake and sweet preparation
55. *Pantibadu, Bidua Panti* and *Ghia parasa*	Consecrated food related services
56. *Amalutoli* and *Purakharada*	Preparation of food ingredients
57. *Tlabadu*	Transportation of cooked food from the kitchen to the temple
58. *Rosapaik* sebakas	Intimation to the sebakas regarding the affairs of the kitchen
59. *Bahara Deula Suar*	Cake preparation in the kitchen of goddess Lakshmi
60. *Rosa Dhopakhalia, Angarua* and *Gobarapania, Dhopakhalia*	Kitchen and oven cleaning

61. *Handi Jogania* & *Tola* sebakas	Earth and earthen article supply
62. *Biribata Samartha*	Blackgram and rice grinding
63. *Kotha Bhoga Jogania*	Supply of new earthen pots to Mahasuara and suara sebaka from Handi Jogania
64. *Panikipata*	Fish cutting, goat butchering during Dasana and daily vegetable cutting
65. *Nikapa* or *Gandhan Nikapa*	Spices work
66. *Biribuha* sebakas	Blackgram and rice supply
67. *Daudibola* sebaka	Rope making
68. *Chunara Garuda* Sebak (*Mahadipa* and *Dwajabandha*)	Ritual services related to God Garuda
69. *Sebata Nijoga*	Service to pilgrims with regard to Hindu rites such as Sankalpa, Sradha and Dana
70. *Paniapata*	Utensil cleaning and water supply
71. *Mandani sebaka*	Canopy fixing on festive occasions
72. *Chaka Apasara Sebaka*	Pillow maintenance
73. *Mulia Suansia*	Supply of wooden materials
74. *Binakara* sebaka	Harp playing

75. *Darpania* and *Bairakhia*	Vessel washing, mirror firing and purnakumbha setting
76. *Kotha Suansia*	*Snan* arrangement for the visiting deities on festive occasions
77. *Mahabhoi*	Milk and milk product supply
78. *Gita Gobinda*	Devotional song recitation from Gita Gobinda
79. *Bhitara Gaani Devadashi*	Ritual service of singing devotional songs and performing dances
80. *Samprada Nijoga*	- do -
81. *Dayanamali*	Flower and Tulsi leaves supply and garland making
82. *Madeli*	Madal and musical instrument playing.
83. *Prasada badu*	Responsibility of sending foods from the temple to the place.
84. *Tatua*	Transportation of foods from the temple to the palace
85. *Patarbandha*	Leaves supply for packing
86 *Vaijayanti* sebaka	*Ghasa* (Musical instrument) playing
87. *Chhatra Nijoga*	Service of holding umbrella and other articles during regular ritual activities
88. *Sankhua*	Conch blowing.

89. *Parbajatra Joganis*	Food material supply from the store to the Mahasuara on festive occasions.
90. *Chitrakara*	Painting of the deities.
91. *Rupakara*	Drawing and painting on the walls of the temple and on the body of the chariot.
92. *Podar* or *Bania*	Jewellery making
93. *Tamarabisoi*	Copper plate supply on the day of Snana Purnima
94. *Karatia*	Timber works of the chariots
95. *Bentabindha Paik*	Ritual of arrow shooting in accordance with a myth
96. *Patarabisoi*	Cloth and dress works of deities.
97. *Kalabettia*	Chariot decoration
98. *Darji*	Tailoring works
99. *Kumbhara Bisoi*	Supply of earthen vessels for consecrated food preparation
100. *Rathabhoi*	Labourer's work in construction of chariots sheds and canopies
101. *Malachula* Seba	Garland making
102. *Banua*	Fire works

103. *Chakra Dihudia & Anasara Chuna Seba*	Responsibility of showing lighted candle in the procession and wheat grinding.
104. *Ojha Maharana* Seba	Blacksmithy
105. *Ghanta* Seba	Gond beating
106. *Ghantua*	Occasional gong beating
107. *Ratha Dahuka* sebaka	Singing songs on the car during car festival
108. *Badhei* Sebaka	Carpentry
109. *Vaidya*	Herbal medicine supply to the deities at the time of illness.
110. *Amunia chhatars*	Leading the food offerings procession with erected umbrellas.
111. *Chhamu dihudi*	Candle lighting
112. *Chapabehera*	Boat plying during *Chandan Jatra* and *Kaliyadalana*.
113. *Chapadelei*	Boat playing
114. *Mapasaita Karan* of *Mahaprasada* Seba	Supervision of the food distribution among the sebakas.
115. *Taddau Karan, Bhandar karan, Changada Karan* (*Sitta Karan*)	Record keeping maintenance of almanac supervisor of daily round services of the temple and festivals.

116. *Baiti Karan*	Accounts maintenance regarding income from flag and gift offerings on the Lion's platform.
117. *Kotha Karan*	Accounts maintenance regarding income from flag and gift offerings upto the Lion's platform.
118. *Carcaita Karan*	Inspection of the service of the sebakas
119. *Dayanapatri*	Ritual service related to Dayanachori festival
120. *Caulabachha Karan*	Service of refining and grinding rice and mung
121. Service rendered on personal basis	Ritual service based on individual capacity (whisk service)
122. *Deul Karana*	Inspection of the regular ritual services sebakas, festivals and distribution of Khei etc.

Festivals observed in Puri round the year

Mainly 12 such festivals are observed in Shrimandir at Puri round the year. There is a Sloka in Sanskrit which mentions these 12 festivals. The sloka is as follows.

"Manchasnanang Rathabaragathii Sayanang Chayane Dway
Parswabruthi Sayan Nibruti Prabrutaihi Pusyapuja
Dola Jatra Damanaka Mahotakhsa Puja Trutia
Chaibang Jatra Bidhini Gadita Dwadasaita Narendra"

In other words these 12 festivals are :

1. *Snana Jatra* : Month of Jestta on full moon day.
2. *Rath Jatra* : Month of Asadha Sukla Dwitiya (the second day of the bright fortnight of the month of *Asadha*)
3. *Sayana Jatra* : On the 11th day of bright fortnight in the month of Asadha.
4. *Dakshinayan Jatra* : On the day the sun begins to more to the equinox.
5. *Parswaparibartan* : On the 11th day of bright fortnight in the month of Bhadrava.
6. *Uthapana* : On the 11th day of bright fortnight in the month of *Kartik*.
7. *Prabarana Sasti* : On the 5th day of the bright fortnight in the month of *Margasira*.
8. *Pusyapuja* : On the full moon day in the month of *Pausa*.
9. *Uttarayana* : On the Makara Sankranti day when the sun moves towards the southern equinox.

10. *Dol Jatra*	:	Representative deities are taken out to Dol Vedi for the swing festival.
11. *Damanaka Chhaturdasi*	:	Festival observed in honour Damanaka (a deity)
12. *Akshya tritia*	:	The construction of the Chariots (cars) begins after Vanajaga ceremony is performed.

From the point of view of the pilgrims coming to Puri in large number the festivals such as Rath Jatra, Dol Jatra, and Akshya Tritiya are famous and important. The 12 festivals are described by K.C. Mishra in the Cult of Jagannath, published by Firma K.L. Mukhopadhaya Cal 1971.

In addition to these 12 important festivals many other festivals are observed in the Shri-Mandir from the period from Mesa Sankranti to Mina Sankranti.

Wards and Sahis and Sahi Jatras

Wards and Sahis

Puri town has many *Sahis* (streets), some of which are larger and older and others are of later developments as extensions of original ones. The old records maintained by the temple scribe show that there were seven main sahis. They are Bali sahi, Dolamandap sahi, Goudabada sahi, Harachandi sahi, Kundeibenta Sahi, Markendeswar sahi and Matimandapa sahi. The other sahis and localities are Baddei sahi, Balagandi sahi, Baseli sahi, Chadaganga sahi, Dandinals sahi, Daita Sahi, Dhanakathi sahi, Ganamala sahi, Gudia sahi, Gurruntee sahi, Karagouri sahi, Kalikadebi sahi, Karati sahi, Kapal mochana, Khatua sahi, Khuntia sahi, Kumuti sahi, Manikarnika sahi, Mausima, Pathuria sahi, Patna Jenapur, Patna Jagannathpur, Patna Balabhadra Ballava, Patna Matipada, Patna balisahi,

Patna Parrhee sahi, Patna Kumbharpada, Patna Tikarpada and Talichha sahi.

As pointed out above the sahis which are situated close to the Jagannath temple are inhabited by the sebakas of the temple and there are also minor temples, monastic houses, lodging houses, sacred trees and tanks, gymnastic centres or youth organizations called *Jagaghar* and *Akhada* scattered in different *sahis* throughout the town.

Sahi organization

Each of the main seven *sahis* has four headmen designated as Sahi Naik. They have assistants of barber caste who are called *Bhandari*. Among the young and adult men of the each sahi 16 able bodied adult men are chosen as *Bhendias* (*bhendia* means a strong and stout young men). The *Bhendias* work as wrestling instructors of *Jagaghars*, the club houses located in the sahis where the young and adult men practise gymanstic performances. Several *jagaghars* combine and function under the control of a bigger organization called *Akhada*.

The members of a *Jagaghar* are called *Sanga* (comrades). One who wants to be a *sanga* of a *jagaghar* should perform a ritual in which vermillion is anointed to the Mahabir, the presiding deity of the jagaghar and provide feast to the members. The nonmembers can learn gymnastic fits at the *jagaghar*, but they cannot be taken as members of it.

The *Naiks* of a *sahi* play an important role in organizing dance, drama and cultural performances related to various themes of sacred scriptures. Just as the Sebakas of the Jagannath temple have specific duties to perform as assigned by the Gajapati Raja of Puri and codified in the service record (*Karmani*) the Naiks of Sahis were also similarly assigned certain responsibilities which were also specified in the record of services. The nature of works which are entrusted to the Naiks is reproduced below from the service record.

"Four *sebaka* brahmins will remain in charge of *Naiks* in each sahi. They will be the head of all sebakas, royats, shop keepers and others of the sahi. All people of the sahi should cooperate with the Naiks so that they can function most effectively. Each household of sebaka community will pay a fee to the Naiks. Similarly the royats will also pay tax (Karachali) to them. A fee of one anna per rupee will be levied on each sale transaction of homestead land, orchard, etc. and given to the *Naiks.* They will set up a centre for cultural performance (*Akhada*) and enroll the Brahmin children in the centre and engage dance and drama experts to teach music and dance to these children. The expert drummers (*Madeli*) may also be appointed to teach them how to play on drums and help them to perform drama on themes selected from sacred scriptures and also narrations (Bachanika) on those subjects. The instructors giving training on these cultural performances will be given new cloths every month".

"The Naiks will see that fiestas and festivals such as birth ceremony of Krishna (Krishna janma) starting from the birth upto killing Kansa (Kansa Badha) and birth of Rama (Rama janma) are performed in the Sahis. In the case of Rama Janma all festivals starting from his birth to the killing of Ravana and thereafter to coronation ceremony will have to be performed. Similarly festivals connected with Baban Janma, Bali Raja and Sutanata during Devi parab will be performed. The divine play which is an aesthetic performance between Krishna and Radha and Gopies popularly known as *Rasalila* of the types such as Brindaban bihar, Basanta Rasa, Sarad Rasa etc., should be performed. During these festivals fire works, lighting of torches and candles beating of drums, singing of songs, decorations in multicoloured cloths of the pandals and places of worship will have to be arranged. When the Gajapati Raja is present in the palace at Bali Sahi in Puri the *Naiks* will show all these cultural performances to the Raja at the palace and thereafter proceed to the temple where they will repeat the same performances.

As per the orders of the Raja the concerned parties will be given saris. The required quantity of oil used for lighting purposes will be supplied to them".

"On the Siva Ratri the *Naiks* will arrange performances of the type called Ananda Nata at the temple of Astasambhu. They will also provide labourers (*Bethia*) as recruited from different sahis to draw the cars upto the temple. Whatever contributions and incomes are received from festivals will be given to the *Naiks* for their personal use. If there will be shortage of funds which are required for the performances of such fiestas and festivals the *Naiks* will meet that amount from their pocket".

It is necessary to give a detailed account of organizations of some important sahis. The description is started with Markendaswar sahi.

Markendaswar Sahi

The first king of Ananta Verma Chodaganga Dev of Ganga dynasty built the temple of Sri Markedaswar Dev and adjoining minor temples during the middle part of the 11th century and established a settlement there. In this settlement he got the Devadasis settled and as population increased subsidiary hamlets sprang up near the main settlement. The most important hamlets which were later on called as Sahis are Chudanga Sahi, Hadagadia sahi, Banambar sahi, Ratha sahi, Bimanbadu sahi and Baseli sahi.

In the Markendaswar sahi and its subsidiary sahis now live such categories of sebakas as *Biman Badu, Paniapata, Kottasuaansia, Dalabehera, Supakar, Pandasamanta, Jatri Panda* (Jatri) and among others who live there such castes as *Khandayat, Teli, Mahanty, Tanti* and *Gudia* are important. The sebakas of *Kottasuansia, Paniapata* and *Dalabehera* belong to *Khandayat* caste, Ballava seba to *Gudia* group, and *Chakradihudi* and *Khalilagi* sebas to Gola caste.

In Markendaswar sahi there is a *Akhada* called Bhagabati Kotha Akhada under which seven *Jagaghars* are present. They are 1. Rahasa Mahanty, 2. Bhatta jaga, 3. Satabakhara, 4. Badapokhari, 5. Duari jaga, 6. Panda jaga and 7. Bada Mahapatra jaga. Each *jagaghar* is called panchayat having a president and other office bearers. A short description of Duari jaga is given below.

Duari jaga

Raja Chodaganga Dev conferred *'Duari'* title on leading agriculturists and employed them in the temple. The service of a *Duari* is of the nature of checking food stuffs required for preparing bhog and watching at the door of the kitchen and outside it also. He was entitled to hold cane while on duty. Among them there was an important man named Basu Duari who was most favourite of the Raja of Puri. He was a great Tantrik like the then Raja of Puri and therefore in recognization of his *tantrik* qualities a *jagaghar* named as *Duari* was established in Markendaswar sahi. The *Duari jagaghar* or panchayat comprises a President, a vice-president, a Secretary and an Assistant Secretary, a Treasurer and 10 executive members. In all there are 100 members of the Panchayat varying in age within 25-60 years of age-group. The office bearers continue in their respective positions so long as everything goes well in the panchayat. However the office bearers are changed every three years. All members of the panchayat sit at the *jagaghar* and select the office bearers. Unanimity rather than majority vote governs the selection of office bearers. One who becomes a member of the panchayat need not pay any fee. He has only to spend something for anointing the goddess of the panchayat with vermilion.

The *Duari jaga* owns a building and land of Ac. 1.500 adjoining it. The presiding deity Mahabir is the owner of the homestead land and other lands of *jagaghar*. It has also a beautiful garden called *Ramitota* which belongs to the goddess Ramchandi attached to the *jagaghar.* The temple of Ramachandi which is 15ft. in height with a platform of 30ft. x 40 ft. which is attached to it and a pond are located in the garden. A priest is appointed by the Sangas of *jagaghar* to worship the goddess.

Dasara is observed at Ramchandi and a feast is prepared on the last Tuesday of the month of *Chaitra.* All the *Sangas* perform these festivals together. A sum of Rs. 200/- is spent on the feast. Public contribution is also used in the performance of festivals and preparation of feast.

The *jagaghar* has an annual income of Rs. 1400/- from various sources such as sale proceeds of cashew nut, coconut, polanga (a kind of seed yielding oil), fruits and fuel, and from fish reared in the tank and miscellaneous sources. Besides these sources they all collect in kind and cash from the passers-by who pass through the road by the side of which the *jagaghar* is located. The people carrying cartloads of fuelwood along that road give some fuelwood to the *jagaghar.* Similarly the brick makers who pass by that road donate some bricks and those with thatching straw put some bundles of straw while passing through the road. Several cases are referred to *jagaghar* for arbitration, and the persons involved in such cases have to pay fees which are deposited in the fund of *jagaghar* and the party considered guilty is generally fined by the members of *jagaghar.* These fines are collected then and there and deposited in the funds of *jagaghar.*

There are also several other sources from which the jagaghar earns some income. For example, when the tank called *Markeanda* located in the sahi is renovated by a contractor some amount is collected from him. The major portion of this amount is credited to the panchayat's fund and some amount is distributed among its members. Close to the tank live many fishermen of *Gokha* caste. When they are engaged to catch fish in the Markanda tank they give one fourth of the catch to the *jagaghar.*

The cases in which there is nothing confidential are adjudicated in the place where Mahabir is installed and those which are of confidential nature are tried in the temple of goddess Ramchandi.

The *Jagaghar* has to perform certain rituals connected with the temple of Sri Jagannath. It has to offer *Panti bhog* to Sri Sudarsan on the day of *Gamha Purnima* and on *Chakrabula Ekadasi* to Sri Krishna on the *Kaliadalana Ekadasi*, to Badi Nrusingh on the 9th day of Swing festival, and to goddess Lakshmi on the day of Rusi Panchami. According to the sacred scriptures Markanda Rusi is the manager of the store of the goddess Lakshmi. He renders accounts of the store to the goddesss on the Rusi Panchami day, Mung, fried rice, cucumber, green coconut, etc, are offered to the deities in the panti bhog and a sum of Rs. 100/- is spent on this account.

As pointed out above the jagaghar has a good mango grove and the mangoes from this garden are offered to the deities and consumed by the members of the panchayat. Some times some mangoes are also distributed among the people of the sahi.

The members observe the birthday of Sri Mahabir on *Pana Sankranti* and spend about Rs. 100/- on this occasion. Similarly they also observe Asokastami for which the members meet all the expenses out of their own pocket.

The *jagaghar* takes up new constructions and undertake repairing of the existing buildings and temples, renovates the tanks and maintains the garden properly. The buildings under its procession are all electrified for which a sum of Rs. 200/- is paid and the rent for the land amounting Rs. 10/- is paid to the Government.

The *jagaghar* has a spacious building used for gymnasium. The male members who are agnates of the members of the panchayat are allowed to attend physical training at this place. There is sufficient room for 10 people to practise physical exercise daily. Those who take part in gymnastic exercise also learn the skills of playing on drums particularly the type known as *Pakhaja* which is very popular among the sebakas.

There are two instructors for imparting physical training, one music teacher and an instrumentalist teaching the trainees the art of singing and playing on musical instruments and drums. All these instructors belong to Markendaswar sahi. The instructors hold their classes at the *jagaghar* two hours in the morning and two hours in the afternoon. The Government of Orissa had given a grant of Rs. 2000/- to the panchayat towards the expenses of musical instruments.

In the Markendaswar sahi the following items of cultural shows are performed.

1. *Putanabadha* (A demon names Putana who was trying to feed poison to Sri Krishna was killed by him).

2. *Jamuna Gadhua* (bathing in the river Jamuna). This is a scene of Gopis taking bath in the Jamuna river).

3. *Sri Krishna janma* (birth of Sri Krishna).

In the fiestas performed in the Sahi (Sahi jata) the following categories of actors take part most prominently.

1. *Sandhiasi* : The young boys dressed in half pants (*Janghia*), white caps and holding sword show various accrobatic and gymnastic performances.

2. *Naga* : A man is dressed like a *Paik*. The things which make up the dress of a Paik are knife held in hand, shield (*Dhala*) tied to the arm, sword (*talabar*) held in hand, battle axe (*Katuri*), arm band (*Bahuti*), bells (*Ghanti*), tied to thigh and waist, tiger's skin (*Baghachhala*), tiger' nail (*Bagha nakha*), gun (*Bandhuka*), head gear (*Handia*).

3. *Meda* : *Meda* is a wooden structure decorated beautifully with coloured clothes and other materials and having seats

for the deities to be installed and for men to sit and dance, etc. The meda is named after the deity which is being installed in it or after the occasion on which it is prepared. Thus there are Durga meda (meda for Siva and Durga), Kalika meda (meda for goddess Kali), Nrusingh meda (meda for Sri Nrusingh).

4. *Sattara* : A *Sattara* does not wear any head gear. He uses sticks to produce rhythm while singing. He sings only devotional songs.

Holding a banner (*nisana*) of red cloth which is called Mahibir Nisana a man sits on an elephant and leads the procession comprising the above mentioned actors in the following order - *Sandhiasi, Meda, Palabala,* (recitors of sacred texts), *Kela* and *Keluni* (a man taking the place of Kela caste - an untouchable and his wife) Sattara and Naga. As the procession proceeds the people at interval go on shouting the following couplet.

Mar Pathar Toda Darwaja Kileki Dewal
(Throw stone, break open door, pull down wall)
Raban, sala Gharme Chhupe Dikho Inka Hal
(Wife's brother Ravana hides himself in the house and see his plight)

The procession starts from the *jagaghar*. All people accompanying the procession have *darsan* of *Patitapaban* and go out of the temple through the southern gate. They proceed along the Lokanath road and come to the *Bada Akhada jagaghar* where they take rest and undress themselves. From there they come to the place where Sri Sanketaswar temple is located. It is located at a *ghat* and from this ghat they sail by boat to the mouth of Harachandi. In the boat the boys will be dancing and some people will be grinding *bhanga* an intoxicant mixed in water to drink. It is most popular drink among the sebakas. From the mouth of Harachandi they proceed to a place called Narasingh Patna. It is at this place that the garland of order of

Sri Jagannath is offered to the goddess Harachandi. The *Mahaprasad* carried with them is also offered to the goddess. A goat is sacrificed and offered to the goddess. Thereafter they return to Narasingh Patna belonging to the Pandit math. They stay there for two days and spend time in eating and drinking. Varieties of food, fish and mutton are cooked and eaten and the time is spent in great merriment. The party returns to Puri after two days.

As regards other *Jagaghar* every one has a history of origin and used to perform festivals with equal elaborations as is done by the *Duari jagaghar*. But for the last two decades or so some of them have altogether stopped performing such fiestas. The *Jagaghars* such as *Panda jega* and *Satabakara* have been performing Ashokastami and *Bhatta jega* continues the festival or Nrusingh chaturdasi.

In other sahis there are similar Akhadas and Jagaghars. They have each a history of origin, organizational arrangements, specific fiestas and festivals to perform and ritual associations with the temple. However, under the influence of modern times the festivities and other functions such as physical training and musical performances show a great deal of attenuation in most cases.

The different sahis are not separate entities. They are connected with one another in various ways. One of the media through which they are more intimately associated with one another is the festive ceremonies which are performed in different sahis. These are called *Sahijatra* (festivals of sahis). For a better understanding of the inter relationship between the sahis it is necessary to give an account of the *sahijatra*.

The *sahijatra* starts from the 9th days of the bright half of the month of *chaitra*. The seven principal sahis of Puri perform these festivals in cooperation with one another. On the 9th day of the bright half of the month of *Chaitra* a festive procession comprising Rama, Lakshman, Bharat, Satrughna and Sita with Rusyasrunga starts from the *Akhada* of Kalikadebi sahi. It is on this day that the birth ceremony of Rama is observed in the temple. The party proceeds to the temple and after having *darshan* of Sri Jagannath who is adorned with the dress of Rama and receiving the garland of order (Agnya Mala) from Sri Jagannath leaves the temple and visits different maths and collects some contribution from each of them and then visits some important houses and also collects some contribution from them and thereafter returns to their sahi.

On the 10th day another festive party called *Nakakana* (nose and ear) starts from Harachandi sahi. The people comprising the party represent the demons. They dress themselves like demons and start from the *Akhada* of Harachandi sahi. Dancing and singing in accompaniment of music they enter the Bali sahi and from there they proceed to the temple and then finally reach Jagannath Ballava Math. At this math they undress themselves and there that day's part of the festival is finished.

On the 11th day the epic hero Parsuram starts his journey from the *Akhada* of Harachandi Sahi. No other castes except the sebakas can play the part of Parsuram and the privilege of being dressed like Parsuram is confined to three or four families of Harachandi Sahi and it is these families which act as Parsuram on a hereditary basis. However a change has come about in this regard. In the last 8 to 10 years other people having good physique are acting as Parsuram.

The Parsuram visits the houses of noted families and recites his valor and deeds and collects contributions from them. He does this for two days and on the last day after having darsan of Sri Jagannath goes to Jagannath Ballava Math where he is killed. These are all theatrical actions, nothing real. For this purpose three members of the *Akhada* of Markandaswar Sahi dressed as Rama, Lakshman and Sita proceed from their *sahi* to Jagannath Ballava Math through the temple of Sri Jagannath and fight with Parsuram and kill him. It is known that the acting of Parsuram was not originally of the Harachandi sahi. But three decades back the Matimandap sahi had transferred this festival on sale from their *Akhada* to that of Harachandi sahi.

6

Pilgrimage to Puri in History and Contemporary Period

Puri as a Pilgrim Centre

Before describing about the pilgrimage to Puri in the past and in contemporary period it is necessary to go into the question of since when did Puri became a famous pilgrim centre and the idol became so celebrated as to attract hundreds of Pilgrims from different parts of the country. The antiquity of Puri and the cult of Jagannath are still shrouded in history. In specific terms to fix the time of the importance of Jagannath in Puri town is quite impossible. Puri was known in the past as *Purusottama Khetra*, because the presiding deity of this *khetra* was formerly known as *Purusottama* and by virtue of the name and fame of this deity the Purusottama Khetra has been enjoying a position as one of the foremost religious centres of India. Besides this name Purusotama Khetra the city is also known as *Niladri*, *Sri Khetra*, *Sankha Khetra*, *Jamnika Khetra* and *Martya Baikuntha*. So great is the majesty of the presiding deity which goes by the name Jagannath that all people are equal before him, and all social distinction of caste and creed and nationality disappear in the presence of his greatness and sanctity. The cult of Jagannath is considered to be the embodiment of various sects and therefore Puri is considered to be *Sarva Dharma Samanwaya Dhama* which is taken as one of the seven *Mokshapuris* or salvation city of the Hindu faith.

As mentioned above the history of Purusottama Khetra or the cult of Purusottama Jagannath is of great antiquity. The *Kapila Sanhita* refers to the Purusottama Khetra as the one that takes away sin. The *Matsya Purana* which is one of the oldest *puranas* has a reference to Purusottam but there is no mention of Jagannath. But the Puranas which came later on make references to Jagannath as a presiding deity of the Purusottama Khetra.

Jagannath makes his first appearance in history in 318 A.D., when the priests fled away with his image to escape the wrath of *Raktabahu* and his army. After about 150 years later the holy log of the image of Jagannath was recovered by a noble prince. Murari Mishra has given reference to Lord Purusottama who was being worshipped on the seashore. That there was an earlier temple of Jagannath at *Purusottama Khetra* prior to the present one built by Chodaganga Deb in 12th Century A.D. One point which requires mention regarding the antiquity of Purusottama Jagannath is that Anncharlott Eschmann, Hermann Kulke and Gaya Charan Tripathi have mentioned in the book the Cult of Jagannath and the Regional Tradition of Orissa that "the entire early period of 600 years from the 4th century to the beginning of the 10th century A.D. there is not even the slightest hint in any inscriptional or archaeological sources of the existence of a Purusottama Khetra in Orissa or of a Jagannath temple on the seashore. But in the '*tirthayatra*' section of *Vanaparva* of Mahabharata there is a mention of *Svayambhu Lokesvara* and the *Vedi*, a famous spot in Puri itself, thus testifying to the antiquity of Puri as a place on the pilgrim's route"[1] L.S.S. O' Malley in Bihar and Orissa district Gazetters, Puri has mentioned, "The Jagannath Pilgrimage appears to be at least eight centuries old, for in an inscription dating back in 1137 A.D. We find mention of a pilgrim who went to the sacred Purusottama Khetra and gave away his wealth in charity on the noisy shore of the sea"[2]. Throughout these centuries the magnificence of the temple, with its elaborate rituals, the liberal royal patronage is enjoyed, the development of Vaishnavism, the catholicity of worship it inculcated, have combined in attracting attention to Jagannath and year after year a steady stream of pilgrims has flowed to the temple by the sea inspite of the great difficulties of the journey.

Thus it shows that pilgrimage to Puri was of great antiquity. No inscriptions refer to the present temple, the construction of which probably started after 1135 A.D. The Madala Panji's tradition is that an older dilapidated temple was pulled down in order to build the present temple. Thus there existed a famous Purusottama temple in Puri during the Somavansi rule Mahasivagupta Yayati Kesari II (cir AD 1023-1040) 11th century and it was widely known since the middle of the 11th century.[1] As stated above under the liberal royal patronage of the dynasties which followed the temple became famous and widely known as a great pilgrim centre which was visited by thousands of pilgrims from different parts of the country. For example, Ananga Bhima Dev III (1198-1223) built the present Jagannath temple and appointed different categories of ritual functionaries called *chhatisa nijog* performing different ritual services in the *sebapuja* of the Lord Jagannath.

After the rulers of Ganga dynasty came Kesari dynasty, Surya dynasty, and Bhoi dynasty which succeeded Somavansi rulers in succession donated vast landed properties, established Sasan villages and donated precious stones, Jewellery and ornaments, etc. which enhanced the fame of the deities and the temple and attracted thousands of pilgrims from different parts of the country during festivals and on many ritual occasions throughout the year.

This famous temple of Lord Jagannath also known as Sri Mandir stands on the holy ground of *Sri Khetra* or *Purusottam Khetra* and also described as *Sankha Khetra*. Located between Lat. $19^{0}18'$ and 17"N and Long. $85^{0}51'$ and 39"E, this majestic edifice is 214.66 feet in height from the ground level standing on a raised platform of stone (area 420000 sqft.) and surrounded by an outwall known as *Meghanada Pacheri* of 665 ft in length and six metres in height as well as by an inner wall *Kurma Bedha* of 420 feet in length. The sanctum-sanctorum contains the *Ratna Bedi* (throne of chlorite) and over this five-feet high platform are seated the three deities Balaram, Subhadra and Jagannath. Within the inner compound there are several shrines, small temples, sacred trees and other sacred places which the pilgrims visit during their pilgrimage to Puri. The Kendupatna copper plates give credit to Codaganga (1078-1147 A.D.) as the builder of the present temple of Lord Jagannath.

One word may be mentioned regarding how and when the *Purusottama Khetra* came to be known and called as Puri. The Europeans referred to it as "*Jekanat*" or "*Jaggarnat*". After the British conquest the town was sometimes called "*Jaggarnath-Poore*". Mr. W.Hamilton in his description of Hindustan (1820) mentioned the place as "*Jaggarnati*", "*Jaggarnathpoor*" and "Poore". Sterling in his account of Orissa (1824) used both "Jagarnnath-Poore" and simply "Pooree". Later the term Pooree was abbreviated and changed to simply Puri which is being used since the last half of the 19th century.

L.S.S.O' Malley in Bihar and Orissa District Gazetteers Puri (1929) mentioned "The Jagarnnath Pilgrimage appears to be at least eight centuries old (p. 124). It is certain that after the construction of the present temple of Jagannath during the period of Anantavarman Codaganga Deva sometime between 1135 A.D. and Mid-12th century A.D., the pilgrimage to Puri must have increased considerably. That there was an earlier temple of Jagannath at Purusottam Khetra prior to the present one built by Chodaganga Deva in 12th century AD is proved by the mention of Davayatana of God Purusottama in Krishna Mishra's Prabodha Chandrodaya Natakam (c. 1078 AD). Thus it is probable that pilgrimage to Puri may have taken place much earlier to 12th Cen. AD.

In any case the pilgrimage to Puri is something of great antiquity and it is impossible to deal with this subject since that time. Considering the limitations of time and financial provisions the study is confined to a period beginning from the Mughol rule through Maratha administration to the British Raj extended to the present time. The description of pilgrimage during the first two periods, that is, the Mughol and Maratha periods is sketchy whereas that of the later periods, that is, the British rule and post British contemporary period has been somewhat elaborately dealt with.

The Pilgrims

As already mentioned that Pilgrimage to reputed holy places have ever been so popular in India, but no pilgrimage was ever so extensively practiced and so generally famed as that of pilgrimage to Jagannath. The legend relating to discovery of Jagannath by *Bidyapati* in a forest where *Biswabasu* was worshipping him and the construction of temple in the seashore at Puri for instalation of the deity in the temple. Consecration of the temple and the deity by Brahma himself who came down to Puri on invitation from the then Raja *Indradyumna* and royal patronage that the Puri temple received from the Hindu kings from one dynasty to another are some of the circumstances which made the idol most sacred and celebrated and widely known in the country. Thousands and thousands of pilgrims including famous saints like Sankaracharya, Chaitanya, Ramanuja, Kabir, Nanaka and many others of different sects came on pilgrimage to Puri during festivals and other ritual occasions which are observed at Puri. For the last 10 centuries covering the period of Ganga dynasty up to the present day the temple has stood in the shore of Bay of Bengal, with the Lord of Universe, Lord Jagannath. Here is the national temple whither thousands and thousands of pilgrims coming from every part of the country even from abroad flock together to worship Lord Jagannath. Groome, one of the Collector of Puri appointed by the British Government in the year 1803 has given an elaborate account of the pilgrims resorting to the temple of Jagannath.

The pilgrims used to come from different directions. Those coming from the north passed through a place called *Khunta* on the border of Mayurbhanj state and continued upto Atharanalla at the entrance of Poorshuttam or Puri. The pilgrims coming from the south were entering the holy city through Lokanath. These entry points such as the Atharanalla Ghat and Lokanath Ghat were set up enabling the officers stationed at those places to collect the tax from the pilgrims. The number of pilgrims coming on pilgrimage to Puri runs to thousands. Of all the festivals the Car festival attract thousands of pilgrims from all corners of the country. Various authors have estimated the number of pilgrims who visited Puri during Car festival and all other festivals from the early period of British rule up to the present time the yearwise figures have been given in the Annexure XII.

Types of pilgrims

There are many types of pilgrims depending upon their economic condition, sect affiliation, nativity. An account of different types of pilgrims is given below.

1. ***Panchakosi Jatri***

   These pilgrims belong to Puri town and the neighbouring areas covering the villages within 5 *Kosas* (10 kms.). Specifically the area covers upto Pipli in the north Konark in the east. Brahmagiri in the west. Of course the area which comes under *Panchakosi* may be more than 5 *Kosas*. The pilgrims of *Panchakosi* have no specified Pandas nor they used to pay any pilgrim tax in the past.

2. ***Pancha tirtha Jatri***

   The pilgrims belonging to this category were untouchables. They came only to go to *panchtirthas* located in Puri town. The places under Panchatirthas are 1) *Markanda*, 2) *Swetaganga*, 3) *Mahodadhi*, 4) *Chakratirtha*, 5) *Indradyumna*. They used to pay only

Rs. 4/- towards the pilgrim tax and had *Darshan* of the *panchtirthas* with the help of *Choukidars*.

3. ***Desi Jatri***

The pilgrims coming from the area which covers the Baitarani river in Jajpur district were called *Desi Jatri*. They are also exempted from the pilgrim tax.

4. ***Lal Jatri***

The Jatris belonging to this category are the richest of all categories of the pilgrims. When they were coming via Atharanalla they used to pay tax at the rate of Rs. 10/- per head and Rs. 6/- per head if they came via Lokanath ghat. They were allowed to stay at Puri for a period of 30 days. The permit ticket which was issued to them were of red colour. They were permitted to go to the temple holding *Chamar* (whisk) in day time and *Masal* (torch) at night.

5. ***Nim lal Jatri***

The pilgrims used to pay tax at the rate of Rs. 5/- per head if they came from North via Atharanalla and Rs. 3/ - if they came from south Via Lokanath ghat.

6. ***Bhurunga Jatri***

The pilgrims used to pay tax at the rate of Rs. 2/- per head if they came via Atharanalla. They were permitted to stay in Puri town for only 4 days.

7. ***Khairati Jatri***

The pilgrims who are local people, Government servants, poor people, destitutes, diseased, police, sipahi, and messengers, belong to this category and they were exempted from payment of any tax.

8. ***Gangajali Jatri***

The pilgrims of this category used to carry water from the rive Ganges and pour them on the deity Lokanath and then have *darshan* of the Lord Jagannath and there after go back home. They were exempted from payment of any tax.

9. ***Bairagi Jatri***

The *Sanyasi*, diseased, destitutes, and those having no shelter anywhere like wandering *sanyasis*, a mad persons who come under this category did not have to make any payment of taxes.

10. ***Dandabhanga Jatri***

The *Jatri* of this category covers the journey not by walking but by means prostrating his body on the road and then getting up and again prostrating. This way he covers the distance from the point he left for pilgrimage until he reached his destination, that is, Puri.

11. ***Pousa Gaya Jatri and Gangasar Jatri***

After offering manes to the ancestors at Gaya the pilgrims visit Puri on pilgrimage to have *darshan* of the Lord Jagannath.

12. ***Mala Jatri***

The pilgrims belonging to different parts of the country and even some of them coming from abroad come on pilgrimage to Puri. Generally the pilgrims take help of *Jatri Pandas* and *Jatri Gumasthas* for *Darshan* of the deity and for going round *Sri Kshetra* to touch upon the sacred places and sacred objects. For the services rendered by the *Pandas* and their assistance, they make some payments to them according to their means. But these categories of pilgrims do not take any help from the Pandas nor they pay anything to them. Therefore the Pandas have given them as name as Malajatri or dead pilgrims.

Like the above mentioned divisions of the pilgrims there were also divisions according to their nativity. There divisions are -

1. *Jaleswar Jatri* : Those *Jatris* coming from the northern localities of the Mahanadi river were designated as such.

2. Southern *Mahajatri* : The pilgrims coming from Singhbhum, Gujarat, Agartala, Gaurakumuti, Kendujharia, Budia, Bundeli were called southern *mahajatri*.

3. Western *Jatri* : The *Jatris* coming under this category belonged to Marahatta, Nagpur, Garhmandala, Chhatisgarh, Sambalpur, Ranpur, Kamatelenga, Shri Baishnaba, Kalahandi, Bastar, Raipur, Jaypur, Raygada, Gunpur, Paratikali, Tarala, Badakhemundi, Jarada, Manjusa, Mahuri, Sorada, Seragarh, Ghumsar.

For collection of taxes and for regulation of tax collection centres were established at Narsinghpur, Jobra, Gundichaghar, Mangalaghat, Lokanath ghat, Atharanala, and Puri sadar office. Besides these centres Khunta of Mayurbhanj was also a place where a collection centre was established permit cards were issued to the *Jatris* for entry into Puri town. Also exit cards were issued while leaving Puri town. This permit card issued for their return journey was called *Khalasi* letter.

Prof. Prafulla Chakrabarti, K.C. Malhotra and Ila Pal had undertaken a study on Puri Pilgrims in the year 1978. This study gives details about area of origin of pilgrims etc. is reproduced under Annexure 17. This study is also included in the list of Reference Literature.

The pilgrims of different categories were interviewed during field investigation and the data collected from them are mentioned below. For lack of space only one pilgrim of each category has been mentioned below to illustrate the point.

Pilgrims and their visit to Puri during the Car Festival and other festivals - Personal interview with some selected pilgrims

The pilgrims are classified into various categories depending upon their nativity and sect affiliations and special characters. The interviews with each category of the pilgrims are presented below in the English version of their speech in their mother tongue.

1. ***Panchakosi Jatri*** :
   (Jatri belonging to the locality within a radius of 5 Kosas (10 kms).

The area under reference is located with Pipli village in the north (at a distance of 50kms from Puri), with Konark in the east (at a distance of 60 kms from Puri) with Brahmagiri in the West (at a distance of 30 kms). In reality the area which is called Panchakosi is not within a radius of 10 kms. It is located within a radius on an average of 40 kms to 60 kms.

The pilgrims belong to the clean castes like Brahmin, Kshatriya, Vaishya, and Sudra. The pilgrims do not have any hereditary Pandas. Any Panda available during their visit to Puri serves them and takes care of them, offers bhog on their behalf to the deities, makes necessary arrangement for their visit to different holy places located in and around Puri town, takes care of their boarding and lodging at Puri if they halt for sometime at Puri. The pilgrims of Panchakosia category are not so much well to do to make lucrative payments to the Pandas as the pilgrims of higher means do and their stay at Puri is not very long. It does not exceed a day. Since Puri is at a walking distance from most of their village they leave Puri the same day they came to Puri.

2. ***Pancha tirtha jatri :***
   (Pilgrims coming on a visit to cover Panchatirthas - five minor pilgrim centres located in Puri town).

The pilgrim of this category who was interviewed is Haria Bhoi by name of 38 years of age. He is a male pilgrim of Bauri by Caste. He belongs to the Bhoi ward of Biranarasinghpur Sasan village situated in the bank of Bhargavi river flowing on the north of the Puri town at a distance of 12 kilometres from Puri town. He came on bicycle by road from his village 12 other persons from his village accompanied him all by bicycle which took one and a half hour one way and their stay at Puri covers a day. All these people of younger age group belonging to the age range between 20 years and 35 years.

They visited such places as Markanda tank, Swetaganga, Sea, Indradyumna temple and tank, Sunar Gouranga, Chakratirtha, Narendra tank, the well called *Deddasura Bhaibohu* (husband's elder brother-younger brother's wife) and Swargadwar (Gateway to heaven). These pilgrims have no specified Pandas attached to them traditionally on a hereditary basis and they reside on the Verandah of the shops on the *Bada danda* (great grand road).

They came to perform hair cutting ceremony and their total expense at Puri was of Rs. 72/- (Food worth Rs. 60 + charges of hair cutting ceremony of Rs. 12/-).

The main purpose of visit to Puri was to observe Snana Jatra (bathing festival) going round at Puri, and fulfilment of wishes. They expressed that they belong to untouchable caste and therefore do not enter the temple out of fear. Those who want to see Lord Jagannath they come to Puri on the Snana Purnima day and have *darsan* of the Lord on the Snana Mandap by standing in the grand road. But they satisfy themselves by having darsan of *Patitapabana* at the eastern gate of lion's gate.

3. *Nimna Lal Jatri*

The name of the pilgrim was Dwaraka Nath Jha, Professor of Banaras University. He was Brahmin by caste and of 48 years of age. Those who accompanied him were 4 other Professors, 3 lady professors and 5 students. They travelled by train from Benaras to Puri and stayed at Puri for 3 days. During their stay at Puri they had *darshan* of Lord Jagannath in the temple, Gundichaghar, Swargadwar, Shri Lokanath and Chakratirtha, Jagannath Sanskrit University and Sadasiva Central Sanskrit Vidyapittam.

Their Jatri Panda was Shrinath Khuntia of Harachandi Sahi, Puri. They came by themselves and engaged Shrinath Khuntia at Puri to help them in going round the town. They also stayed in the Jatri Panda pilgrimshed located near the western gate of the temple. They spent about Rs. 21,200 on different items of expenses such as travelling requiring Rs. 8000/ - Annadana Atika worth Rs. 7000/- food expenses of Rs. 3200/ - and the Misc expenses of Rs. 3000/-.

They came to Puri to spend sometime at leisure and visiting some new places. What they said about their experience at Puri are narrated below. They said that the people gave much importance to visit Puri on pilgrimage and have *darshan* of the Lord Jagannath. They had the opportunity of having *darshan* of Biswanath at Benaras. But the *darshan* of Lord Jagannath was rare. By staying in the pilgrim shed of Shrinath Khuntia they had the chance of eating dried sweets and *mahaprasad*. They saw the two educational institutions - Shri Jagannath Sanskrit University and Sadasiva Sanskrit Vidyapittam located at Puri.

The sanitary condition of the town appears to be unsatisfactory. But the sea shore is most enjoyable and comfort giving. We heard that the Jatri Panda were misbehaving and illtreating the pilgrims. But out experience at Puri does not prove it. The Panda who is attached to us is a perfect gentleman and well behaved. The Panda made all arrangements for seeing the

Car festival without any difficulty and without any trouble. They had opportunity to have darshan of Lord Jagannath twice at Gundichaghar.

Nimna Lal Jatri :

The name of the pilgrim was Suvendu Goyal of 54 years of age and milkman by caste, belonging to Rajasthan. The other pilgrims who accompanied him are 51 in number. Of them 38 persons were adults of both male and female persons, 7 boys and 6 girls. They hired a bus and came to Puri via Cuttak and Bhubaneswar where they halted two days. They took 4 days in the journey and had plans to spend 4 days at Puri. They came to see the Jagannath temple, Gundichaghar, Sunargouranga, Chakratirtha, Swargadwara and Shrilokanath.

Their Jatri Panda was one who was Aujun Sarangi by name of Baseli Sahi, Puri. They came on invitation by Jatri Panda. They settled at the pilgrim shed of the Jatri Panda, and some of them also stayed at the Jyoti hotel. In the journey and stay at Puri they incurred expenses to the extent of Rs. 4000/-.

The purpose of their visit was to witness the car festival and visit other places of religious importance. The experience he gained and other matters which he narrated are given below.

To visit different pilgrim centres located in different parts of country was hobby of this man. This year he had a good crop and he got constant profit out of his business. Therefore he did not meet any difficulty in arranging the funds required for his pilgrimage. He contacted some interested persons of his neighbourhood. The bus owner was also interested in coming to Puri because he had not seen the place before. Therefore he was eager to give his bus on rent to come on a visit to Puri. At Puri we got down near *Gundichaghar* where the bus was kept. Since the souchalaya maintained by Puri Municipality was present at the place where they kept the bus and there was Indradyumna tank near by they had no difficulty in taking bath at Puri.

Next day the *Jatri Gumasta* of their *Jatri Panda* took them and made all arrangement for their stay in the pilgrimshed of their *Jatri Panda*. As there was no sufficient accommodation 17 persons of the group stayed in the hotel and lodging houses. The Jatri Panda made all arrangements for their visit to different places at Puri and neighbouring areas. He also made arrangements for offering *Annadana Atika* for which they paid Rs. 500/- to the Jatri Panda. They liked to spend hours at the sea beach and loved to stay one or two days more at Puri which was very much attractive to them.

Desi Jatri : (Pilgrims of our Country)

His name is Manabendra Maiti of 40 years of age, a male pilgrim of scribe caste of Udalay, Mayurbhanj district, Orissa.

He came by a reserve bus with fifty six other passengers who also came on pilgrimage. They spent overnight at Barabati in Cuttack town and resumed their journey to Puri early morning next day. Of the 56 passengers - 35 persons were adults. 14 persons were boys and girls and older persons were 7 in number. They all stayed at Puri for 7days and visited such places as Konark, Sakhigopal, Piplii, Raghurajpur, Jagannath temple, Shri Lokanath, Panchatirtha, Swargadwara, Chakratirtha, Alarnath, Satapada, Chilika, Sidhamahabir, different maths, Gundichaghar (Mausima).

The pilgrim party was assisted in their visit to different places as mentioned above and in their stay at Puri by the Jatri Panda Purna Chandra Tiadi. The Jatri Panda went to their native place and told them to pay their visit to Puri on pilgrimage. On reaching Puri they were provided accommodation in the pilgrimshed maintained by the Panda. It is estimated that each of the pilgrims on an average spent about Rs. 2000/- in the pilgrimage.

The objective of their visit to Puri to witness the car festival and have *darshan* of the Lord Jagannath, to visit the near by sacred places and fulfillment of their desire.

The journey was comfortable because they travelled in a reserve bus. The owner of the bus belongs to Puri town and therefore he could find out a suitable Jatri Panda for the pilgrims. He also found out a pilgrimshed for the pilgrims and made all necessary arrangements for their boarding and lodging. As the sanitary arrangements were not adequate in the lodging they took bath in the tanks present in the Puri town. The Jatri Panda gave his personal attention to travel to visit different places in and around Puri.

The pilgrims arranged in the shed for cooking their food and sleeping at night. After attending to their ablutions early morning they used to go out to have *darshan* of the deities in the temples, *maths* and other places. They also visited different tanks and sacred sites located in the Puri town. Puri appeared to them like a heaven upon earth and felt that both the day time and night was alike. One day they faced some trouble regarding payment to a Panda. But when they told him that they were under the care of so and so Jatri Panda the trouble was subsided.

It was the experience of these pilgrims that the people of Puri were unable to understand the Oriya language which were speaking and they felt that there was difference in the dialect they spoke and that the local people of Puri speak.

Dandapaka jatri

Dandapaka Jatri (the pilgrim who covered the journey to Puri by prostrating on the ground and then getting up and again prostrating the whole distance from starting place to Puri town).

The name of the pilgrim who covered the distance in this way was Rajendra Kumar Biswal. His age was 23 years and he was a farmer by caste. He belonged to Delang of Puri district. He covered the journey from his native place by prostrating and advancing towards Puri. He covered the distance in 12 days and his father and elder brother accompanied him to Puri. He spent only one day at Puri.

During his stay at Puri he went round many sacred places including Shrimandir, Shri Lokanath, Panchatirtha. He had no Jatri Panda to assist him and he is stayed in Goeinka Dharmasala. He spent a sum of Rs. 600/- on the following items. (1) Food Rs. 400/- (2) Offering to Gods Rs. 100/- (3) Cloths Rs. 100/-. Total Rs. 600/-.

The purpose of his journey of pilgrimage to Puri was to fulfill his desire. Being the only son of his parents and because of his young age his father and his uncle's son accompanied him in his journey to Puri. They carried his food, his clothes and other belongings and walked the distance along with him. Early morning on the day he started his journey. He took his bath and was determined to cover the distance by means of prostration. He put on a new cloth and prayed to Lord Jagannath and started his prostration. For some hours in the beginning he felt uneasy but later on he did not feel any trouble nor any difficulty. He walked by prostration in the day time and took complete rest at night. He took rest on the way in such places where there were shops. When he reached at Batamangala he got courage and strength to cover the remaining distance by prostration. When he was crossing Atharanalla he recalled the vocational song recited by a devoted person Saria by name.

From a distance he saw the Jagannath temple and felt that he was getting relief gradually. Next day he left *Batamangala* and started his journey towards Puri. On the way many devoted persons asked him why he had undertaken his journey by prostration. He replied to all that it was the desire of the Lord Jagannath.

On reaching the grand road he came across two Gumastas of the category of Dhulia Gumastha. They gave him a advice as to what he should do in order to fulfil his desire. On reaching the Lion's gate he had *darshan* of *Patitapabana*. Then he went to *Sweta Ganga* and had his bath there. Thereafter he went to the temple through the southern gate. A Jatri Panda offered to the deities whatever food stuff he gave. The Panda was so kind enough that he arranged Mahaprasad out of his own pocket for him and other two persons who accompanied him. He gave the Panda Rs. 5/- who accepted it with great reluctance. Being pleased with him for what he did to have *darshan* of the Lord Jagannath he gave him a token help of Rs. 50/- to spend on his way back home.

Jaleswar Jatri

The name of the pilgrim who was interviewed was Gangadhar Pani of 70 years old. He was Brahmin by caste of Bhograi village of Baleswar district. He came by bus upto Baleswar railway station and from there Via Naraj took another train to reach Puri. It took nearly two days in the journey from his home to the Puri town. The persons who accompanied him consisted of 4 newly married couples, 8 family persons, 5 housewives, 3 widows, 2 old persons, and 7 children- a total of 33 persons.

All of them stayed for 3 days at Puri and during their stay at Puri they went into the Jagannath temple to have *darshan* of the deities. They also visited Shri Lokanath, Panchatirtha, Swargadwara, Girinanabanta math. Their Jatri Panda was Manoranjan Sinhari who brought them to Puri on pilgrimage. They were divided into different groups and stayed in different places of their choice. Some of them stayed in Paradise hotel, some at Goenka dharmasala, and at Panjabi math, some of them preferred to stay in the pilgrim shed belonging to their Jatri Panda Manoranjan Sinhari. They incurred expenses to the extent of Rs. 8750/- under different items such as Rail ticket - Rs. 4500/-, Bus fare Rs. 450/-, Lodging expenses Rs. 300/-, Food Rs. 3000/-, Total Rs. 8750/-.

The purpose of undertaking the journey to Puri was to witness the Car festival and go round Puri to see different places and fulfil their wishes.

On getting down at the Puri rail station many Pandas asked them to which Jatri Pandas did they belong. They had known that they belonged to the Sarangi house as their Jatri Panda. They searched for the *Gumastha* of Sarangi, but finding none of the Sarangi family they followed the Gumastha of Sinhari who told them that he would take care of them in the matter of providing lodging house to them and accompany them in their visit, to different sacred places at Puri. He arranged a mini bus for them and took them in that place and helped them to stay at 3 places. The well to do families of their group stayed in Dharmasalas. Although they stayed in different groups at different places they used to get together at one place and all together go to visit different places and have *darshan* of the deities. One day they went to the temple of Lord Jagannath and at that place came across their real Jatri Panda Sarangi by name. Sarangi told them that he was their real Jatri Panda. But being grateful to Sinhari they continued to remain with him and took his assistance in all matters.

As per their economic condition they deposited fees for Annadana Atika and got receipts from the office. Sinhari was well behaved and under his care they spent 8 days at Puri. In the meantime two persons of their group found shortage of funds with them to meet the expenses for their return journey. Sinhari assured them to meet their expenses for purchasing rail tickets. These two persons promised that they would send the money to him by M.O on reaching their village. They had plans to visit a few important places outside the Puri town, and make some purchases of some articles like bangles, conchshell, dried consecrated cooked rice, and some dry sweets.

Jaleswar Jatri :

The pilgrim's name was Dinabandhu Sen of 72 years old and of Khandayat caste belonging to Soro of Balesore district. He came by a reserve bus and halted one day at Bhubaneswar. His journey from home to Puri was of two day duration. 22 persons accompanied him in the pilgrimage. There were 8 adult males, 5 adult females, 6 boys and 3 children. They spent two days at Puri.

During their stay at Puri the places they visited are *Shri.nandir* (the temple of Lord Jagannath), Gundichaghar, Shri Lokanath, Chakratirtha, Swargadwara, Jagannath Bhalava Matha, Konark and Sidha Mahabir. The Jatri Panda who was associated with the group was Sinhari Bhuban Mohan Kar who is a resident of Puri town. The Jatri Panda visited their native place and invited them to come on a pilgrimage to Puri during car festival. The members comprising the group stayed at different places in Puri town. These places are Kanheyalal Dharmasala, Lokanath lodging house and Jyoti hotel. The total amount of expenses they met during their visit on pilgrimage to Puri was of the order of Rs. 5,100/- broken of into the following items, 1) Bus fare Rs. 3000/- 2) Lodging and food expenses Rs. 2100/-. Total Rs. 5,100/-.

The purpose of their visit was to witness the Car festival and visit to different sacred centres in and around Puri town. During their visit to Puri they had some experience which they narrated during interview, the narration is as follows.

On reaching Puri town and getting down from the bus they went straight to Narendra tank where they took their bath. The Jatri Panda took them round and helped them to show different pilgrim spots. At Shri Lokanath the sebakas created trouble and misbehaved with them. The pilgrims thought which it was not good to pick up quarrels with the sebakas at Puri. Therefore they kept quiet and paid them what ever they demanded from them.

It was our observation that the Leprosy patients who were sitting in line in front of the temple demanded some money and spoke in bad language if they were not complied with their demand.

While staying at Puri they took their food in a hotel for two days. But in other days they took Shri *Mahaprasad* and dry sweets. They saw the Car festival to their hearts content. They offered coconut to the deities while the cars were moving towards Gundichaghar. They used to go to the temple in the evening and have *darshan* of deities at Gundichaghar. On this occasion they had the opportunity to come across many pious people with whom they had lots of discussions. Some persons of the group were expert in performing *Nadia Kirtan* and they got themselves merged in performing *Sankirtana*. The people around the place they enjoyed their Sankirtana with rapt attention. The performance was so charming that people gathered around them and as the crowd swelled up the police began to disperse them. In memory of the visit of the pilgrims to Puri they purchased the photos of the deities, some utensils available in Puri town, conchshells and dried consecrated cooked rice (Nirmalya). Then they started their return journey to their home villages.

Gangajali Jatri

Name of the Jatri	:	Bijaya Kumar Behura
Age	:	28 years
Sex	:	Male
Caste	:	Milkman
Village	:	Rasola
District	:	Dhenkanal
Mode of Travel	:	Upto Cuttack by bus and from Cuttck to Puri on foot. From Gadagadia ghat of river Mahanadi carried the river water by means of carrier hanging from shoulder walked the distance from the ghat to Puri.
Days travelled	:	Two days
Accompanied persons	:	A group of 13 youngmen together each carrying water proceeded on foot to Puri.
Days spent at Puri	:	Three days

Places visited	:	Shri Lokanath and Shri Mandir
Jatri Panda	:	None
Place at Puri where stayed	:	Lions Gate, Puri
Expenses	:	Food Rs. 200/-. Rituals and fees Rs. 100/-.
Purpose	:	Fulfilment of desire and religious objective

Experience

The distance of 100 kms from Cuttack to Puri covered by walking. Inspiration was given to him by Gadagadeswar when the vessels were dipped into the river and filled with water and carried by means of a carrier held hanging on the shoulder. He took rest for sometime at Batamangala and took the consecrated food at that place. Thereafter he proceeded forward and reached Shri Lokanath in time. He paid Rs. 10/- to the Sebayat for offering the water he carried to Shri Lokanath - Sebayat was told what his name was and what was his *gotra*. After knowing these information he uttered these things loudly and asked him to pour water. Then insence, lamp and food were offered. After the water was offered and he put on some other clothes and circumambulated the compound of the temple. After performing all rituals all the people of the group gathered together at one place outside the temple compound. They proceeded to the temple of the Lord Jagannath, had *darshan* of the deities and then took *Mahaprasad* and then they started their journey back by bus to their native place.

Pilgrimage to Puri, Pandas and their Pilgrim Business

Many years back there was no road communication to Puri. But thousands of pilgrims from different parts of the country used to come on pilgrimage to see the car festivals and the Jagannath temple at Puri. Those coming from North India used to take routes via-Bihar and Chhotanagpur and those coming from eastern India come via Lakshmanabati and Cuttack. Those coming from southern India used to come via Ganjam through coastal area and Chilika lake. Many of them had to come by boat through Hoogly, Baleswar, Masalipatna, Similipatna, Barrua, Chilka lake.

In order to develop road communication the British authorities started the construction of the Jagannath road in 1822 to 1826. The Raja of Calcutta Sukhamaya Deb douated about one and a half lakh of rupees. In spite of lack of good communication about 53 thousands of pilgrims visited Puri on Pilgrimage in the year 1839. This number increased to 1.12.000 in 1842, and it further increased to 2,10,000 in the year 1861 during the car festival. Inspite of such difficulties of road communication the Pandas and their Gumasthas used to go out 5 to 6 months before the festival took place to their respective areas and villages to meet their pilgrims, spread the Jagannath cult and invite them to come to Puri during the coming car festival. Thousands and thousands of pilgrims used to come to Puri on foot covering hundreds of miles from their respective villages through forests and rough and rugged terrain. As a result of such arduous journey many pilgrims had to sustain injuries in their body and also meet death on the way Mr. John beams, the then Collector of Balaswar had a descriptive eye witness account of the pilgrims journey on Calcutta-Madras Trunk Road to Puri to witness the Car festival in the year 1860. This descriptive account is available in a book called Memories of Bengal civilian. (See Annexure XIII for details).

A list of the important Pandas and their pilgrim ilakas (areas)

	Name of Jatri Panda	Native place	Area under their jurisdiction
1/1	Ramachandra Gochhikara	Harachandi Sahi	Gujarat
2/2	Artatrana Mahasuara	Harachandi Sahi	Maharastra
3/3	Balabhadra Gochhikara	Harachandi Sahi	Hariyana
7/4	Ramachandra Pratihari Pancha Bhai Gobardhana	Harachandi Sahi	Jhansi Lalita Bina, Kari
8/5	Lokanath Pratihari (Kabara Ghoda)	Harachandi Sahi	Banda, Himrpur, Sindubad
13/6	Lokanath Gangadhara Mahapatra	Harachandi Sahi	Rayagada, Saranga, Bilaspur, Raypur
14/7	,nata Mahapatra	Harachandi Sahi	Nepal, Assam
15/8	Banamali Mahapatra	Harachandi Sahi	Manipur 45%
17/9	Shrinath Khuntia	Harachandi Sahi	Allahabad, Lucknow
21/10	Dwarikanath Khuntia	Harachandi Sahi	Allahabad
26/11	Ramanath Khuntia	Harachandi Sahi	Bankuda Grama
31/12	Balakrushna Mahapatra	Harachandi Sahi	Sambalpur
34/13	Ramanarayana Khuntia	Harachandi Sahi	2 or 3 district Rajasthan
5/14	Kalijuga Damodara Pratihari		Punjab, Jammu
22/15	Jayaram Sinhari		
6/16	Bade Harihara (Guru Estate) Rabi Narayana Guru Prasana Guru	Goudabada Sahi	Bihar
33/17	Mahadeba Pujapanda	Gudia Sahi	Berhampur
10/18	Telenga Padhiari	Balisahi	South India
11/19	Narasingh Nath Daltapati	Dolamandap Sahi	Medinipur
20/20	Gopal Khuntia	Dolamandap Sahi	West Bengal
23/21	Kashinath Sinhari	Dolamandap Sahi	Kanpur town
24/22	Chintamani Sinhari	Dolamandap Sahi	Chari sampradaya
25/23	Niranjana Sinhari	Dolamandap Sahi	West Bengal, Banki (Orissa)
28/24	Jagannath Puspalaka	Dolamandapa Sahi	Angul (Orissa)
12/25	Raghunath Sinhari	Talucha Sahi	Chhatisgarh

	Name of Jatri Panda	Native place	Area under their jurisdiction
27/26	Raghunath kar	Talucha Sahi	Madhya Pradesh
32/27	Bhubana Mohana Kar	Hajuri Lane	Athagada
16/28	Chandan Hajuri	Harachandi Sahi	Pradap Gada
18/29	Arjuna Sadangi	Baseli Sahi	Rajasthan
19/30	Mahabir Khuntia	Markendeswar sahi	West Bengal
29/31	Bhagabana Mahapatra	Balisahi Bahari lane	Dhenkanal
4/32	Chhota Gobardhana Jagannath Mahapatra	Gochikara Sahi	Delhi
8/33	Kashinath/Biswanath Padhiari (Choudha bhai babda)	Bhind, Morena	Gowallior
30/34	Chintamani Kar	Talucha Sahi	Talcher

7
Life of the Pilgrims at Puri

Being a famous Vaisnavite Tirtha of the 12th century Puri, originally known as Purushottam Kshetra or Jagannath *Dham*, attracts thousands of pilgrims from all Indo-Aryan regions of the country. Their number runs to millions during the car festival. The earliest record of pilgrimage to Puri dates back to 1137 A.D. A pilgrim visited this sacred centre in that year and gave away all his wealth to the temple.

The Panda and Pratihari sebakas have divided different areas of the country among themselves and visit those areas with *Nirmalya* (rice grains half cooked in the temple kitchen), and *Mahaprasad* call upon their clients and give them prasad and bring them to Puri on a short visit in pilgrimage during festivities such as car festival, *Chandan* and *Dol jatra*. The prosperous and influential Pandas have employed agents or *Gumasthas* to perform journey on their behalf and fetch the pilgrims to Puri.

The assistants of the Pandas are of two classes : *Deswari* or *Batua* who go out to different parts of the country and fetch their pilgrims and *Ghatua* who are pilgrim touts remaining at Puri and contacting pilgrims at the railway station and at other points of entry into Puri town.

The British Government levied a tax on the pilgrims reporting to the temple of Sri Jagannath under the Regulation IV, 1806 A.D. which has been furnished in the Annexure VIII.

Later the Regulation V, 1806 A.D. was passed for checking persons who evaded payment of the tax. The text of the Regulation is given in Annexure IX.

In Regulation IV, 1809 A.D. which is given in Annexure X, the entry points were specified and accordingly the pilgrims were admitted into Puri through these points. Two avenues for the admission of the pilgrims were specified, that is Atharanalla Ghat on the north and Lokanath Ghat on the south-west of Puri town. According to the categories to which the pilgrims belong the amount of the tax to be paid by each class of pilgrims, duration of their stay and access to the temple etc., were specified in the Regulation.

In the year 1840 the East India Company felt that the money received in the form of Pilgrim Tax was to a certain extent the price of a State sanction to idolatry and accordingly the company abolished the Pilgrim Tax and by passing the Act X, 1840 the temple authorities were forbidden to impose any restrictions upon the pilgrims for admission into Puri town and into the temple to pay homage to the deities (Annexure XI).

From a very early time the pilgrims from different directions of the compass representing different parts of the country have been visiting in thousands on pilgrimage to Puri. According to them Puri is nothing but a heaven upon earth. In specific terms what they believe about Puri has already been mentioned elsewhere. Thousands of Pilgrims coming from far off and near by places witness the car festival at Puri. The scene of multitudinous of pilgrims during car festival has been vividly described by David B. Smith, M.D. Sanitary Commissioner for Bengal during his visit to Puri in 1868. The narrative of his visit is as follows :

"I had been anxious to get to this celebrated place before dark; but this I found to be impossible. My first view of the city was by starlight. As I passed up its principal street-the "*Burra Dund*" which is nearly a mile long and very broad, I observed, chiefly at the far end of it, many thousands of pilgrims lying on the ground, sleeping quietly; there was no noise; here and there a small wick lamp was burning, which had been lit by one of a party of individuals lying huddled together, a little apart from the rest of the slumbering crowd. The scene was peculiarly impressive. Those numberless men and women, enjoying much-needed repose, had come together from every point of the compass, many of them from very distant places, all actuated by the one burning desire to reach Juggernauth. Here at last they had accomplished their desire, and wearied with the accumulated fatigue of many marches, they lay in perfect stillness on the bare ground, Not a sound was to be heard; the stars yielded faint light, and before me I saw, as if in dreamland, an army of religious enthusiasts, who, in the fervour of a fanatical creed, had completed a pilgrimage which, to the Hindoo mind, is the surest viaticum to a happier state of being."

While narrating the hardship and strain the pilgrims had undergone in their journey Smith had further said.

"During the Rath Jatra festival, those who come together are for the most part Bengalees, of whom a very large proportion are women. While I was passing along the crowd I observed a party of up-country men, I spoke to them, and found that they were Punjabees who had just come down all the way from Hazara, some 2,000 miles. They told me that they had been travelling four and five months, that they were going to stay a day or two at Juggernauth, and then at once return to their homes. Shakespear's words were recalled to my mind :

"A true-hearted pilgrim does not fear to
measure kingdoms with his feeble-steps"

More vivid and pathetic was the description of Sir W.W. Hunter regarding the journey of the pilgrims to Puri. A paragraph from his description is quotated below.

"The great spiritual army marched in hundreds sometimes thousands of miles along burning roads, across unbridged rivers, and through pestilent regions of jungle and swamps. Those who kept to the road had spent their strength long before the holy city was reached. The sturdy women of Hindustan braved it out and sang songs till they dropped; but the weaker females of Bengal limped piteously along with bleeding feet in silence, broken only by deep sighs and an occasional sob. Many a sickly girl died upon the road; and by the time they reached Puri, the whole party had their feet bound up in rags, plastered with dirt and blood (Puri District Gazetteer, 1929, by L.S.S. O'Malley p. 128)".

The pilgrims pour into Puri from all directions most of them waling the distance from home to Puri. As road communications developed people came by bullock carts, along the Jagannath Trunk Road and also by rail. In this connection a paragraph from the Puri District Gazetteer, 1929, by L.S.S.O'Malley, p. 125 is reproduced below.

"At that time the Bengal pilgrims had to tramp all the way from Uluberia to Puri on the Jagannath Trunk Road. Only the wealthier classes travelling in bullock carts or palanquins, while pilgrims from the south used to come by road along the strip of land between the Chilika lake and the Bay, or in a few cases by boats across the Chilika lake. During the last thirty years of the nineteenth century the difficulties of the journey were much decreased, as it was possible to go from Calcutta by sea-going steamers to Chandabali in the Balasore district, and thereafter by the river up to Cuttack, and lastly by road to Puri. Now-a-days most pilgrims travel by rail direct to the sacred town. Even after the roads were developed some pilgrims are even now seen measuring their length prostrate along the road, all the way from their home for scores of miles.

The pilgrim-Pandas and their agents take care of the pilgrims at Puri. The pilgrims of different areas are attached to different Pandas. As soon as the pilgrims arrive at Puri their respective Pandas lodge them in Dharmasalas and lodging houses, arrange for supply of mahaprasad daily and depute men to show them round particularly the sacred places. Those pilgrims who land up at Puri without escort by any pilgrim-guides or agents of Pandas fall into difficulties. They are questioned by the Pandas, and the registers maintained by the

Pandas are looked into to trace out the ancestors or any relations of these pilgrims. These registers are called Panda's book in which the names of pilgrims and details about their native places and date of visit to Puri are recorded. When no record of a pilgrim is traced out there is often a brawl, a fight between two Pandas each claiming the pilgrim as his client and in the long run the mightier wins the case. In this connection David B. Smith has also given a pathetic description in his report on Pilgrimage to Puri.

The pilgrimage to Puri as observed by Smith not only entailed incalculable misery, suffering and loss of life, in the journey but it was also a history of disease and death which the Pilgrims met at Puri. Under what unhygienic and insanitary conditions the pilgrims were crammed into the lodging houses in the earlier days will be clearly understood from the following paragraphs which are reproduced from the Smith's report p.3 to p. 5.

The pilgrims at Pooree are so densely crowded in every apartment, that it is simply impossible to admit more inmates; not only the corners and the centre of a lodging house are occupied, but the entire space was full of pilgrims. One Dr. Mouat has described one of these terrible places :-

In the lodging-houses they are crowded to such an extent, that I was shown one apartment, in the best pilgrim hotel of the place, in which eighty persons were said to have passed the night. It was thirteen feet long, ten feet five inches broad, with side walls six feet and a half in height, and a low pent roof over it. It had but one entrance, and no ventilation worthy of note. It was dark, dirty and dismal when quite empty, and must have been a rest house during the festivals. In this house, in a similar room, occurred the first case of cholera of the last outbreak. If this be the normal state of the best lodging-house in the broad main street of Pooree, it is not difficult to imagine the condition of the worst, in the narrow, confined, undrained, back-slums of the town-for there are lower depths even in this abode of filth and corruption".

Most of the Pandas have houses of their own for the reception of pilgrims. When these are fully occupied, other places are rented, at high charges, in which pilgrims are crowded almost to suffocation. In apartments containing 50 or 100 people, there is very little light, less pure air, and no ventilation".

The following is an extract from the diary of the Deputy Inspector General of Police, for the week ending 16th November, 1867 :-

"The District Superintendent writes :- I went into a house in the town this afternoon; above 45 pilgrims were putting up, men and women; the place had only two doors, no windows (one of the doors was locked). This place measured 12 by 20 feet, certainly not more; and in this place no less than 45 persons were crammed. The stench was overpowering and the heat like an oven; no wonder the people are attacked with cholera; and unless some law is passed to prevent these Pandas overcrowding their houses with pilgrims, not only cholera but other diseases are sure to be generated".

Mr. Raban, the Magistrate and Collector of Pooree, thus alludes to this subject in his admirable Report to the Commissioner of Cuttack (No. 93 T dated 19th February, 1968) : - "The poorer up-country pilgrims submit to crowed rooms : but the Oriya pilgrims crowd into a room till it would be difficult to introduce another person. I visited one room filled with Oriyas from Kimedy, in the Madras Presidency; the room was so crowded that it was difficult to move, yet several of the people were singing, and one was actually cooking for the rest at a large fire, which filled the room with smoke. This was an extreme case, but I satisfied myself, by visiting a number of houses, that the people are crowded in a manner prejudicial to health, and calling for special legislation. Many of the houses afford very fair accommodation for limited numbers, but are quite unfit for the reception of the number that crowd into them. A third class railway carriage, filled with native passengers, gives a very fair idea of the extent of the crowding; and it must be recollected that these people sleep in these crowded rooms, which are no better provided with ventilation that the ordinary kind of houses in this country".

"Giving heed to these observations of eye-witnesses, and remembering that a single individual breathes 1616 cubic feet of air in an hour, and that in that time he should be supplied with a fresh supply equal to nearly 2,000 cubic feet, we are in a position to estimate the dreadfully abnormal conditions of the interiors of Pooree lodging-houses".

Shocked by the alarming report of Dr. Smith and others a bill was brought before the Lieutenant Governor's council on the 15th December 1866 for better regulation of lodging houses at Puri. The most important points mentioned in the bill were the following suggestions for the improvement in sanitary conditions, the suggestions are 1) The appointment of a Health Officer and the management of the lodging houses only by license holders, 2) imposition of fines on lodging houses only by license holders, imposition of fines on lodging house keepers not taking out a license and keeping the lodging house in insanitary conditions and periodic inspection of lodging house in sanitary conditions and 3) periodic inspection of lodging houses by health officer.

Subsequently a committee called Pilgrim Committee was formed with the Collector/Magistrate and leading persons of the town, representatives of sebaka communities and Mahantas of selected monasteries to control and regulate pilgrim traffic. The arrangements made by the committee are as follows :

1. The district Magistrate shall issue licenses to such number of persons as he thinks fit to act or be employed as a Panda remaining in charge of lodging houses. The District Magistrate may delegate this power to any of his subordinate officers.

2. Any Sebak or person connected with the *seba puja* or worship of Jagannath is entitled to act or be employed as a Panda provided he be of good character.

3. Any respectable person of good character may be employed by any *Panda* as his *Gumasta* or agent and may take out a license to act as such through his employer.

4. The licence granted to a Panda shall ordinarily be for life and shall be chargeable with a fee of Rs. 15/-.

5. The *Gumastas* can be divided into two classes :-

   a) *Deswari* or *Batua* that is, those that go out to differnt parts of India to fetch pilgrims.

   b) *Ghatua,* that is, those who meet and tout for pilgrims at Puri and neighbouring railway stations.

   As a rule these two classes are quite distinct from each other, and separate licenses might be granted to them according to the nature of the duties which they have to perform. The license granted to a *Gumasta* of either kind shall be tenable for one year and shall be chargeable with a fee of Rs. 1/-. Every Panda shall be bound to have the license of his gumastas renewed every year.

6. The licenses granted to Pandas and gumastas of the 2 classes shall be respectively in the prescribed form.

7. An advisory committee consisting of some reputed persons shall be formed to help and cooperate with the district magistrate in the issue of these licenses.

8. All applications for licenses should be made to this Committee. The committee will consider these applications and if the applicant be found suitable forward it with their recommendation to the District Magistrate for granting a license. If they are of opinion that the applicant is not worthy of getting the license the committee will send back the application with their reasons to the District Magistrate.

9. When any Gumasta desires to leave his employer and get employed under someone else, he shall obtain a transfer certificate from his employer. If his employer refused to grant the certificate without reasonable cause

he shall apply to the Committee who will enquire from his employer and recommend such action on his application as they think fit.

10. An officer of a rank equivalent to that of sub-Deputy Collector shall be employed by the District Magistrate to supervise and control the work.

11. It shall be duty of this officer as far as possible to meet all trains and see that no person acts as a Panda or as a *Gumasta* without a licence and that the licenced persons abide by the conditions of their license. He shall decide on the spot all disputes arising between rival Pandas and report all cases of misconduct on their part.

12. A Register giving details about all licensed Pandas and *Gumastas* shall be kept by this officer and all changes shall be noted therein.

The break out of Cholera was a regular feature in Puri due to unhygienic and insanitary conditions which were prevalent in the earlier days. The root cause of cholera was the eating of bad food. All the pilgrims consume mahaprasad when they are at Puri during festivities. Mahaprasad is good when fresh, but it becomes stale after some hours like all other types of cooked food.

In the report of the Pilgrim Committee the matter regarding the eating of *Mahaprasad* featured prominently. What the members observed in this regard are quoted below.

The distinctive feature of the pilgrimage to Puri is the Mahaprasad, the sacred food which has been consecrated by offering to the Lord Jagannath and other deities. The *Mahaprasad* is considered as sacred that all may eat this food together irrespective of caste distinctions. To eat the Mahaprasad is one of the chief rites of the pilgrimage and no pious Hindu in good health would think of cooking his own food while at Puri. The conditions under which this food is cooked and sold are obviously of great importance with reference to the public health. Sometimes the pilgrims do not get fresh *Mahaprasad* and has to eat stale stuff and this is the main reason for the out break of Cholera, diarrhoea and other enteric troubles. The committee recommended certain measures to be taken strictly so that pollution of food should be controlled and occurrence of epidemics would be minimised. (See Annexure XIV for a narration about the epidemic)

a) The wells are insufficiently protected and at least one of them in the *Ananda Bazar* is much used by the pilgrims who come to eat the *Mahaprasad*. It would be a great improvement if these wells could all be covered over and have pumps attached. This we understand is impossible as there are very strong objections. We would recommend that the wells should have their cylinders thoroughly plastered with cement and that they should be provided with efficiently drained plinths, with parapets around their mouths and with pulleys, ropes and buckets for drawing water.

b) The kitchens are good but the drains outside are defective and attract flies. Between the drains and the kitchen is a space which is much used as a urinal. It is important that there should be no stagnation in the drains as the sullage from the kitchen consists almost wholly of rice washings which decompose quickly. It was recommended that they should be constructed with glazed earthenware pipes laid in cement or of other impervious material such as Indian patent stone. They should also be placed close to the kitchen walls to avoid the intervening space being polluted.

c) Near the kitchens are some houses for the cooks and other servants. The houses do not belong to the temple, but it would be an improvement if these are acquired and removed, new houses of a good pattern being built in their place. The area around these houses and between them and the kitchens might also be paved with advantage.

d) Several areas within the temple are polluted and suitable steps should be taken to stop pollution.

8
Concluding Remarks

Pilgrimage to Puri

Pilgrimage is a world wide phenomenon. There is perhaps no country in the world in which devotees have not at one time or another gone on pilgrimage to some holy and sacred places of their choice to fulfil their desire for achieving something of pious nature. The delightful spirit which impels a person to undertake a journey to a sacred and holy place for the fulfilment of his desire to present his vows and offerings to the deities and some other heavenly objects is universal. The belief in the virtues of pilgrimage, the passionate desire for a *Darshan* of the divine object, the reverence with which the object of his choice is looked upon generates a kind of readiness and willingness to undertake a journey no matter what hardship, austere penance, dangers and difficulties he may endure en route to reach the place of his destination. The Indian Hindu pilgrims are no exception in their yearning after holy places particularly their passionate desire to visit the Purusottam Kshetra for their *darshan* to the Lord Jagannath.

Day and night throughout every month of the year particularly in the month of June-July during the Car festival of the Lord Jagannath thousands of pilgrims coming from every part of the country throng at Puri to witness the Car festival and to offer there prayer and offerings to the Lord Jagannath, to take bath in the holy tanks, to circumambulate around the holy shrines, tanks and trees and bathe in the sea and partake the holy food Mahaprasad and finally praying the Lord for their salvation.

The troops of devotees covering miles on foot where there was no road and rail communication reach Puri fatigued and with blood stained feet in time to have *darshan* of the Lord Jagannath his elder brother Balabhadra and their sister Subhadra seated in their respective Cars to meet these wearied devotees and showering on them their blessings. An account of W.W. Hunter regarding the Pilgrim Hunters going to different parts of the country and including the pilgrims to come on a visit to Puri is reproduced below.

"The great spiritual army that thus marches hundreds, and sometimes thousands of miles, along burning roads, across unbridged rivers, and through pestilent regions of jungle and swamp, is annually recruited with as much tact and regularity as is bestowed on any military force. Attached to the temple is a body of emissaries, called pilgrim-hunters, or pilgrim guides, according as a friendly or a hostile view is taken of their functions, numbering about 3000 men, who visit every province and district of India in search of devotees. Each of the leading priests keeps up a separate set of these men, sending them to the province of which he enjoys the spiritual charge, and claiming the profits of the disciples they bring in. They wander about from village to village within their allotted beats, preaching pilgrimage as the liberation from sin, and sometimes using arguments as worldly, and drawing pictures as overstrained, as those by which the flagging devotion of Europe was lashed into zeal during the later crusades."

"The arrival of pilgrim-hunter is a memorable event in the still life of an Indian village. There is no mistaking the man. The half-bald shaven head, the tunic of coarse dirty cloth, the cap drawn over the ears, the palm leaf umbrella, the knapsack on the back, and the quid of narcotic leaf which he chews and rolls in his cheek as he strides forward, proclaim the emissary of Jagannath. He seldom shines in public exhortation, but waits till the men have gone out to the fields, and then makes a round of visits to the women. Skilled in every artifice of persuasion, he works upon the religious fears and the worldly hopes of the female mind; and by the time the unsuspecting husbands come home from their work, every house has its fair apostle of pilgrimage. The elder women and some of the aged fathers of the hamlet long to see the face of the merciful god who will remit the sins of a life, and are content to lay their bones within his precincts. Religious motives of a less emphatic sort influence the majority. The hopes of worldly reward for a good deed swell the number. The fashionableness of pilgrimage, and that social self-complacency which springs from being in the mode, attract the frivolous. The young are hooked by the novelty of a journey through strange lands. Poor widows catch at anything to relieve the tedium of their blighted existence; and barren wives long to pickup the child-giving berries of the banyan tree within the sacred enclosure, and to pour out the petition of their souls before the kindly god.

Dr. Smith, the Sanitary Commissioner in his report on Pilgrimage to Juggernauth (Jagannath) in 1868 has mentioned that the number of pilgrims during the Car festival in July 1825 was 225,000 (vide "India's cries to British Humanity " by J. Peggs, Late Missionary at Cuttack, London, 183-page 221). He has added that "I think there can be but every little doubt that the annual attendance generally at Pooree has much fallen off of late years. It is probable that 50,000 is quite equal to the present average. In former times it was much higher."

The journey to Puri took months and the haltage at Puri was for a couple of days. The Jatri Pandas and their assistants used to visit the native places of their pilgrims and bring them to Puri in festivities. At Puri the Pandas take care of lodging, boarding and sight seeing and visiting to sacred shrines and holy places and charge them for the expenses they incur for such arrangements. Almost every year there occurs the breakout of cholera at Puri during Car festival because the unhygienic condition of in which the pilgrims live in pilgrimsheds at Puri and the stale and contaminated food they eat are mainly responsible for the breakout of cholera. Moreover the long distance they travel and the difficulties and sufferings they endure make them sick and miserable. Both of these hardship en route to Puri and the unhygienic living condition and contaminated food consumption while at Puri add to the misery of the pilgrims. Many writers have remarked that pilgrimage is nothing but a string of disease and death. But after the road communication was improved and necessary steps taken for the improvement of sanitation and of lodging and boarding facilities at Puri many difficulties and epidemics were minimized.

The pilgrims were charged a tax for their entry into the Puri town during festivities. Two entry points one at Loknath Ghat and the other at Atharanalla ghat were fixed and the officials were stationed at both these entry points to collect tax from the pilgrims. In addition to these main entry points there were also minor entry points fixed at various places along the routes which the pilgrims travelled. The pilgrims were classified into different categories on the basis of their nativity and economic condition. The classification of the pilgrimage is as follows.

1. Lal Jatree :

   These Jatrees were affluent coming from the north paid Rs. 10/- at Atharanalla and Rs. 6/- at Loknath ghat. They had also to pay Rs. 2/- for the Pandas and Pratiharis. They were given red tickets and therefore they were called Lal Jatri. They were permitted to stay at Puri for 30 days. He was also allowed to use Chauris in day time and Masala at night and a Panda would accompany him while going to the temple. He was also allowed to take his family members along with him while going to the temple.

2. Nim lal Jatree

   A Nim Lal Jatree paid Rs. 5/- while coming from the North and passing through Atharanalla ghat and Rs. 3/- while coming from the south and passing through the Lokanath ghat. The Nim Lal Jatree was allowed to stay at Puri for seven days.

3. Bhurrang Jatree

Those pilgrims who paid Rs. 2/- as tax and annas sixty as fee were called Bhurrang Jatree. They paid the same amount at either ghat.

4. Panch Tirtha

The jatrees of this category visited Panch Tirthas located in the Puri town under the charge of a Panda called Bada Panda. After visiting the Tirthas on payment of Rs. 4/- they were given a certificate which they produce at the office of the Collector of Pilgrim Tax to get permission to perform the customary ceremonies at the gate of the temple within 16 days.

5. Dandapaka Jatri

The devotee or a pilgrim completes his journey from the starting point to the Jagannath temple by laying himself down at every step measuring the round by the length of his body as a penance or merit to please his god. The jatri is generally as *Dandabhanga Jatree.*

6. Gangajali Jatri

The pilgrims of the category carries water of the Ganges or any sacred river to be poured on the Lokanath deity at Lokanath ghat and there after he comes to the Jagannath temple for *darshan* of Lord Jagannath.

7. V.I.P. Jatree

The zamindars, rich persons, renowned persons and persons of nobilities used to come on a visit to worship Lord Jagannath and the pilgrims of these categories used to be given all help for their journey and stay at Puri comfortably. Great attention is paid to them by the officials so that they visit the temple and worship the Lord Jagannath.

8. Khairati Jatree

Those pilgrims who came under the category of Khairati Jatree and exempted from the payment of pilgrim tax were the principal *Suthuds* whose business it was to induce the Hindoos from all parts of the country to perform pilgrimage to Puri. Similarly *Patta daurias* who supplied silken ropes by which the idols were hoisted into their respective cars. Several pensioners of former Government servants were exempted from payment of any tax. The professional musicians and singers were exempted from duties. The sick and *Kangalas* or poor persons were exempted from payment of duties. The Bairagis or the *Sadhus* and *Sanyasis* were exempted from payment of pilgrim tax on religious grounds. The Mathadharis and their assistants came under the categories of Bairagi. Groeme's report gives a list of those persons who came under the categories of *Khairati* pilgrims who did not make any payment to the Government.

9. Panchakosi Jatree

The pilgrims who belonged to villages which were situated in the area lying between Pipli in the north and Manikapatna in the south covering about 10 kms. around Puri were exempted from paying any tax including pilgrim tax.

10. Government servants

The government servants of the categories of sepoys of the company, the servants of the European officials, and the clerks (*Amala*) of Puri collectorate, residents of Puri, Kangalas or destitutes were exempted from payment of the pilgrim tax.

The collection of pilgrim tax from the pilgrims was in vogue during the Mughol period. It was also present during the Maratha rule. During the British Government the system was streamlined. But when the Christians and missionaries objected to the collection of pilgrim tax by the British Government the system of collection of tax from the pilgrims was abolished towards the middle part of the 19th century and since then there is no custom of the collection of tax from the pilgrims. The details of the pilgrims and the tax they used to pay and hygienic condition at Puri are given in Annexure XV.

One word may be mentioned about Puri as a famous pilgrim centre. Some famous sages and saints have said that Utkala Desa, the glorious country is considered to be the realm established by the gods. Of all the regions of the earth India is considered to be the noblest and of all the countries and of India Utkal boasts the highest renounces. From end to end it is one vast region of pilgrimage. Orissa is divided into four great regions of pilgrimage. From the moment the pilgrim passes the Baitarani river, or the high road 40 miles North-East of Cuttack, he treads on the holy ground. A narrative of the visit of David B. Smith, M.D. Sanitary Commissioner for Bengal gives a picture of Pilgrimage to Puri in Annexure XVI.

Speaking in particular about this holy land a pilgrim leaves the land behind him where this worldly beings live. Before him beyond this worldly land extends to the other world by land of heaven. On the southern side of the Baitarani river rises shrines after shrines to Siva, the All-Destroyer. On its very bank the pilgrim beholds the house of Yama, the king of the dead, in the typical Baitarani river.

On leaving the stream, he enters Jajpur, literally the city of sacrifice, the head quarters of the region of pilgrimage, sacred to Parvati, the wife of the all-destroyer to the south-east is the region of pilgrimage, sacred to the sun, now scarcely visited with its matchless majestic sun temple in ruins in the Bay of Bengal. To the south west is the region of pilgrimage dedicated to Siva with its city of temples and the sacred bank Bindu Sagar all popularly called Ekamra or Bhubaneswar. Beyond this, nearly due south is the region of pilgrimage abode of Vishnu, known to every one throughout India and to every nation on earth as the abode of Purusottam the lord of the World otherwise known as Shrikshetra or Sankha Khetra or Jagannath dham which was sanctified by no less a divine being than Brahma one of the Holy Trinity in the golden era. Besides the Shri Mandir the home of Nilamadhaba in the Nilachal hills lying on the seashore there are hundreds of monasteries and shrines established by Sadhus, Sages and Sanyasis like Sankar, Ramanuja, Chaitanya, Nanaka, Kabir and many devotees of other sects around the Jagannath temple at the centre and more than 300 sacred shrines around this centre within the inner compound wall and many important shrines and other sacred places within the outer compound wall (Meghanada Pacheri) there are hundreds of temples of minor deities, monasteries, panch tirtha, 1) Markand temple with Markand tank, 2) Sweta Ganga (another sacred tank), 3) Chakra tirtha, a temple of a deity which is adorned with the garlands which were put on by the Lord Jagannath on the day called Nrusingh Chaturthi) and the 4) Indradyumna (both the tank and the temple) and 5) the Sea (Bay of Bengal outside the Temple compound).

Besides these sacred places there are many other important shrines, tanks, trees, and holy spots which are dotted in the area covering the Sankha Kshetra. The map gives location of the sacred spots which are mentioned in the list with 115 different sacred places which the pilgrims try to circumambulate during their visit to Puri.

Besides these sacred places located mainly in three concentric zones, there are many other shrines and places which are connected in some way and other with the Lord Jagannath and its surrounding shrines and sacred institutions. A preliminary enumeration of these spots, which are situated within a radius of 10 kms. around the sacred complex, that is in and around the outer compound wall (Meghanada Pacheri) of the great temple of Lord Jagannath, comes roughly to 100 sacred places. In other words the boundary of the *Sankha Kshetra* is confined to the *Atharanalla* in the North, the Sea in the South, the Siva temple of *Jambeswar* and *Sidhamahabir* in the east and the Siva temple of Lokanath in the west, the goddess *Batamangala* in the North-East, the goddesss *Batamangala* in the North-West, the *Swargadwara* in the South-West, and the *Chakra tirtha* in the South-East. The places which are associated with the core of Sacred complex that is *Sankha Kshetra* are mostly outside the *Sankha Kshetra.*

There are many *Sahis* or Wards all radiating from the Jagannath temple in all directions. The main *Sahis* are *Bali sahi*, *Dolamandap sahi*, *Goudabada sahi*, *Harachandi sahi*, *Kundeibenta Sahi*, *Markendeswar sahi* and *Matimandapa sahi.* Besides these main Sahis there are as many as 35 *Sahis* which are branches of or subordinate to the main sahis. These sahis are composed of ritual functionaries of the temple, painters, stone carvers, ayurvedic practitioners, astrologers, sanskrit pandits, and people of other castes carrying on other professions such as sweetmeat makers, tailors, cobblers, grocery shop owners, businessman etc.

The main sahis have each an organisation which is under the charge of headman called *Sahi Naik*, their assistants called *Sahi Bhandaries*, and youth organisations called *Akhada* with important people of the Sahi as members who arrange performance of *Sahi jatras* or fiestas which are performed on different occasions. The gymnastic clubs which are called *Jagaghar* are associated with the *Akhadas.* The youths of the *Sahi* practice gymnastic exercises at the *Jagaghar.* Each *Sahi* has also a presiding deity which is installed at the *Jagaghar* and the youths who otherwise known as *Sanga* (comrades) arrange ritual performances on different occasions. Youths of the *Sahi* receive training for gymnastic performances, singing songs and playing on musical instruments. A youth who wants to be a *Sanga* offers consecrated food to the presiding deity Mahavir by name and anoints vermilion on the body of the deity and feeds the comrades of the Jagaghar.

The *Jagaghar* owns some landed property on which the *Jagaghar* is built and the presiding deity is installed. It also owns a garden of mango trees. There is a temple in this grove and the deity Ramachandra by name is worshipped in this temples. At the back of the temple a tank is present and it is meant for pisciculture. The members of the *Jagaghar* observe some ritual like *Dashara* festival which is observed to worship *Ramchandi*. In this month of *Chaitra* on the tast Tuesday of the month a feast is arranged and all the members meet the expenses incurred for the feast and rituals performed at the presiding deity Mahabir and Ramachandi. The grocery shop owners donate whatever spices and other ingredients are required on this occasion and the persons passing by the *Jagaghar* with their cartloads contribute whatever quantity of fuel is required to cook food for the feast.

Similarly the brickmakers contribute some bricks whenever they pass by the *Jagaghar* with their carts with bricks. The persons who pass by the *Jagaghar* with cart loads of thatching materials such as straw bundles contribute some bundles of straw. With these donation the members meet their requirements for the performance of the festivals, construction or repair of the houses of Jagaghar.

The *Jagaghar* gets income from the following sources.

1) Sale proceeds of cashewnuts.
2) Sale proceeds of fishery from the tank
3) Sale proceeds of coconuts
4) Sale proceeds of Polang seeds for extracting oil
5) Sale proceeds of fruits and
6) Sale proceeds of fuel wood

Sometimes the members get some income from arbitration of disputes which are referred to them by the aggrieved parties. On the whole the Jagaghar is a sort of informal cooperation organisation which functions for socio-cultural purposes exclusively on the basis of self help whenever the pilgrims visit Puri town they make it a point to go round some Sahis and observe the theatrical and dramatic performances and *sahijatras* (dance and music and theatrical performances held in different sahis). Moreover they do not make any special efforts to witness these activities held at *Jagaghar* because they reside in the pilgrimsheds which are maintained by the *Jatri pandas* who live in these *Sahis*.

Besides these institutions and feasts, fiestas, and festivals performed in these institutions round the year, many festivals are performed in the Jagannath temple which are intimately associated with the Sebapuja of the Lord Jagannath and his elder brother Balabhadra and their sister Subhadra.

Mainly 12 such festivals are observed in Shrimandir at Puri round the year. There is a Sloka in Sanskrit which mentions these 12 festivals. The sloka is as follows.

"Manchasnanang Rathabaragathii Sayanang Chayane Dway
Parswabruthi Sayan Nibruti Prabrutaihi Pusyapuja
Dola Jatra Damanaka Mahotakhsa Puja Trutia
Chaibang Jatra Bidhini Gadita Dwadasaita Narendra"

In other words these 12 festivals are :

1. *Snana Jatra* : Month of *Jestha* on full moon day.
2. *Rath Jatra* : Month of *Asadha Sukla Dwitiya* (the second day of the bright fortnight of the month of *Asadha*)
3. *Sayana Jatra* : On the 11th day of bright fortnight in the month of *Asadha*.
4. *Dakshinayan Jatra* : On the day the sun begins to more to the equinox.
5. *Parswaparibartan* : On the 11th day of bright fortnight in the month of *Bhadrava*.
6. *Uthapana* : On the 11th day of bright fortnight in the month of *Kartik*.
7. *Prabarana Sasti* : On the 5th day of the bright fortnight in the month of *Margasira*.
8. *Pusyapuja* : On the full moon day in the month of *Pausa*.
9. *Uttarayana* : On the *Makara Sankranti* day when the sun moves towards the southern equinox.

10. *Dol Jatra*	:	Representative deities are taken out to Dol Vedi for the swing festival.
11. *Damanaka Chhaturdasi*	:	Festival observed in honour *Damanaka* (a deity)
12. *Akshya tritia*	:	The construction of the Chariots (cars) begins after *Vanajaga* ceremony is performed.

In addition to these 12 important festivals many other festivals are observed in the Shri Mandir from the period from *Mesa Sankranti* to *Mina Sankranti*. These festivals are listed below.

The Almanac shows that there is some festival or other almost everyday round the year and there is flow of pilgrims to Puri almost everyday throughout the year. That is why even the minor festivals are as important as the major ones from the point of view of pilgrimage to Puri.

Festivals of Lord Shri Jagannath

1. *Maha Visuba-Pana Sankranti*
2. *Shri Rama Navami*
3. *Basantik Mahanavami*
4. *Akshyaya Trititya*
5. *Niladri Mahoday*
6. *Nrusingha Janma*
7. *Bhaunri*
8. *Rukmini Haran Ekadasi*
9. *Chamapka Dwadasi*
10. *Snan Purnima*
11. *Netrotsaba*
12. *Shri Gundicha*
13. *Bahuda Ratha*
14. *Sayan Ekadasi*
15. *Niladri Bije*
16. *Karkata Sankranti*

17. *Chitalagi Amabasya*
18. *Jhulan*
19. *Gahma Purnima*
20. *Shri Krishna Janmastami*
21. *Nanda Utsaba*
22. *Banabhoji Besa*
23. *Kali Dalan Besa*
24. *Pralambasura Besa*
25. *Krishna Balaram Besa*
26. *Satapuri Amabasya*
27. *Hadhastami*
28. *Paraswa Paribartan, Ekadasi*
29. *Baman Janma*
30. *Ananta Brata*
31. *Durga Puja*
32. *Dasahara*
33. *Kumar Purnima*
34. *Uttahan Ekadasi*
35. *Rasa Purnima*
36. *Prathamastami*
37. *Odhan Shasi*
38. *Panda Nursingha Bije*
39. *Dhanu Sankranti*
40. *Bakula Amabasya*
41. *Pusyabhiseka*
42. *Makar Sankranti*
43. *Basanta Panchami*
44. *Magha Saptami*
45. *Bhaimi Ekadasi*
46. *Gajodharan Besha*
47. *Shiba Ratri*
48. *Phagoo Dasami*
49. *Dola Purnima*

The research project comprises several themes with points of focus representing different aspects of the study. These aspects are closely related and a dislocation in any of them has severe repercussions throughout the whole nexus. The institutional inter linkage of the Sacred Complex is shown in the chart.

1. Gradual economic impoverishment leading to disintegration of culture institutions and attenuation and mismanagement of palace and temple rituals (Seba Puja).

2. Bureaucratization and monetization of ritual services resulting in proxy and sale transactions and irregularity in the performance of ritual services.

3. Inflationary spiral causing economic diversification in Sebaka community and deterioration in both quality and quantity of consecrated foods.

4. Reforms in Land system leading to litigation between tenants and ritual functionaries and impoverishment of sacred institutions.

5. Government interference in Seba Puja and changing attitude of the public resulting in conflict between Raja Superintendent and Administrative representatives and changes in people's image of God-king relationship.

To sum up, all these forces have combined to destroy the morals of the Ritual Functionaries, to alienate the Monasteries, Brahman Sasans and Militia community, to weaken the royal power and to disintegrate the sacred complex. Further, this study has implications for broader inquiries into some of the processes of secularization in modern Hinduism.

Annexures

Annexure I

Important Tourism Places in India with names of places and State

Pilgrim Centre

Amarnath (Cave Temple)	Jammu & Kashmir
Yamanotri	Uttaranchal
Gangotri	Uttaranchal
Badarinath	Uttaranchal
Kedarnath	Uttaranchal
Haridwar	Uttaranchal
Mathura	Uttar Pradesh
Ayodha	Uttar Pradesh
Allahabad	Uttar Pradesh
Patna	Bihar
Gaya	Bihar
Baidyanath Dham	Jharkhand
Dwarka	Gujarat
Ujjain	Madhya Pradesh
Nashik	Maharashtra
Amarkantak	Chattisgarh
Tirupati	Tamil Nadu
Thuthukkudi	Tamil Nadu
Rameswaram	Tamil Nadu

Temples

Sun Temple, Martand	Jammu & Kashmir
Waishnodevi Temple	Jammu & Kashmir

Kangra, Historic Temple	Himachal Pradesh
Amritsar, Golden Temple	Punjab
Ahichhattra, Historic Temple	Uttar Pradesh
Chittaurgarh, Temple of Virji	Rajasthan
Abu, Dilwara Temple	Rajasthan
Khajuraho	Madhya Pradesh
Deogarh, Vishnu Temple	Madhya Pradesh
Varanasi	Uttar Pradesh
Guwahati, Kamakhya Temple	Assam
Dwarka, Ancient Temples	Gujarat
Junagarh, Jain Temple	Gujarat
Palitana	Gujarat
Somnath Temple	Gujarat
Lingaraj Temple, Bhubaneswar	Orissa
Chalukya Temple, Bijapur	Karnataka
Palampet	Andhra Pradesh
Warangal	Andhra Pradesh
Konark	Orissa
Puri, Jagannath Temple	Orissa
Patadkal, Chalukyan Temple	Karnataka
Badami, Chalukyan Temple	Karnataka
Panaji	Goa
Lakkundi	Karnataka
Sringeri	Karnataka
Halebid, Hoysala Temple	Karnataka
Belur, Hoysala Temple	Karnataka
Hampi	Karnataka
Tadpatri	Andhra Pradesh
Kolar	Karnataka
Bangalore, Jain Temples	Karnataka
Kanchipuram	Tamil Nadu
Vellore	Tamil Nadu
Shri Rangapattana	Karnataka
Mysore	Karnataka
Shravan Belgola	Karnataka
Mamallapuram	Tamil Nadu
Chidambaram	Tamil Nadu

Thuthukkudi	Tamil Nadu
Tiruchchirapalli	Tamil Nadu
Thanjavur	Tamil Nadu
Mudurai	Tamil Nadu
Thiruvanthapuram	Kerala
Kanyakumari	Tamil Nadu

Holiday Resort

Srinagar	Jammu & Kashmir
Gulmarg	Jammu & Kashmir
Pahalgam	Jammu & Kashmir
Dalhousie	Himachal Pradesh
Mussouri	Uttaranchal

Hill Stations

Dalhousie	Himachal Pradesh
Manali	Himachal Pradesh
Mussouri	Uttaranchal
Darjeeling	West Bengal
Mudumalai	Tamilnadu
Tiruchirapalli	Tamilnadu

Health Station

Shimla	Himachal Pradesh
Ranikhet	Uttaranchal
Almora	Uttaranchal
Abu	Rajasthan
Darjeeling	West Bengal
Shillong	Meghalaya
Pachmarhi	Madhya Pradesh
Ranchi	Jharkhand
Mahabaleswar	Maharashtra
Vishakhapatnam	Andhra Pradesh
Puri	Orissa
Gopalpur	Orissa
Mudumalai	Tamilnadu

Sanctuary

Place	State
Jim Corbett National Park	Uttaranchal
Bharatpur	Rajasthan
Kaziranga	Assam
Sasan Gir	Gujarat
Vedantagal	Tamilnadu
Bandipur	Kerala
Udagamadalam	Tamilnadu
Kaladi	Kerala

Buddhist Remains

Place	State
Kasia	Uttar Pradesh
Sarnath	Uttar Pradesh
Varanasi	Uttar Pradesh
Baraut	Uttar Pradesh
Nalanda	Bihar
Rajgir	Jharkhand
Sanchi	Madhya Pradesh
Jabalpur	Madhya Pradesh
Nagarjunakonda	Andhra Pradesh
Amaravati	Andhra Pradesh

Monuments

Place	State
Bikaner	Rajasthan
Jodhpur	Rajasthan
Alwar	Rajasthan
Ujjain	Madhya Pradesh
Ahmadabad	Gujarat

Museum

Place	State
Dehra Dun	Uttaranchal
Jaipur	Rajasthan
Jodhpur	Rajasthan
Mathura	Uttar Pradesh
Lucknow	Uttar Pradesh

Sarnath	Uttar Pradesh
Varanasi	Uttar Pradesh
Guwahati	Assam
Vadodara	Gujurat
Sanchi	Madhya Pradesh
Jabalpur	Madhya Pradesh
Calcutta	West Bengal
Mumbai	Maharashtra
Pune	Maharashtra
Hyderabad	Andhra Pradesh
Nagarjunakonda	Andhra Pradesh
Amaravati	Andhra Pradesh
Konark	Orissa
Shrirangapattnam	Karnataka
Chennai	Tamilnadu
Thanjavur	Tamilnadu
Thiruvanthapuram	Kerala

Famous Temple

Martand	Jammu & Kashmir
Waishnodevi	Jammu and Kashmir
Amritsar	Punjab
Abu	Rajasthan
Gwalior	Madhya Pradesh
Allahabad	Uttar Pradesh
Junagarh	Gujarat
Bhubaneswar	Orissa
Palampet	Andhra Pradesh
Konark	Orissa
Puri	Orissa
Helebid	Karnataka
Belur	Karnataka
Bangalore	Karnataka
Kanchipuram	Tamilnadu
Shravan Belgola	Karnataka
Mysore	Karnataka

Chidambaram	Tamilnadu
Thanjavur	Tamilnadu
Kumbakonam	Tamilnadu
Madurai	Tamilnadu
Thiruvanthapuram	Kerala
Kannyakumari	Tamilnadu

Historic Place

Delhi	Hariyana
Jaipur	Rajasthan
Chittaurgarh	Rajasthan
Agra	Uttar Pradesh
Bhubaneswar	Orissa
Mumbai	Maharashtra
Hyderabad	Andhra Pradesh
Bangalore	Karnataka

Rock-cut caves and sculptures

Bagh	Madhya Pradesh
Junagarh	Gujarat
Ajanta	Maharashtra
Allora	Maharashtra
Jajpur	Orissa
Bhubaneswar	Orissa
Aurangabad	Maharashtra
Elephanta	Maharashtra
Karli	Maharashtra
Aivalli	Karnataka
Badami	Karnataka
Helebid	Karnataka
Belur	Karnataka
Vellore	Karnataka
Mamallapuram	Tamilnadu

Annexure II

Details about the Holy and Sacred Characteristics

Once upon a time many sages and *sadhus* congregated in one place and asked the *Suta* (Almighty God) (*Bhagawan*) how are the *Tirthas* like and which *Tirtha* occupies the top most position so far as its sacredness and catholicity is concerned. What the *Suta* said in this respect are presented below.

This descriptive part of sacred centres is extracted from the 1st chapter of the book called Niladri Mohadaya written by Dr. Brajakishore Swain of Sadgrantha Niketana. The relevant parts of chapter 1 dealing with sacred places (Kshetras) are reproduced below in translated forms.

Of all the *Kshetras* and *Tirthas Shri Purusottama Kshetra* is the most famous and has occupied the top most position in the ritual world. This *Purusottama Kshetra* is most sacred destroyer of all darkness of ignorance giver of all that is good and holy. These qualities are present in the mountain called *Nilaparbata* which is located in a place between the Rusikulya river and the Baitarani river.

This Tirtha is located in the North of the sea and south of Mahanadi river covering the area close to the sea coast. The sacredness of this spot is spread around the area covering 10 Jojonas. Every inch of this area is most sacred.

Beginning from the distant part of this area upto Nilachal the area is so sacred that only sages and sadhus and pious persons can have access to this sacred spot. Those having a pious heart and have taken bath in the Baitarani river and have *darshan* of Biraja goddess in the bank of Baitarani river can have access to Ekamarakanana (Bhubaneswar) famous for the *Lord Lingaraj.* Those having visited *Ekamarakanana* after their bath in *Bindusagar* can have access to the temple of Lord Lingaraj (*Nilakantha*) for *darshan* and these visitors will also be able to go to Arka Kshetra and have *darshan* of *Suryadev* in Konark temple in *Arka Kshetra.* The pilgrim who visits Arka Kshetra takes bath in the Chandravaga river and have darshan of the rising Suryadev (the rising sun). Those who have prayed for piety and religious virtues by taking bath in these rivers and having darshan of Biraja goddess and Lord Lingaraj and *Suryadev* are entitled to visit *Shri Purusottama Kshetra.*

A person becomes free from all vices by having *darshan* of *Shri Purusottama* at *Nilaparbata* which is located in the area which is of the shape of a Sanka (shape of a conch shell). As it is of the shape of a *Sankha* the *Kshetra* is otherwise called *Sankha Kshetra.* Its coverage is 5 Kosa in extent and is situated on the sea shore. The *Nilaparbata* occupies the Naval of Conch shell. Those who circumambulate the surrounding area covering three kosas on foot become free of all vices.

Those having the greatest dedication to Lord Jagannath they can visit this *Kshetra* which is a *Kshetra* of all *Kshetras* and which is a very rare Kshetra in crores of universe.

Since *Shri Purusottama Kshetra* which covers an area of three Kosas touches the sea, therefore the sea becomes famous as *Tirtharaja* (king of tirthas).

In this conch shell shaped virtuous *Kshetra* there is a reservoir called *Rohinkunda.* The water of this reservoir is so sacred that one who touches the water becomes free from all vices and becomes virtuous. North of this reservoir there is a tree called *Kalpa brukshya*. A person who sits in under the tree and touches the tree becomes free from all vices. At the root of the tree lies the *Ratna Singhasan* studded with most attractive jewels and it is on this *Singhasana* that the *Nilamadhava* (Jagannath) is seated. On both sides of this deity there are two goddesses namely *Dhara* (goddesss of earth-*Bhudevi*) and *Laxmi* (goddess of wealth *Shridevi*).

At a distance 100 cubits in the western corner the deity called *Madhaba* is installed. South of this deity *Nrusingh* another deity is present. To the north of *Nrusingh* temple there lies the deity called *Khetrapala*, otherwise known as *Kama*. It is near this place that the goddess *Bimala* is present. At some distance a sacred spot called *Manikarnika* tirtha is present, and near by is the *Siva* temple of *Kapolomochan*. On the sea shore there is another Siva temple in which *Jambeswar* is installed.

Another Lord *Sambhu* called *Kondumuni* whose worship gives immense virtuous results which are not received to this extent even by worshipping crores of Lingas is present in the north-eastern corner of the *kshetra*.

In the compound of *Jambeswar* temple there is goddesss such as *Chandi* and in front of her there lies another temple in which goddess *Kalika* is present. She is present in the south of *Chandi* temple and installed as a worshipper of *Vishnu*. In the back region of *Vishnu*, *Kalpa brukshya*, sea shore and *Kalika* temple there lies *Sweta Ganga*. In the south there lies fish like incarnation of *Vishnu* and whitish *Siva* temple. The place between this *Vishnu* and *Siva* is most sacred and many sages and sadhus spend time in this place.

The south facing *Ganesha* is present in the south of Bateswar which is situated near *Kalpa brukshya* and Sarbamangala. The most powerful deity called *Marichika* is installed in the east of *Nilaparbata*.

The *Rudra* called *Eysenaswar* is present in the North-eastern corner of the place where *Madhaba* (Vishnu) is present. The goddess *Devi Ardhasani* and *Kapalamochana* are present in the east.

The Lord *Hari* has given protection to the middle portion of *Sankha Kshetra*. The Siva namely *Nilakantha* is present at the apical region of *Sankha Kshetra* and *Sarbamangala* is installed at the back of the *Sankha Kshetra*.

Lord Siva namely *Markendeya* is present in the north-western corner of *Purusottama Kshetra*. In the name of *Markendeya* a tank has been dug and it is called *Markendeya* tank. After bathing in this tank the pilgrims worship *Markendeswar*. Like this the *Purusottama Kshetra* is full of many important *kshetras* including many trees, creepers, and sacred tanks, temples and places of beauty. The sacred centres are scattered all over the *Tirthasthana*. The gods and goddess come down from heaven to this *Kshetra* for worshipping *Shri Nilamadhaba* or Shri Jagannath who is decorated everyday with fragrant flowers.

To the west of this kshetra lies a hamlet inhabited by *Savaras* which is called *Sabarpalli*. In this hamlet the king of *Sabaras Viswavasu* by name lives and he provides the consecrated food to Lord Jagannath everyday. It is this Sabar king who goes to the place where *Nilamadhaba* is installed to pay homage to the deity. This *Purusottama Kshetra* is most sacred in the 14 universes or worlds.

Once a crow being thirsty reached *Rohinikunda* and saw Madhaba being reflected in the water of the tank while seeing the lord and drinking water from *Rohinikunda* its body was transformed with *Sankha*, (Conch shell) *Chakra* (discus), *Gada* (Club) and *Padma* (Lotus), held in its hands and in his transformed body the crow flew straight to heaven.

As regards the sacredness of *Shri Purusottama* one or two words may be mentioned here. The *Purusottama kshetra* is so sacred that those who die in this place they become free from rebirth and go to heaven without being tortured by the *Yamaraj*.

Addressing to the *Yamraj* as his son Lord *Vishnu* said that *Yamaraj* exercises his control over all places in the world but he has no right to enter the *Purusottama kshetra* and also its adjoining areas lying within a radius of 5 Kosas. Who ever dies in *Purusottama kshetra* whether it is a human being or an animal or an insect do not reborn again. They become free to go to heaven where they settle down with other heavenly bodies. The *Swargadwara* (gateway to heaven) a place on the sea shore is the place where the dead bodies are consummated.

A similar account of *Shri Purusottama Kshetra* has been given in *Utkal Khanda* of *Shri Purusottama Mahatma* (1st Part) published by Shri Chaitanya Ch. Das.

Annexure III
Catholicity of Orissa and Puri

The aspect of Catholicity of Orissa and Puri is reproduced from the Chapter-III on the Jagannath published in Asiatic Society.

"For two thousand years Orissa has been the holy land of the Hindus. The ancient texts love to dwell on its sanctity. It is 'the land that taketh away sin'[1]. It is 'the realm established by the gods'; and its Sanskrit name, *Utkala-desa*, literally the glorious country, has crystallized the devotional regard of forty generations[2]. 'Of all the regions of the earth', says an inspired sage in explaining the various places of pilgrimage to his pupils. 'India is the noblest; and of all the countries of India'. *Utkala* boasts the highest renown. From end to end it is one vast region of pilgrimage[3]. Its happy inhabitants live secure of a reception into the world of spirits; and even those who visit it, and bathe in its sacred rivers, obtain remission of their sins, though they may weigh like mountains. Who shall adequately describe its sacred streams, its holy places, its fragrant flowers and exquisite

1 *Sarva papa haran desa' Kapila Sanhita*, cap. 2

2 Mr. John Becames Magistrate of Balasore, the first Bengal civilian who has brought scholarship to bear on the NEO-Aryan languages of India, believes that *Utkala* means the outlying strip i.e. lying beyond the Gangetic valley, from ut+kala = Katila=cut off. He has got the Balasore Pandits to accept this signification, but the Puri priests and all Brahmans that I have talked to on the subject adhere to the meaning.

3 Tirtha. Vol. II

fruits ? Who shall estimate the soul's gain from a sojourn in such a land ? But what is the need for enlarging on the praises of a realm in which the gods themselves love to dwell ?[4]

Continuing about the subject the author said "Orissa is divided into four great regions of pilgrimage. From the moment the pilgrim passes the Baitarani River, on the high road forty miles north-east of Cuttack, he treads on holy ground. Behind him lies the secular world, with its cares for the things of this life; before him is the promised land, which he has been taught to regard as a place of preparation for heaven. On the southern side of the river rises shrine after shrine dedicated to *Siva*, the All-Destroyer. On its very bank he beholds the house of *Yama*, the king of the dead; and as he crosses over, the priest whispers into his ear the last text which is breathed over the dying Hindu at the moment the spirit takes its flight; 'In the dread gloom of *Yama's* halls is the tepid *Baitarani* river[5]. On leaving the stream he enters Jajpur, literally the city of sacrifice, the headquarters of the region of pilgrimage[6], sacred to *Parvati*, the wife of the all-destroyer. To the south-east is the region of pilgrimage sacred to the sun[7], now scarcely visited, with its matchless ruins looking down in desolate beauty across the Bay of Bengal. To the south-west is the region of pilgrimage dedicated to *Siva*[8] with its city of temples, which one clustered, according to native tradition, to the number of seven thousand, around the sacred lake. Beyond this, nearly due south, is the region of pilgrimage beloved of *Vishnu*, known to every hamlet throughout India, and to every civilised nation on earth, as the abode of *Jagannath*, the Lord of the World"[9].

The author continued writing further as "There is not a Fiscal division in Orissa without its community of cenobites, scarcely a village without fertile abbey lands, and not a single

4 *Kapila Sanhita*, Stirling's account of Orissa proper, Asiatic Research, vol. XV.p.166.
5 *Yamalaye mahaghore tapta Baitarani nadi*
6 *Parvati kshetra*
7 *Arka*, or *Padma Kshetra*
8 *Kshetra*
9 Bishnu or Purushottama Kshetra

ancient family which has not devoted its best acres of land to the gods. Hundreds of monasteries dot the province, and enjoy an aggregate rent role of $ 50,000 a year[10]. Every town is filled with temples and every hamlet has its shrines. This lavish devotion extends into the hill country. In going up the Mahanadi, I noticed that each rocky islet, or wooded crag that rose from its banks, was crowned, not, as upon the Rhine, by the castle of a noble but by a temple dedicated to some god. Even foreigners feel that they are treading on hallowed ground; and the villagers still tell how the image-breaking Musalmans retired abashed before the sanctity of Orissa. "This country is no fit subject for conquest, or for schemes of human ambition', exclaimed the victorious general of Akbar in 1580; 'it belongs to the gods, and from end to end is one region of pilgrimage"[11].

What was mentioned next was, "This national reverence for holy places has been for ages concentrated on the city of Puri sacred to Vishnu under his title of *Jagannath*, the Lord of the World. As the outlying position of Orissa long saved it from conquest, and from that dilapidation of ancient Hindu shrines and rites which marks the Muhammadan line of through India, so Puri, built upon its extreme south-eastern shore, and protected on the one side by the surf, and on the other by swamps and inundations, is the corner of Orissa which has been most left to itself. On these inhospitable sands, Hindu religion and Hindu superstition have stood at bay for eighteen centuries against the world. Here is the national temple whither the people flock to worship from every province of India. Here is the *Swarga-dwara*, the Gate of Heaven, whither thousands of pilgrims come to die, lulled to their last sleep by the roar of the eternal ocean. Twenty generations of devout Hindus have gone through life, haunted with a perpetual yearing to visit this shrine. On its fever-stricken sand-hills a nation's adoring love has been lavished. They are Puri, 'the City' of its religious aspirations on

10 Report of Committee to inquire into the Maths of Orissa, dated 25th March 1869, Para, 15.
11 Stirling, as Res. XV, 167, 291

earth; they are Purushottama, the dwelling of *Vishnu*, 'the Best of Men' they are the symbolical blue mountain; they are the mystic navel of the earth. Even *Siva* is unable to comprehend its glory; how feeble, then, the efforts of mortal men"[12].

"This is the place which is frequented by pilgrims throughout the year from every part of the country. Quoted from the chapter V of History of the Jagannath Temple in the 19th century by Prabhat Mukherjee, Firma KLM Pvt. Limited 1977 it is said, "Pilgrimage to reputed holy places have ever been so popular in India. But no pilgrimage was ever so extensively practised and so generally famed as that of pilgrimage to *Jagannath* Puri. By what fortuitous circumstances that idol became so celebrated, it is difficult to imagine"[13].

It may added that, "It is to this place Puri and to this temple and the idol of *Jagannath* for several centuries Hindoos have thronged-weary, footsore and feverish, yet ever patient under fatigue and hardship-to get the sight of their god, which they believe obliterates the transgressions of a whole life. Their belief being what it is, we can scarcely wonder at that invincible enthusiasm which urges them to a place so sacred"[14].

What Sutton has said, "Orissa is to India what Jerusalem was to the land of Israel. It is the holy land of the Hindoos. As the Israelites went up to worship at Mount Zion, so do the inhabitants of the various provinces of India go on pilgrimage to the great temple of Juggernath. The car festival of Juggernath is the greatest meeting place of the Hindoos of all India"[15].

N.K. Bose had said, "The worship of *Jagannath* is for the highest minds among the Hindus, a pure system of Theism. To

---

12 Vernacular tract sold to pilgrims at the door of the temple, Amos Sutton's Orissa, p. 124

13 History of the Jagannath Temple in the 19th Century by Prabhat Mukherjee, Firma KLM Pvt. Ltd. 1977 at para 1 in p. 138.

14 Rev. Lacroix-Calcutta Christian observer : 1849

15 Sutton : Orissa and its evangelization (1850), p.8

the polytheistic multitude it offers the infinite phases of divinity as objects of worship and provide for their delectation, an infinite number of rituals and ceremonials. In a word, it supplies the spiritual requirements of different classes of Hindus in different stages of their intellectual development. Under its broad and receptive roof, doctrines, the most divergent, find a resting place".

Speaking further what he has added "*Jagannath* is an unsectarian name. All Hindu sects worship at its shrine. The followers of a Sankaracharya, Ramananda, Kabir, Chaitanya and Nanak are to be seen doing homage to the great god. Even the Jains of the Digambar sect flock to the Temple at a certain season of the year. The common link of all these sects is their belief in the supremacy of *Jagannath*"[16].

About this matter Smith has said, "These numberless men and women had come together from every bit of the compass many of them from very distant places-all actuated by one burning desire, to reach Juggernath. Here at last they accomplished their desire and weary with the accumulated fatigue of many marches, they lay in perfect still ness on the ground-an army or religious enthusiasts, who in the fervour of a fanatical cred, had completed a pilgrimage, which, in the Hindoo mind, is the surest viaticum to a happier state of being"[17].

In the chapter III on *Jagannath* of Asiatic Society Hunter has mentioned, "this great yearning after *Jagannath* is to some extent the outcome of centuries of companionship in suffering between the people and their god. In every disaster of Orissa, Jagannath has borne his share. In every flight of the people before an invading power, he has been their connade. The priests, indeed, put the claims of their god upon higher ground. 'In the first boundless space', they say, 'dwelt the Great God, whom men call *Narayan*, or *parameswar*, or *Jagannath*'. But

16 N.K. Bose (Collector of Puri), Calcutta Review 1891

17 David B. Smith : Pilgrimage to Juggernath (1868)

without venturing beyond this world's history, the first indistinct dawn of Orissa tradition discloses Puri as the refuge of an exiled creed. In the uncertain dawn of Indian tradition, the highly spiritual doctrines of Buddha obtained shelter here, and the Golden Tooth of the founder remained for centuries at Puri, then the Jerusalem of the Buddhists, as it has for centuries been of the Hindus".

"*Jagannath* makes his first historical appearance in the year 318 A.D., when the priests fled with the sacred image, and left an empty city to Red-arm and his buccaneers. For 150 years it remained buried in the western jungles, till a pious prince drove out the foreigners, and brought back the sacred Log. Three times has it been buried in the Chilika Lake; and whether the invaders were pirates from the sea, or the devouring cavalry of Afghanistan, the first thing that the people saved was their god".

"Nor was Lord *Jagannath*, although hurried away helpless in a covered cart, unable to defend himself by spiritual arms. In 1558 the Musalman general tracked him to his hiding-place, and digging him up, carried him off on an elephant to the Ganges. There he determined to make an end of the god of Orissa, and threw him on a blazing pile of wood. In the same moment the vaunting Musalman's limbs dropped off and he fell dead. A looker - on snatched the image unharmed from the fir- and cast it into the river. Holy Mother Ganges knew the god, and floated him safely down her stream, till a priest who had followed *Jagannath* into exile, rescued him from the river, and extracting the immortal part from his bosom, brought it safely back to Orissa".

"But the true source of *Jagannath's* undying hold upon the Hindu race consists in the fact that he is the god of the people. As long as his towers rise upon the Puri sands, so long will there be in India a perpetual and visible protest of the equality of man before God. His apostles penetrate to every hamlet of Hindustan preaching the sacrament of the Holy Food. The poor outcaste learns that there is a city on the far eastern shore in which high and low eat together. In his own village, if he accidentally touches the clothes of a man of good caste, he has committed a crime, and his outraged superior has to wash away the pollution before he can partake of food of approach his god. In some parts of the country the lowest castes are not permitted to build within the towns, and their miserable hovels cluster amid heaps of broken potsherds and dunghills on the outskirts. Throughout the southern part of the continent it used to be a law, that no man of these degraded castes might enter the village before nine in the morning or after four in the evening, lest the slanting rays of the sun should cast his shadow across the path of Brahman. But in the presence of the Lord of the World priest and peasant are equal. The rice that has once been placed before the god can never cease to be pure, or lose its reflected sanctity. In the courts of *Jagannath*, and outside the Lion Gate, 100,000 pilgrims every year are joined in the sacrament of eating the holy food. The lowest may demand it from or give it to the highest. Its sanctity overleaps all barriers, not only of caste, but of race and hostile faiths; and I have seen a Puri priest put to the test of receiving the food from a Christian's hand".

"Woe to him who denies the divine efficacy of the *Mahaprasad*, the Great offering: A hundred tales among the people warn priestly arrogance of the wrath of a despised god.

There came a proud man from Northern India, who swore that he would look upon the Lord of the World, but that he would eat no leavings of mortal of immortal being. But as he crossed the bridge outside the city his arms and legs fell off, and there he lay on the road-side for two months, till a dog came out of the town eating a fragment of the holy food, and dropped some as he passed. The proud man crawled forward on his stomach, and grubbing with his mouth in the mire, ate the leavings, all slavered from the jaws of the unclean animal. Thereupon the mercy of the good Lord *Jagannath* visited him; new limbs were given to him, and he entered the holy city as a humble disciple 'God's pity' says the chief apostle of Jagannath, 'knows neither family nor tribe. 'Not the learned in the four holy scriptures, but the lowly man who believes, is dear to me; to him be given, and from him be received; let him be reverenced even as I am reverenced".

"Besides this perpetual appeal to the popular instinct, the worship of Jagannath aims at a catholicism which embraces every form of Indian belief, and every Indian conception of the deity. Nothing is too high, and nothing is too low, to find admission into his temple. The fetishism and bloody rites of the aboriginal races, the mild flower-worship of the Vedas, and every compromise between the two, along with the lofty spiritualities of the great Indian Reformers, have here found refuge. The rigid monotheism of *Ramanuja* in the twelfth century, the monastic system of *Ramanand* in the fifteenth, the mystic quietism of *Chaitanya* at the beginning of the sixteenth, and the luxurious' love-worship of the Vallabhacharis towards its close, mingle within the walls of *Jagannath* at this present day. He is *Vishnu*, under whatever form and by whatever title men call upon his name".

"But not content with thus representing *Vishnu* in all his manifestations, the priests have superadded the worship of the other members of the Hindu trinity in their various shapes; and the disciple of every Indian sect can find his beloved rites, and some form of his chosen deity, within the sacred precincts. Scholars tell us that in pre-historic times the Hindu race fell into polytheism by recognising God too vividly in his manifestations and worshipping the work rather than the worker. *Jagannath* represents the final result of the converse process. It exhibits the goal to which a highly intellectual race painfully arrives after ages of polytheism, during which the masses were sunk in darkness, while the higher spirits of each generation have been groping after the one eternal deity. Noble conceptions of the creator, and profound views concerning his dealings with man, are welded together with degrading superstitions, and declare how vain are the efforts of the human intellect to search out God".

"Here, then, is a great phenomenon in the inner history of a nation, over which those who would study the workings of the religious instinct in man's heart will do well to pause. In order to understand what Jagannath now is to the Hindus, it is necessary to learn what he has for ages been. I propose, therefore, to examine stage by stage that complex growth of enchaining superstitions and of yearnings after truth, which, nourished by the pilgrim bones of centuries, and watered by the tears of millions of disciples, now spreads itself out in full-grown luxuriance upon the Puri sands".

"The very origin of *Jagannath* proclaims him not less the god of the *brahmans* than of the low-caste aboriginal races. The various accounts differ less in their substance than in their details. The following story of the Divine Log is one of the most popular legends of Orissa, and was taken down for me upon the spot"[18].

18 Asiatic Society Chapter III, Jagannath, by Hunter

Annexure IV
Hunters description about the Puri Pilgrimage and Vishnuism

W.W. Hunter has given a narration about the pilgrims of Jagannath in Chapter IV of the Asiatic Society. This narration is given in Annexure III.

"This longing after shrines forms a very important feature in the national character of the Hindus. Day and night throughout every month of the year, troops of devotees arrive at Puri, and for 300 miles along the great Orissa road every village has its pilgrim encampment. The parties consist of from 20 to 300 persons. At the time of the great festivals these bands follow so close as to touch each other; and a continuous train of pilgrims, many miles long, may often be seen on the Puri high-road. They march in orderly procession, each party under its spiritual leader. At least five-sixths, and often nine-tenths of them, are females. Now a straggling band of slender, diminutive women, clothed in white muslin and limping sadly along, announces a pilgrim company from Lower Bengal; then a joyous retinue with flowing garments of bright red or blue, trudging stoutly forward, their noses pierced with elaborate rings, their faces freely tatooed and their hands encumbered with bundles of very dirty cloth, proclaims the stalwart female peasantry of Northern Hindustan. Ninety-five out of a hundred are on foot. Mixed with the throng are devotees of various sorts, some covered with ashes, some almost naked, some with matted, yellow stained hair, and almost all with their foreheads-streaked with red or white, a string of beads round their necks, and a stout staff in their hands. Every now and then, covered waggons drawn by the high-humped bullocks of Upper India, or by the smaller breed of Bengal, according to the nationality of the owner, creak past on their wooden wheels. Those from the Northern provinces still bear traces of the licentious Musalman rule, by being jealously shut up. The Bengali husband, on the other hand, keeps his women good-tempered, and renders pilgrimage pleasant, by piercing holes in the waggon-hood, through which dark female eyes constantly peep out. Then a lady in coloured trousers, from some village near Delhi, ambles past on a tiny pony, her husband submissively walking by her side, and a female domestic, with a hamper of Ganges water and a bundle of dirty cloth, bringing up the rear. Next a great train of palankeens, carrying a Calcutta banker and his ladies, sweeps past. I met one consisting of forty palankeens, with 320 bearers and about fifty luggage-carriers, whose monotonous chant made itself heard far off in the silent night. But the greatest spectacle is a north country Raja with his caravan of elephants, camels, led horses, and swordsmen, looking resigned and very helpless in his sedan of state, followed by all the indescribable confusion, dirt, and noises of Indian royalty".

Further he has added, "The great spiritual army that thus marches its hundreds, and sometimes its thousands of miles, along burning roads, across unabridged rivers, and through pestilent regions of jungle and swamp, is annually recruited with as much tact and regularity as is bestowed on any military force. Attached to the temple is body of emissaries, called pilgrim-hunters, or pilgrim-guides, according as a friendly or a hostile view is taken of their functions, numbering about 3000 men, who visit every province and district of India in search of devotees. Each of the leading priests keeps up a separate set of these men, sending them to the province of which he enjoys the spiritual charge, and claiming the profits of the disciples they bring in. They wander about from village to village within their allotted beats, preaching pilgrimage as the liberation from sin, and sometimes using arguments as worldly, and drawing pictures as overstrained, as those by which the flagging devotion of Europe was lashed into zeal during the later crusades".

Mentioning about the pilgrims he has said, "The arrival of a pilgrim-hunter is a memorable event in the still life of an Indian village. There is no mistaking then man. The half-bald shaven head, the tunic of coarse dirty cloth, the cap drawn over the ears, the palm-leaf umbrella, the knapsack on the back, and the quid of narcotic leaf which he chews and rolls in his cheek as the strides forward, proclaim the emissary of Jagannath. He seldom shines in public exhortation, but waits till the men have gone out to the fields, and then makes a round of visits to the women. Skilled in every artifice of persuasion, he works upon the religious fears and the wordly hopes of the female mind; and by the time the unsuspecting husbands come home from their work, every house has its fair apostle of pilgrimage. The elder women and some of the aged fathers of the hamlet long to see the face of the merciful god who will remit the sins of a life and are content to lay their bones within his precincts. Religious motives of a less emphatic sort influence the majority. The hopes of wordly reward for a good deed swell the number. The fashionableness of pilgrimage, and that social self-complacency which springs from being in the mode, attract the frivolous. The young are hooked by the novelty of a journey through strange lands. Poor widows catch at anything to relieve the tedium of their blighted existence; and barren wives long to pick up the child giving berries of the banyan tree within the sacred enclosure, and to pour out the petition of their souls before the kindly god".

Moreover he had added. "The shut-up, aimless life of Indian women gives a peculiar charm to the enterprise. The arrival of a pilgrim-hunter sends a general flutter through the whole zananas of the district, and a hundred little female heads beat wildly against the wires of their cages. In parties of thirty pilgrims I seldom counted more than five men, and sometimes not more than three. The best authorities I have consulted give the proportion of males at ten per cent, and one native writer puts them at lease than five in a hundred. The first part of the journey is pleasant enough. Change of scene, new countries new races, new languages, and a world of new customs and sights, await the travellers from Upper India. A good part of the distance is now accomplished by railway, and the northern pilgrims can thus get over their first 1000, or even 1400 miles, if they chose to travel straight through, in three days. But generally they walk from 300 to 600 miles and long before they have reached the holy city their strength is spent. The sturdy women of Hindustan brave it out, and sing songs till they drop; but the weaker females of Bengal limp piteously along with bleeding feet in silence, broken only by deep sights and an occasional sob. The pilgrim-hunter tries to keep up their spirits and insists with a necessary obduracy, on their doing a full day's journey every day, in order that they may reach in time for the festival. Many a sickly girls dies upon the road, and by the time they reach Puri, the whole party has its feet bound up in rags, plastered with dirt and blood. I have counted bands in which nine out of every ten were lame".

He has further added, "But, once within sight of the holy city, the pains and miseries of the journey are forgotten. They hurry across the ancient Marhatta bridge with songs and ejaculations, and rushing towards one of the great artificial lakes, plunge beneath its sacred waters in a transport of religious emotion. The dirty bundles of rags now yield their inner treasures of spotless cotton, and the pilgrims, refreshed and robed in clean garments, proceed to the temple. The pilgrim-hunter makes over the flock to his priestly employer and every hour discloses some new ideal of solemn spectacle. As they pass the Lion Gate a man of the sweeper caste strikes them with his broom to purify them of their sins, and forces them to promise, on pain of losing all the benefits of pilgrimage, not to disclose the events of the journey or the secrets of the shrine".

Adding more about the pilgrims he has said "In a few days the excitement subsides. At first nothing can exceed their liberality to their spiritual guide. But thoughts of the slender provision remaining for the return journey soon begin to cool their munificence, and the ghostly man's attentions slacken in proportion. Before a week is over money alterations commence, which in process of time resolve themselves into an acrimonious haggling over every shrine, and the last few days of their stay are generally devoted to schemes for getting out of the holy city with as few more payments as possible".

He has also pointed out "Every day the pilgrims bathe in one of the sacred lakes. These vast artificial sheets of water are embanked with solid masonry, honeycombed by time, and adorned with temples rising from the edge or peeping from beneath masses of rich foliage. At the principal one 5000 bathers may be seen at once. On the masonry banks, which are formed into one continuous flight of steps all the way round, a good mile in length, there is sometimes not an inch of standing room to be had. Here, as in every spot where the common people congregate, the primitive adoration of local divinities and village gods makes its appearance. In this centre of *Vishnu*-worship, half-way down the grand flight of steps to the lake, stands a venerable banyan tree, the abode of an ancient sylvan deity, whom the pilgrims propitiate by sticking red flowers into the crevices of the weather-beaten trunk".

To this he has added, "Not far off is the garden-house of *Jagannath*, whither the three sacred images are drawn during Car festival. I have mentioned that the Chinese travellers in the fifth century describe a similar ceremonial of the Buddhists. But I suspect that both the Buddhists and later worshippers of *Jagannath* caught the idea from those older woodland rites, of which traces survive in every hamlet of Bengal. To this day each district has some secluded spot in the jungle, whither the villagers flock once a year to adore the genius loci, in the shape of a log, or a lump of clay, or a black stone, or the trunk of a tree. I believe the Car Festival is only a very pompous development of this primitive hankering after forest devotions, skillfully incorporated with the incidents of the legendary life of *Krishna*, who was himself essentially a woodland god".

Asiatic society Ch. IV The Pilgrims of Juganuath by W.W. Hunter

Annexure V

Construction of Jagannath Temple

In the last third of the 11th century the Somavansi kingdom began to decline. Daksina Kosala was lost to the Telegu Colas in ca. 1070 A.D. and the kingdom finally collapsed in 1112 A.D., when the southern neighbour Anantavarman Codagangadeva of Kalinga conquered Orissa. He was the medium by which the next strong impulse of Visnuism was introduced in Orissa. It came again from the south.

Anantavarman Codagangadeva

Anantavarman Codagangadeva was, like all his predecessors, a devotee of Siva Gokarneswara. During the first 31 years of his reign he referred to himself as *parama-mahesvara.* But in the Korni plates dated Saka 1034 - 1112 A.D. he changes his attitude and appears to demonstrate religious universality by applying to himself the three juxtaposed titles *parama mahesvara, parama vaisnava, parama brahmanya.* Already his next major charter, the Vishakhapatnam plates dated in Saka 1040 - 1118 A.D. retains only the last two of these titles : it omits parama mahesvara. What led to this change ?

Many scholars have spoken of a 'conversion' of Anantavarman Codanganga deva from Saivism to Visnuism and claimed that it was under the impact of the preaching of Ramanuja (1056-1137) that this conversion took place. In fact, Ramanuja had a tremendous influence, and during his time the

Sri Vaisnava movement spread rapidly into Kalinga and into Orissa. One of the contemporaries of Anantavarman Codangangadeva, the Raja Jaya Bhanjadeva, is also known form his inscription to have joined the Vaisnava religion although he had been a devotee of Siva before.

A perusal of the inscriptions of the time of Anantavarman Codangangadeva has shown that in his case such a conversion did not take place. Privately the king's devotion to Siva was not affected. A large number of "unofficial" inscriptions, especially inscriptions referring to grants made by his brother or by his numerous queens, continue to call him a devotee of Siva (*parama maheswvara*).

On the other hand, the king seems to have been keenly aware of the spiritual trends of his time. He was ready to adjust himself to them and to use them for his own political purposes. As expressed in his above mentioned Korni plates, he was willing to support all who supported him in turn, whether they be Saiva or Vaisnava or others. He later built the huge temple at Puri for the god *Vishnu*, very likely in order to base his power on a rising movement. In his Vishakhapatnam plates which were taken as a proof of his conversion, he suppressed the reference to his devotion of Siva because the donation was made to a devotee of *Vishnu*, a certain Madhava who belonged to a Vaisnava family. In donations to *Siva* temples such as the temple at *Draksarama* or the *Nilakanthesvara* temple at *Bobbili* a similar policy was followed, i.e. the king was only represented as devotee of Siva. Therefore, instead of proving a conversion, the inscriptions only show that on the occasion of gifts to temples or private persons the king refrained from hurting the feelings of his subjects.

Some other important facts emerge from the inscriptions. The first refers to the *Madhukesvara* temple at Mukhalingam which was the main temple in the capital of Eastern Ganga kings up to 1135A.D. *Madhukesvara* was the actual state deity of Gangas, replacing the family god *Gokarnesvara* on the Mahendra mountain for practical purposes, because the latter was too difficult of access. That the temple served as a kind of legal archieve of the state is evident even inscriptions recording gifts to other temples or to private persons were inserted into the walls or incised on the pillars of this temple for easy reference.

With this "official status" of the *Madhukesvara* temple in mind one should consider the following facts.

An important and auspicious event in the religious calendar of the Vaisnavas the so-called *mahadvadasi* also known as *devotsava-dvadasi* or *utthana-dvadasi* which is celebrated on the 12th *tithi* of the bright fortnight in the month of *Kartika* when *Visnu* is supposed to rise from his sleep, was observed in the temple of *Madhukesvara*. Donations, mainly of a perpetual lamp, were made to the god on this occasion. The inscriptions recording such gifts on *mahadvadasi* occur from Saka 1030=1108 A.D. onwards. From the same year onwards the name of one Prolacari (Prolacarya) who seems to have been a Vaisnava priest appears in the inscriptions of the temple. He was appointed in the Madhukesvara temple for several years. Later he was transferred to the Nilisvara (Nilakanthesvara) temple at Bobbili where his name occurs for eleven more years from Saka 1044 to Saka 1055 = 1122=1133 A.D.

An earlier inscription of Saka 1005-1083 A.D. mentions already a *pujari* of *Madhukesvara* with the name *Narayanabhatta*. His connection with Visnuism is likely but less certain.

A Visnu image was installed (in a separate shrine ?) in the Madhukesvara temple and dancing girls were appointed for it.

These details show that at least as early as 1108 A.D., i.e. four years earlier than the first mention of his Vaisnava leanings in the Korni plates, Anantavarman Codangangadeva did already exhibit a policy of religious inclusiveness in the sense of a coexistence and combination of Siva-and Visnu worship in his main temple. Moreover, the god *Madhukesvara* is twice invoked as *Jagato-natha*, a name which comes very close to the later title *Jagannatha*. Both times the name occurs in a Vaisnava setting. In saka 1030-1108 A.D. queen *Somala-mahadevi*, one of the wives of Anantaverman Codagangadeva, offers a lamp on the occasion of *mahadvadasi* to *Madhukesvara Jagato-natha*: *praddad akhandam mahadvadasyam madhukesvaraya jagato nathaya dipam*. Already 28 years earlier, in Saka 1002-1080 A.D. i.e. less than 2½ years after Anantavarman Codanganga's accession to the throne, a man with the Vaisnava name Janarddana gave a lamp in memory of his father to *Madhukesvaraya jagatannathaya*.

Thus it appears that the religious policy of the king which he consciously applied by the choice of his priests at least from 1108 and made generally known in 1112, was in accordance with the actual trend of religion as practised in the main temple of his own capital from the very beginning of his reign.

The temple of *Madhukesvara* remained important under Codagangadeva's eldest son Kamarnavadeva. But being cut off from the centre administration which had been moved to the north, it gradually declined in the time of the later rulers. It is possible that the title *Jagato-natha* (Jagannatha) for the main god of the imperial Gangas, although introduced in Puri at a later period had a firm root in the family tradition and was transferred to Puri from Mukhalingam when the latter had completely lost its significance for the religion of the state.

Finally the influence of his queens on Anantavarman Codagangadeva should not be neglected. His chief queen was Jayamgonda Codadevi, the daughter of Viracoda who was the 3rd son of the great king Kulottunga Cola. Viracoda erected a temple for *Visnu-Purusottama* at Sarpavaram while he was viceroy in Vengi (1078-1084 and 1088-1092 A.D.). Nine inscriptions in this temple, recording mainly grants by Anantavarman Codagangadeva's younger brother Permadideva and his wives, refer to the god as *Purusottama*. Therefore a temple of Purusottama, built by Anantavarman Codagangadeva's father-in-law, existed in the East Godavari

District since the last quarter of the 11th century, about fifty years prior to the earliest date for the completion of the *Purusottama* temple in Puri. The preconceived notion that the only temple of *Purusottama* in the coastal area of Eastern India was at Puri, which has biased all modern works on the history of *Jagannatha*, is wrong.

All this goes to show that Codaganga's religious policy was not the outcome of an isolated decision. He was pushed on by a general trend which has been set in motion by the *Serivaisnava* movement. He promoted this movement at Srikurmam from 1113 A.D. onwards. Later, when he built his own *Purusottama* temple at Puri, this temple had to reflect the greatness of his power and prestige, since his kingdom now extended from the Godavari in the south-west to the mouth of the Ganges in the north-east. The main tower was probably not yet completed before he died in 1147. The other parts of the temple were gradually added by his successors.

Extract from "The Cult of Jagannath and the Regional Tradition of Puri" pg. 22-25.

Annexure VI

Passports issued to dignitaries for their visit on Pilgrimage to Puri

1. Vol. IV. No. 1097 : 7 June 1774 - Sambhaji Ganesh, the Subadar of Orissa, was informed that the family of Raja Rajballabh was going on pilgrimage to Poorsutum Chattar. He was requested that the facilities might be afforded to the pilgrims during their journey.

2. Vol. IV. No. 1224 : 10 June 1774-Dustack was granted in favour of Gopal Gossain who was going on a pilgrimage to Jagannath with travelling requisites.

3. Vol. IV. No. 1367 : 2 November 1774 - Jasrat Khan, the Naib Nazim of Dacca, informed that his Dewan Ram Kunwar was proceeding on a pilgrimage to Puri. He requested that a Dustack might be issued in favour of his Dewan.

4. Vol. IV. No. 1395 - Madhaji Hari, the Subadar of Orissa, was informed that Ram Kanta Ray, the Dewan of Jasrat Khan, was going on a pilgrimage to Sri Jagannath. The Subadar was requested to afford him assistance during the journey.

5. Vol. V. No. 1475 : 13 December 1774-Dustack was granted in favour of Ragalal and twentyfive persons who were proceeding from Calcutta to Jagannath on pilgrimage.

6. Vol. V No. 1658 : 24 March 1775 - Dustack was granted to Rangalal Bishnoo (Vaishnava) and others of Banaras who went to Jagannath. They would return to Banaras by boat from Calcutta.

7. Vol. V. No. 494 : 3 January 1776 - Dustack was granted to Radhagovinda Ray who was going on pilgrimage to Jagannath with 5 or 6 companions.

8. Vol. V. No. 604 : 4 August 1777 - Beniram Pundit notified his intention of proceeding to Jagannath and of his resolution of waiting on the Governor General at Calcutta.

9. Vol. V. No. 1247 : 16 December 1778 - Kashi Rao, Rajaram and Hirdai Ram were intimated that Rao Ananta Ram, the brother of Raja Govinda Ram, was going on a pilgrimage to Jagannath. They were requested to help him in the performance of his religious duties.

10. Vol. V, No. 1386 : 5 March 1779 - A letter from Beniram Pundit. Having taken leave from his master the Maharaja, he, in company of Ramakanta Ray, reached Cuttack on 24th February. The latter had proceeded to Jagannath and the writer had been detained at Cuttack on business with Rajaram Pundit (the Maratha Governor).

11. Vol. VI, No. 927 : 18 December 1783 - Dustack was granted to Ram Sunkar who was proceeding from Calcutta to Jagannath on pilgrimage. He had with him food, clothes, two hundred men and women and fifty horsemen.

12. Vol. VII No. 38 : July 1784 - Mudhoji Bhonsle instructs Rajaram Pundit to pay one lakh of rupees in charity to Motiger and other Gosains who had proceeded towards Cuttack for the performance of religious ceremonies at the temple of Jagannath.

13. Vol. VII, No. 189 : 29 April 1785 - Rajaram Pundit was informed that Shankar and Bishannath were going on pilgrimage to Jagannath with sixty companions. They had

with them twenty horses and same number of coolies. The Governor was requested to give the pilgrims every facility. After pilgrimage they would proceed to Bombay.

14. Vol. VII, No. 201 : 5 May 1785 - Dustack was granted to Sahu Gopal Das, who was going from Banaras to Jagannath. He had with him two hundred men, 15 Bahangees (Palanquins) and 16 bullock carts.

15. Vol. VII. No. 634 : 14 August 1786 - Madhaji Sindhia requested that peremptory orders be issued to the authorities in Orissa to give every facility to the mother of Bissambhar Pundit, one of his worthy dependents, to enable her to perform pilgrimage to Jagannath and other holy places in its neighbourhood.

16. Vol. VII : 4 October 1786 - Baby Ausan Singh requested for a passport for pilgrimage to Jagannath.

17. Vol. VII, No. 1428 : 4 July 1787 - Mohunt Sukhdeo Das of the temple of Jagannath writes that Raja Rajnarayn, the zamindar of Kasijora in the Midnapore district, assigned 960 Bighas of land for bhog to be offered to Jagannath two years ago. His estate had been confiscated by the E.I. Company. The Mohunt had written to the Government to release the aforesaid property which was a charity grant. Rajaram Pundit was officiating Governor-General of Bengal, in this connection. But no action had been taken so far.

History of the Jagannath Temple in the 19th Century by Prabhat Mukherjee, p. 19-21 Firma KLM Pvt. Ltd. Calcutta - 1977.

Annexure VII

Groome's Report giving an account of Pilgrim Tax

60. As the business of collecting Tax's from the pilgrims must unavoidably be entrusted to the natives I have taken great pains to ascertain how it could be transacted so as to entirely prevent, speculation and to ensure pilgrims of every description and domination from unnecessary detention and oppression, but I have not been able to hit upon a plan calculated holy to answer these purposes. It has therefore suggested itself to me that as I can not entirely prevent all the inconveniences of detention oppression and speculation that the best mode is to give as little latitude for it as possible and therefore to have as few places of collection as the nature of circumstances will admit.

61. Having the principle place of collection as formerly at the Atharanulla abuses may be practised as heretofore without the possibility of checking them I could therefore recommend that the only place of collection for pilgrims coming from the northward be at the collector (*Cutcherree*) and the best mode of collecting that appears to me is by having a *Daroga* at Joobra ghat whose business it shall be, when pilgrims arrive there, to make out lists of the number Palanqueens, *Doolis* horseman Hackeries and Pilgrims on foot and to send them to the collector Cutherree but he is to separate those who make objections

to pay the rate which Government may choose to fix, either from inability or any other cause. At the head of the list the *Daroga* must mention the name of the Suthooa and pandas who have brought the pilgrims people of rank who may object to come to the *Cutcherree* for the purpose of paying the tax's may be permitted to pay the amount to the *Daroga* who will send it with the name of the pilgrims to the Collector who will then furnish him with a pass. The pass shall mention the number of pilgrims and their quantity with the name of the Panda to whom they are made over but any pilgrim not taking a Panda may have a pass for himself persons who may object to pay the tax's from inability should be obliged solemnly or *Dhurrum* etc. to declare their not being worth more than five rupees in which case they may pass free but should they have more, they should pay as the collector may think just provided the excess does not exceed the amount fixed by Government. To administer an oath on such an occasion, would be considered an act of violence and confining pilgrims would be contrary to the justice and equity of the British Government. Therefore considering the biogotry of the Hindoo on a pilgrimage, a solemn declaration of this nature may in general be relied on should however any pilgrim came who will neither pay nor make the declaration his pass may be refused him for 2 or 3 days. This measure is proposed in order to give the poor and needy an opportunity of seeing the idol as well as the wealthy and opulent such pilgrims and those exempt as specified in list No. 2 at least such as Government may deem right to allow to continue exempt shall receive a pass with the words "duty free".

62. To check pilgrims who actually come in palanqueens, *Doolies*, on horse back, or in Hackeries, from imposing upon the *Daroga* at Joobra ghat by leaving their conveyances at a short distance from the river it is proposed to have a Daroga at Nirisingpoor Ghaut situated

to the northward of Balasore whose duty it shall be daily to send an account to the Collector of the number of palanqueens, Doolis Horsemen, and Hackeries that pass that Ghat for Jagannath, with the names of the proprietors and the *Sothoos* or *Pundah* in whose charge they are. The reason for this measure is, because I shall here after mention the rates which I propose to be fixed on each description of conveyance and therefore it is intended to prevent pilgrims eluding the rates, to be proposed by quitting the superior for the inferior mode of conveyance.

63. Another Daroga should be stationed at the Authara Nullah to whom all passes must be delivered, on the back of which in order to save time he must affix his seal as a voucher of its having been shown and the pilgrim will return it to the Daroga at Joobra Ghaut on his way back to whom is send it to the Collector. The Daroga of the Autaranullah should likewise send daily by the *dawk* on account of the number of passes delivered on each day with the description of the quality of the pilgrims. The Daroga suffering any Hindoo to enter the town of poorsottam without a pass should be held liable to a fine equal to the amount that would have been paid by the pilgrims suffered to pass and likewise dismission from office.

64. It have always been customary for the pilgrims from Kunka Kojung and of the purganahs adjacent to those territories to proceed by the way of the *Gundicha Mandap* of Babooghaut, where a *Daroga* must be stationed to collect the taxes and which *Daroga* will furnish them with passes. The collections from these pilgrims will not amount to much annually, and it is impossible to device any plan to prevent embezzlement in the *Daroga* stationed there, unless fear of punishment and dismission from office be sufficient.

65. During the rains the pilgrims from the hill forts by the way of Khurda cannot get to the Authara Nullah, therefore a Daroga will be required at Mungala Ghat near the tank of Markhund who will collect and furnish the pilgrims with passes.

66. At Lokenath Ghat a *Daroga* is requisite for the purpose of collecting the duties from pilgrims coming from the southwards.

67. All these *Daroga* should be obliged to send a deity list of pilgrims who they have allowed to pass with the amount of the taxes collected from each and the money must be forwarded to the collector's treasury at the end of every month another use of these *Daroga* will be to prevent pilgrims from Bengal evading the duties at Joobra Ghaut.

68. Near the above *Ghats* there are several fords at which it will be necessary to station *Chuprassees* to prevent people passing. These fords should be under the superintendence of the *Daroga* to which they are nearest and for the purpose of guarding them each *Daroga* will require an establishment they are however specified in the accompanying list No. 17 as likewise the names of the Fords and to what ghat attached.

69. There are objections to fixing high rates to collections from pilgrims of inferior orders as it is the wish and intention of the British Government that no persons should be assessed above this means so as to enable him to pay his devotions with ease and convenience, it would be moreover, oppressive to the lower order to tax them equally with the superior, I have, therefore, specified in list. No. 18 a lower rate of taxation for pilgrims of the former order than hereto-fore collected, and a higher for those of the latter. The increase to the least will not subject them to any inconvenience or deter any of that description from

performing the pilgrimage, but the former high rates for the first prevented many from coming who would otherwise have made a point of it.

70. The rates for pilgrimage from the southwards were always low as a diminution of the tax for those from the north ward has been proposed. I conceive it but justice to decrease that for the pilgrims from the southward as the people from this direction are in general poor.

71. To prevent the delay in enquiring and ascertained the truth of the assertions of the inhabitants of the northern side of the Mahanadee and in collecting different small sums for residents of different villages I recommend that the whole of these people be assessed alike and that all the inhabitants of this side of the Mahanadee except those in the territories of the Gujarats be exempt as heretofore.

72. As the passes for the pilgrimage could be more liable to be forced, and less easily discovered if written I could recommend the passes being pointed with vacancies left for the names, members of pilgrimage and the date of their being issued.

I am & C

Zh. Juggernath

Signed C. Grome Collector
Rev. Department
The 10th June, 1805

C. Grome Collector, Puri to Thomas Fortescue Esqr. Secretary to the Commissioner for the affairs of the Province of Cuttack.

Annexure VIII
Regulation IV of 1806 A.D.

A regulation for levying a tax from pilgrims resorting to the temple of Jagannath, and for the superintendence and management of the temple :- passed by the Governor General in Council, on the 3rd of April 1806; corresponding with the 22nd *Chyte* 1212 Bengal area; the 30th *Chyte* 1213 Fussily; the 22nd *Chyte* 1213 Willaity; the 15th Chyte 1863 Sumbut; and the 13th *Mohurrum* 1221 *Higeree.*

Whereas it is provided by Section XXXI, Regulation XII, 1805, that a tax shall be levied from pilgrims reporting to the temple of Jagannath : And whereas it is effendally necessary that provision should be made for the protection of the pilgrims from undue exactions on the part of the officers of Government or of the temple, and also for the preservation of order, tranquility, and regularity in the town of Jagannath Puri, and its dependencies, and for the trial of civil suits of inconsiderable amount or value within those limits; the following rules have been passed, to be in force from the time of their promulgation.

A.D. 1806 Regulation IV

II. A tax shall be levied on the part of Government (as was heretofore done under the late Marhatta government) on pilgrims resorting to the temple of *Jagannath*. The collection of the tax shall be entrusted to an officer, (being a connected servant of the Company) with the official designation of the collector of the tax on pilgrims at Jagannath. The general superintendence of the collections, and the control of the officers employed in the performance of that duty, shall be vested in the Board of Revenue at Fort Williams.

III. The avenues for the admission of pilgrims to the *Jagannath* shall be confined to two : viz. ghat Atharah Nullah on the North, and ghaut Lokanath on the South of the town of Jaganath Puri.

IV. The tax to be levied at ghaut Atharah Nullah, shall be fixed at ten rupees; and the tax to be levied at Ghat Lokanath, shall be fixed at five rupees, on each persons of the class of pilgrims, commonly called Laal Jautreys; whether such appellation shall have been assumed by the pilgrims themselves, or whether they shall be so denominated by their conductors.

V. The tax on all other pilgrims indiscriminately shall be levied at the rate of two rupees form each person.

VI. The above mentioned rates of tax on pilgrims, are to be considered to include the usual fees of the officers of the temple; and these fees shall in future be paid to them out of the funds which have been, or may be assigned for the support of the temple. Provided, however, that this rule shall not be considered applicable to the officers denominated *Purharees* and *Pundahs*, who shall be entitled to receive, in conformity to established usage, a fee from the pilgrims, according to a table of rates which shall be kept fixed at the temple of Jagannath, and in places adjacent to the temple for general information. The officers attached to the temple are accordingly strictly prohibited from making any demands for money, exclusively of the tax and fees specified in this and the proceeding sections. This restriction however, shall not be construed to preclude the said officers from receiving presents of gifts; the same being voluntarily made. Any deviation from these rules will subject the officer, by whom such offence shall be committed on proof thereof made to the satisfaction of the Board of Revenue, or of the Governor General in Council, (if the nature of the case shall require a reference to Government under the general provisions contained in Regulation V, 1804) to be dismissed from his employment.

VII. It shall be the duty of the Collector of the tax on pilgrims to establish, with the approbation of the Board of Revenue, such rules, as may be necessary for the due collection of the tax for keeping regular and clear accounts of the receipts; for the prevention of embezzlement by the native officers; and for guarding against any evasion of the established tax by the pilgrims.

VIII. It shall likewise be the duty of the Collector to establish, with the sanction of the Board of Revenue and aided by the officers of police, such rules for the admission of pilgrims into the town of Jagannath Puri through the prescribed avenues of ghaut Atharah Nullah and Ghat Lokenath, as may be necessary to guard against accidents and confusion, and to preserve regularity and good order among the great concourse of people resorting to the temple.

IX. In conformity to long and established usage, the following description of persons shall be considered to be exempt from the payment of the tax on pilgrims at Jagannath viz. Byraghies; persons employed in carrying the water of the Ganges to the temple of Jagannath, or to any other Hindu temple; persons residing between the *Byturnee* Nullah and the Ganjam river ; persons resorting to the town of Jagannath Puri for trade, or for any other purpose excepting on pilgrimage. Pilgrims likewise in an actual state of poverty shall be exempted from the payment of the established tax; on declaring, under such form or ceremony as shall be prescribed by the native officers entrusted with the management of the temples that they cannot contribute the prescribed tax of two rupees and that they have not in their immediate possession more money than is absolutely necessary to desray their expenses on their return from pilgrimage.

X. If it should appear that any other class of people was therefore exempted from the payment of the duty levied on pilgrims under the late Marhatta Government, the Collector of the tax shall report the circumstances to the Board of Revenue. That Board shall submit the case with their sentiments on the subject, to the Governor General in Council; who will order such case of people to be in future exempted from the payment of the tax or not, as may appear to him to be proper.

The Governor General in Council likewise reserve to himself the power of granting any temporary and special exemption from the tax in favour of individuals he may consider to be proper.

XI. The superintendence of the temple of Jagannath and its interior economy; the conduct and management of its affairs; and the entire control over the priests, and servants, attached to the idol and to the temple, shall be vested in the assembly of pundits or learned Brahmins, who on all occasions shall be guided by the recorded rules and institutions of the temple, or by long and established usage.

XII. The assembly of pundits shall consist of three members, to be recommended by the collector of the tax on pilgrims, through the Board of Revenue, to the Governor General in Council.

XIII. In the selection of persons to fill that situation, it shall be the particular duty of the collector to consult the opinions or the most respectable Hindus, with respect to the description of persons, from whom the selection ought to be made, and to satisfy that they will exercise the important trust to be committed to them with propriety. Nothing however contained in this or in the foregoing section shall be construed to preclude the Governor General in Council from nominating in the first instance any person to fill the office of Pundit, should be at any time deem it acceptable to exercise that power.

XIV. In all cases of differences of opinion amongst the members the opinion of the majority shall be adopted by the assembly.

XV. The Pundits shall hold their sections so long at they shall continue to conduct themselves with integrity, diligence and property, but nothing contained in this regulation shall prevent the Governor General in Council from removing any person from that situation on proof of misconduct in such person made to the satisfaction of Government.

XVI. To enable the assembly of pundits to perform the duties of their station with greater effect, they are hereby empowered to punish persons subject to their control, for any instance of neglect or misconduct, by imposing small fines upon them not exceeding one month's salary or income, or by suspending the offender from his office, if the offence shall appear to merit that punishment; provided however that, in the former case, the fines so imposed shall be reported to the collector, in order that the amount may be deducted from the suspension of any officer from his employment, a report shall be made to the collector for the decision of the Board of Revenue or of the Governor General in Council, according to the nature and the circumstances of the case, on the principle of the rules contained in Regulation V, 1804.

XVII. If any person attached to the temple of Jagannath shall be guilty of any offence of a criminal nature, which may appear to the assembly of pundits to require any greater punishment than that above stated, the person accused shall be delivered over to the charge of the officers of police, who will proceed against him in the manner prescribed in the general regulations.

XVIII. Such salaries shall be allowed of the funds to be assigned for the support of the temple, to the persons composing the assembly of pundits in Jagannath, and to the other ministers and officers of the temple, as the Governor General in Council may hereafter think proper to fix for their support.

XIX. It shall be the duty of the collector to report to the Board of Revenue whenever vacancies may occur among the ministers and officers of the temple; when that Board will either order the vacancies to be filled, or refer to the case to Government, as may appear to be proper, in conformity to the principle of the rules contained in Regulation V, 1804. In the recommendation of persons to fill such vacancies, the collector is required to attend particularly to the established usages of the temple, and to the religious opinions of the temple, and of the pilgrims who resort to it.

XX. To enable the collector of the tax on pilgrims at *Jagannath*, to perform the duty entrusted to him with effect, he is hereby empowered to levy small fines from any of the ministers officers, or servants, attached to the temple for neglect of duty, or other misconduct. Provided, however that no fine shall be levied exceeding the actual or computed monthly allowance of the person by whom it may be payable. Provided also, that any person, on whom such punishment may be imposed, shall be at liberty, should be deem himself aggrieved, to apply for redress to the Board of Revenue; who will pass such orders on the subject as shall appear to be just and reasonable, and whose decision shall be final.

XXI. The collector of the tax on pilgrims at Jagannath shall be ex-office assistant to the magistrate of the zillah of Cuttack, and shall be competent to exercise all the powers which either are, or at any time may be, vested in the head assistants to the zillah and city magistrates. The person, by whom these powers may be exercised, is required at all times, to give every attention to the religious opinions of the Hindus, and to the particular institutions of the temple of Jagannath, which may be consistent with the general regulations; and with the maintenance of peace and good order at the temple, and its vicinity; and he shall on no account suffer his peons or ministerial officers to enter the precincts of the temple.

XXII. The town of Jagannath Puri, and the country adjacent, shall constitute a police jurisdiction within such limits as may be fixed with the approbation of government; and either one or more of the Dewul *Purchhas*, as the Governor General in Council may direct, shall be appointed to be *darogas* of police within those limits, with the powers vested in the darogahs by Regulation XIII, 1805, and the other regulations thereby extended to Cuttack.

XXIII. It shall be competent for the court of *Sudder Dewanny Adawlut*, to appoint the *Dewul Purchhas* to be commissioners in the town of Jagannath Puri and its dependencies, for the trial of civil suits to a limited amount, under Regulation XL, 1793, and Regulation XLIX, 1803, extended to Cuttack by Regulation XIV, 1805. The Sudder *Dewanny Adawlut* is likewise hereby further authorised to prescribe such rules, as may appear to be necessary for the conduct of the duties of the commissioners, either in rotation or in such other mode, as may appear to be best calculated for the speedy decision of the suits of which the commissioners are empowered to take cognizance, and as may the least interfere with the duties of the temple.

Annexure IX

Regulation V of 1806 AD.

A regulation for preventing persons from evading payment of the tax established by Regulation IV. 1806 passed by the Governor General in Council, on the 17th of April 1806.

Whereas it has been deemed advisable to make further provision for preventing evasion of the payment of the tax established by Reg. IV. 1806 on the part of the persons resorting to the temple of *Jagannath* : And where as it has been like wise judged advisable, to grant an exemption from the payment of the tax in favour of persons of the religious order denominated, sonassies; the following rules have been established to be in force from the time of their promulgation.

II. The application of *holy* jatras being applicable to all classes of Hindoos of substance and respectability, when engaged on a pilgrimage to the temple of *Jagannath* if any person of that description shall endeavour to evade payment of the prescribed tax by assuming an appellation applicable only to the inferior ranks, he shall be compelled not only to make good the difference between the sum actually paid by him and the established tax; but he shall likewise be subject to the payment of a fine equal to double the amount of the tax; provided that, it shall be proved to the satisfaction of the Collector, that such pilgrim ought, in the first instance, to have paid the tax at the rate ordered to be levied from holy *Jatras*; provided however, that it shall not be competent for the Collector to order any personal search or examination to be made of the pilgrims, for the purpose of ascertaining whether any cash be discoverable in their possession.

III. Persons of the religious order, denominated, bonafies, shall be exempted from the payment of the tax, established by reg. IV, 1806, in common with the several descriptions of persons specified in Sec. IX of that regulation.

IV. It being prescribed in section XXI, of the above mentioned regulation, that "the magistrate shall on no account suffer his peons or ministerial officers to enter the precincts of the temple." It is hereby explained that such restriction is only to be considered applicable to persons of that description when employed in serving process, or in the execution of other duty entrusted in them in quality of officers of police, and that the said restriction is not intended to extend to such peons or other officers, whenever they may be desirous of visiting the temple for religious or other purposes.

Annexure X
Regulation IV of 1809 A.D.

A regulation for rescinding Regulation IV and V, 1806; and for substituting rules in lieu of these enacted in the said regulations for levying duties from the pilgrims resorting to Jagannath, and for the superintendence and management of the affairs of the temple - passed by the Governor General in Council, on the 28th April 1809.

Whereas it has appeared that the rules at present in force for levying duties from the pilgrims resorting to Jagannath, and for the superintendence and management of the affairs of the temple have been in some respects attended with difficulty and inconvenience, the Governor General in Council, with a view to afford every facility to the different classes of Hindoos, in the performance of their religious ceremonies, and with a view to the better management of the internal affairs of the temple, has been pleased to rescind Reg. IV, and V of 1806, and to substitute the following rules in lieu of them; and where as under the existing rules, respecting persons exempted from the payment of the tax, frauds have been committed by persons professing themselves to be carriers of water of the Ganges, and by persons resorting to Jagannath under the pretext of purposes other than that of pilgrimage, the Governor General in Council has been pleased to make further provision for the prevention of such frauds in future. The following rules therefore are enacted, and they are to have effect from the date of the promulgation of this regulation.

II. First - The Superintendence of the temple of *Jagannath*; and its interior economy, the conduct and management of its affairs, and the control over the priests, officers, and servants attached to the temple, are hereby vested in the Raja of Khoordah, who on all occasions shall be guided by the recorded rules and institutions of the temple, or by ancient and established usage.

IV. The third *dewl purcha* shall execute the duty of supervision, and it shall also be his duty to give an account to the Collector of the tax; of all offerings and presents made to the idol.

V. A tax shall be levied on the part of the Government. (as was heretofore done under the late Marhatta Government and as has also been done under the British Government since the conquest of the province of Cuttack) on pilgrims resorting to the temple of Jagannath. The collection of the tax shall be entrusted to an officer with the official designation of the Collector of the tax on pilgrims. But that officer is to be subject to the authority of the Collector of Cuttack. The general superintendence of the collections, and the control of the officers employed in the performance of that duty shall be vested in the Board of Revenue at Fort William.

VI. The avenues for the admission of pilgrims shall be confined to two, viz : Ghaut Athara Nuallah on the north and Ghaut Lokanath on the south west of the town of Jagannath Puri.

VII. 1st - The pilgrims liable to the tax shall be divided into 4 classes, as follows :

1st class	-	or Laul Jatries
2nd class	-	or Nium Lauls
3rd class	-	or Bhurrungs

4th class - or Punj Tirthees, comprehending the following descriptions of low caste who are not permitted to enter the temple :

1. *Lolee* or *Kusbee*, 2. *Soonree*, 3. *Machoowas*, 4. *Numosooder* or *Chandal*, 5. *Ghookee*, 6. *Gazur*, 7. *Bangdee*, 8. *Jeogee*, 9. *Kahar*, 10. *Ranjbansee*, 11. *Peerally*, 12. *Chamar*, 13. *Dhome*, 14. *Paun*, 15. *Teor*, 16. *Bhoonimalee*, 17. *Haddee*.

2nd - The following are the rates of tax payable by the different classes.

Pilgrims of the 1st class coming from the North and passing the Atturah Nullah Ghat to pay a tax of Rs. 10/- and coming from south and passing Lokannath Ghat Rs. 6/-.

Pilgrims of the second class coming from the north and passing the Atturah Nullah Ghaut, to pay Rs. 5/- and coming from the south and passing Lokannath Ghat Rs. 3/-.

Pilgrims of the 4th class passing either of the ghauts, to pay Rs. 2/-.

3rd - A pilgrim of the 1st class is to be allowed free access to the temple during 30 days, and he is to be attended by a *purharree* or *panda*, at all times he may enter the temple. But if he should wish to be exempted from the attendance of those officers, by the payment of a further sum of Rs. 10/- to the Collector and by the surrender of his pass, he shall be entitled to a *purwannah* authorizing him to visit the temple, at all times when the gates are open whether attended by a purharee or Panda or otherwise, and he shall further be allowed to perform his religious ceremonies for an unlimited time so long as he may wish to remain in the town.

4th - A pilgrim of the second class who may visit the temple at the time of the Ratha Jatra, shall be allowed to the temple during 10 days. But if he should visit the temple at the time of the Dola Jatras or at any other period of the year, excepting at the time of the Ratha Jatra, he is to be allowed access to the temple for a period of 7 days only, and he must be at all times attended by a Panda or purharree, when visiting the temple.

5th - A pilgrim of the 3rd class shall be allowed access to the temple at the time of *Ratha jatra*, during 5 days; but any other time he will only be allowed to visit the temple during 4 days, and he must be attended by a panda or purharee on all occasions.

6th - A pilgrim of the 4th class shall be allowed to perform the customary ceremonies without the temple, during 16 days, attended by the *bat peeada* of the Collector of tax at *Jagannath*.

7th - It shall be obtainal to all descriptions of persons entitled to visit the interior of the temple, to enroll themselves under whichever class they may prefer, on payment of the prescribed rate of tax.

Second - The Raja of Khoordah and his successors shall hold the charge vested in them by the above clause, so long as they shall continue to conduct themselves with integrity, diligence and propriety : but nothing contained in the regulation shall be construed to preclude the Governor General in Council, from removing the present Raja, or any of his successors from the superintendence of the temple, on proof of misconduct in such persons made to the satisfaction of Government.

Third - To enable the Supdt. of temple to perform the duty of his station with efficiency, he is hereby authorised to punish persons subject to his control, for any instance of neglect or misconduct by imposing small fines upon them, not exceeding one month's salary, or income or by removing the offender (if not one of the three head *purchhas*) from his office, if the offence shall appear to merit that punishment. The amount of any fines imposed under this clause are to be carried to the account of Government by the *suttaishuzzary purchhas*.

III. 1st - The three *dewl purchhas* are to be appointed by the Collector of Cuttack, subject to the confirmation of Government, and they are not to be removed from their officers, without the sanction of the Governor General in Council. These officers, however, are to execute the functions of their officers under the direction of the Raja and they are required to obey his orders punctually..

2nd - In the event, however, of any orders being issued by the Raja, inconsistent with recorded rules and institituris of the temple, or with its ancient and established usages, it shall be the duty of *purchhas* to represent the circumstances of the case to the Collector of the tax, for the final orders of the Governor General in Council, if it is necessary for the restoration of good order, and the prevention of disputes and irregularities.

VIII. 1st - With a view to facilitate access to the temple, and to remove all difficulties from the way of the pilgrims passing the ghauts, printed certificates shall be prepared which shall be procurable on the payment of the fixed tax at the offices of the Secretary to the Board of Commissioners and Sec. to the Board of Revenue, the Collectors of Cuttack and Ganjam, and at the two ghauts.

2nd - The following are the forms of the certificate to be granted to the different pilgrims :

Form No. 1

A.B. inhabitant of .... in the district of .... having this day paid into this office, the sum of sicca rupees .... is entitled to pass through the .... ghaut, without further interruption, as a laul jatree or pilgrim of the first class to the cutcherry of the Collector of tax at Jagannath. On producing this certificate to the said collector, he is further entitled to receive a pass, and to have access to the temple during thirty days.

Names or designation of attendance	Amount of tax paid by them respectively	Period for which they are to visit the temple

Form No. 2

.... as a *bhurrung*, or pilgrim of the third class .... access to the temple during 5 days, at the time of *Ratha Jatra* or during 4 days at any other time.

Form No. 3

.... as a *bhurrung*, or pilgrim of the third class .... access to the temple during 5 days, at the time of *Ratha Jatra* or during 4 days at any other time.

Form No. 4

.... as a *punj tirthee* a pilgrim of 4th class .... to receive a pass and to perform the customary ceremonies without gates of the temple during 16 days.

3rd - In case a pilgrim of the 1st class may be desirous of visiting the temple with his family and attendants such family and attendants not exceeding 20 persons, will be admitted to remain in the town so long as their master does, provided they shall in the first instance pay the prescribed tax, either as *bhurrungs* or *nuimlolls*, but they will not be allowed to enter into the temple for a long period of time, than they may be respectively entitled to consideration of the tax paid by them : in cases therefore where a pilgrim may be desirous of having his attendants, and family, allowed to remain with him as long as he remains himself, the tax for such persons either as *bhurrungs* or *nuimlolls* must be paid at the time he takes out his own certificate and the officer furnishing the certificate is to state the names, or designation of the family and attendants, the tax paid account of each of them and the No. of days during which they will respectively be allowed to perform their religious ceremonies, and such persons shall be allowed to remain in the town, as long as their master does.

4th - The certificates shall be dated and attested with the official seal and signature of the officer granting them, who shall also fill up the blank spaces, with the name of the pilgrims (or if female, her designation) the place of his or her habitation, the rate of the tax, and in the instance of pilgrims of the two 1st classes, name of ghaut, through which they will pass.

IX. No interruption by the *daroga* at the ghaut to the pilgrim holding the certificates.

X. 1st - If a pilgrim is unnecessarily delayed at the ghaut the *daroga* shall be fined in a sum not exceeding his salary for 3 months and also to be dismissed from his office.

2nd - Regarding slight offences daroga shall be fined.

3rd - It is to be the particular duty of the Collector of *Jagannath* to superintend the conduct of the *darogas* at the ghauts and to take special care that the pilgrims are not impeded, delayed or molested in any manner.

XI. 1st. - On the pilgrims having passed the ghauts, these of the 1st, 2nd and 3rd classes are to apply to the collector of Jagannath for a license of access to the temple and it shall be the duty of the collector on the receipt of the certificate from the pilgrims to grant to them a license according to the following from :

A.B. inhabitant of ....in the district of .... is entitled to perform the customary ceremonies under charge of .... during ....days, i.e., from .... of the month of .... and for that period you will afford to the holder here of free access to the temple of Jagannath. At the expiration of the period granted you will return this license into the office of the Collector of tax. A license of the form following will be granted by the collector of tax, on the receipt of the certificate from a pilgrim of the 4th class addressed to his *Nazir*.

Form of License

A.B. inhabitant of .... in the district of .... is entitled to perform the customary ceremonies without the entitled to perform the customary ceremonies without the temple gates under charge of .... *bat Peeada*, during .... days the isatgesay, from the .... of the month of .... to the .... day .... of the month of .... at the expiration of which period, the license shall be returned to the Collector of tax.

XIII. As in case of sickness a pilgrim may be prevented from performing his religious ceremonies during the number of days allowed to him, if might operate as a hardship if such person were compelled to quit the town immediately after the expiration of the prescribed time. The collector of the tax therefore shall in such cases be competent to extend the period, for such further time, as may be deemed reasonable by him, the Collector however is of course to observe due caution in the exercise of his authority.

XIV. The Collector of tax at Jagannath shall keep a register of all license granted by him, insert the dates of, and the periods, for which they may be in force, which will enable him to ascertain at all times whether any panda or *purharree* shall have neglected to return the license into the office as required. It shall be the duty of every *panda* or *purharree*, to return the license of the pilgrim under his charge, on the expiration of the period for which they have been granted, in default where of the panda or purharree shall be subject to such fine as on consideration of the circumstances of the case, the Collector of the tax may deem necessary : the amount of the fine shall in no case exceed the amount of tax paid by the 1st class of pilgrims.

XVI. 1st & 2nd - When any pilgrim shall continue to reside in the town on application from the Collector of the tax, it shall be the duty of the police daroga expel such persons from town.

XVIII. 1st - The following descriptions of persons shall be considered to be exempt from the payment of the tax on pilgrims at Jagannath math viz : *Byraghies*, *Sonassees*, *dundies*, *burmacharies*, *mohants*, *gosamis*, *khomartus*, *Nagas*, persons born within the Byturnee Nulha and the Ganjam river or who have resided with their families for a period of 10 years, within the above limits, persons employed in carrying the water of the Ganges to *Jagannath* math, and actually pouring the water over the idol at Lokennath, and persons resorting to the town of Jagannath Puri for trade or any other purpose excepting on pilgrimage.

XIX. With respect to persons resorting to Jagannath for the purpose of trade, or any other purpose, but that of pilgrimage, they are to be admitted to pass the ghauts without the payment of the tax, at all times of the year, excepting for 12 days from the commencement of the *Rath Jatra*. During that time no persons excepting such as may be exempted as *Kangals*, or carriers of the water of the Ganges or on account of their residence, or religious caste shall be admitted within the ghauts without the payment of the tax.

Annexure XI

Act No. X of 1840

Passed by the Right Hon'ble the Governor General of India in Council on the 20th April, 1840.

An act for the abolition of certain pilgrim taxes and for the superintendence of the temple of Jagannath.

I. Where as it is considered proper to abolish the exaction of all taxes or fees upon pilgrims resorting to Allahabad, Gaya and Jagannath, and to transfer the charge of the affairs of the Jagannath temple exclusively to a competent Hindu Supdt. under a full responsibility to the established courts of justice, for the redress of any violence or wrong, upon the application of any party interested.

It is hereby enacted that so much of section 31 Reg. XII of 1805 as provides for the continuance of the duties levied from pilgrims at Jagannath.

So much of section 4 Reg. XVIII of 1793 as provides for the continuance of the duties levied on pilgrims at Gaya and other places of pilgrimage.

II. And it is hereby enacted, that the superintendence of the Temple of Jagannath and its interior economy, the conduct, and management of its affairs, and the control over the priests officers, and servants attached to the

Temple, shall continue vested in the Rajah of Khoordha for the time being; provided always that the said Rajas and all persons connected with the said Temple shall on all occasions be guided by the record rules and institutions of the Temple, or by ancient and established usage, so far as the same may be consistent with the provisions of this act.

III. And it is hereby enacted, that the said Raja of Khoordha shall not receive or allow to be received by any person connected with the said temple, any payment other than such voluntary donations as may be freely offered, from any person, resorting to the said Temple, for the performance of religious ceremonies.

IV. And it is hereby declared and enacted that the said Raja, and all priests, officers and servants attached to the same temple are and shall be liable to be sued or prosecuted by any party interested, in any civil or criminal court of competent jurisdiction for any breach of trust, or official misfeasance, committed in the conduct of their duties or for any extortion or illegal violence exercised upon pilgrims or others under colour of the authority conveyed by this act.

Calcutta 1840 - Printed at the Bengal Military Orphan Press by G.H. Huttmann.

Annexure XII
Festivals

Festivals of the Jagannath Temple

It is essential, according to the *Dharmasastras*, to perform *yatras* or festivals for the installed deities. When *yatras* or festivals are held, the people of remote parts of the country coming to witness them, often find pleasure in seeing the deities in procession. There may be devotees who are old, invalid and diseased and thus do not have the access to the Shrine. All these people may be eager to have a *darshan* of the lords. To satisfy such people, festivals are observed. (Brddha Harita Smrti and Agamas). It is also stated that the performance of festivals in the temples removes fear of fire, famine, flood and epidemic. (Brddha Harita Smrti, Ch. Vi, Slokas 1-6).

These festivals may be celebrated for five, seven or nine days. At times they may continue even for six months or a year[3]. In the Jagannatha Temple several *utsavas* and *yatras* are observed. During these *utsavas* yatras the *Archa images* are often taken out in processions. This system of taking out the installed deities is called *Mulabera*, which is, however, a speciality in this temple. We are going to describe the twelve main *yatras;* the rest will only be simply named at the end.

According to Niladrimahodaya, Lord Jagannatha was born during the month of *Jyestha* on *Purnima* or the full-moon day. Sriharsa in his "*Naishadha Garita*" (XV 89) refers to this festival of *Purusottama*. So on that day the Snana Jatra is performed. The images of *Jagannatha*, *Balabhadra* and *Subhadra*, along with the image of Sudarsana, are brought in procession to the *Snana Vedi*.

The procession is called *Pahandi* or *Pahandi-Vijaya*. Scholars have given different interpretations of this term "*Pahandi*". Some maintain that it has come from the term "*Praspanda*" meaning movement. Some others are inclined to interpret it as a derivation from *Pandya Vijaya*. The *Snanavedi* (bathing platform) is decorated with pictures of jewel-trees and flower gardens. Flags, *toranas* etc. are also put up. The images are decorated with beautiful flowers. All kinds of perfumes, *dhupas* etc. are then offered. As the '*Pahandi*' of the deities takes place to the accompaniment of music and beating of drums produced by various indigenous musical instruments, thousands of people jostle to have a glimpse of them. On the previous day 108 golden and copper pots filled with water brought from the well of *Sitala* are preserved in the *Bhogamandapa*. On the *Snana Purnima* day, these vessels are brought to the *Snanavedi*. This ritual is called "*Jaladhibasa*". First the images are offered red powder and then they are taken to the *Snanavedi*. During this time, the bodies of the images are covered with silken clothes. Then water is poured, the rituals are performed and the *Pavamana* Hymns are chanted. After the bath, the deities are dressed in such a way that together they appear like the image of *Ganesa*. This is called *Gajanana Vesa*. It is said that a staunch devotee of God *Ganesa* and a profound scholar of South India visited Puri and he was rewarded by the king for his scholarship. That was the time of *Snana Yatra*. The king asked the scholar to accompany him to see Lord Jagannatha which the scholar refused under the pretext that he would not worship any God other than Ganesa. Somehow he was persuaded and brought before the *Snana Vedi*. To the surprise of all, Lord Jagannatha gave *Darsan* to the scholar in the form of Ganesa. Therefore during the *Snana Yatra*, when the sacred bath is performed, the deities are dressed like Ganesa. Various reasons for the *Ganesa Vesa* (dress) are assigned. After the sacred bath the colours of the images are generally washed away. Seeing the wooden images without proper colouring the devotees may not have the appropriate devotional attitude and in fact may feel a sinful repugnance. For that reason, the images are dressed as *Ganesa* in such a way that the devotees hardly observe the discolouration resulting from the *Abhiseka*.

This is the first Annual *Yatra* of Jagannatha. Generally the deity *Ganesa* is worshipped at the beginning of every religious rite and ritualistic worship. Because of this reason, Lord Jagannatha is decorated as *Ganesa* during this time. Often *Ganesa* is considered as a form of Vishnu.

After the *Snana Yatra*, the images of Jagannatha and others are kept away from public view for fifteen days without proper daily worship and they are kept on the *Ratna Vedi* inside the temple. This is the period which is called *"Anabasara"* meaning improper time for worship. Already we have stated above that the images are discoloured as a result of the sacred bath. During these fifteen days the *"Daitas"* (who are the descendants of *Viswabasu*, the Savar Chief) colour the images .and make suitable decorations. The period of colouring and decorations of the images is divided into seven short periods, each of two days' duration, and a short period of one day for finalising the colouring is kept apart. Thus the period covers a fortnight. On the 16th day the images become fit for being worshipped in their new forms after renovation. The festival of the first appearance of the Lord Jagannatha to his devotees is called *Netrotsaba* or *Navayavan* (new life). According to the *Silpasastras* and *Agamas*, the images become suitable for worship only after the performance of the rites of "*Caksurunmilana*" or the opening of the eyes. During "*Anabasara*", the "*Daitas*" offer to the deities only fruits and water mixed with cheese. According to them the deities do not keep well and therefore they take rest for the period. In fact they are considered to be ill and are treated by the *Raja Vaidya* or the King Physician with a specific medicine.

Now let us describe the famous *Ratha Yatra* or the Car-festival which is observed on the Asadha Sukla *Dwitya* i.e. the second day of the bright fortnight of the month of Asadha.

The celebration of *Ratha Yatra* during the rainy season is significant. The sages are of opinion that the term '*barsa*' (year) has been literally derived from the term '*barsa*' or rain and this prolific rainy season leads and represents all the seasons of the year. Rain appears as the harbinger of hilarity and vitality of humanity. In "*Satapatha Brahmana*" (III.2) the rainy season is wonderfully admired. Hence the Car-festival is being celebrated in rainy season.

The rainy season is symbolic and microcosmic of all other seasons of the year. The eastern wind in this season symbolises *spring*, the rain showers naturally denote the rainy season where the lightning flashes in it produce the autumnal effect, the break in rain indicates '*hemanta*' and above all, the alternate currency of heat and cold reminds one of summer and winter. Hence the rainy season represents all aspects of the natural seasons and appears as an entire organic whole. In the said work (*Satapatha Brahmana* - IV.2), an interesting legend regarding the origin of the *Ratha* is to be found. The car of the lord was in heaven long back. It was not to be noticed on earth. The legend says, the car originated on earth right from the battle between *Indra* (the king of heaven) and the demon *Brutrasura*. When *Indra* violently flung the weapon of lightning on the body of the demon, the weapon was divided into four parts. The third part was metamorphosed into a chariot. Possibly the term '*Ratha*' or chariot gained currency on earth since that day and gradually the process of its making was initiated. *Indra* is taken to be lord of rains and thunder. As the car is supposed to have been created out of his weapon, the car-festival at the beginning of the rainy season is mythically justified.

Besides '*Nandighosa*' the car of the Lord Jagannatha (Plate No. 39) has another name called the "*Garudadhwaja*". As has been already stated, the car of Lord Balabhadra is named as "*Taladhwaja*". The mystery behind the formation of this car is still unsolved. Baladeva is the incarnation of "*Sesa*", the holy *infinite* serpent on whom lord Visnu takes rest. It is said that Lord Balabhadra places a mirror of wisdom on His altar below and receives a view of the entire universe through that. As the mirror is placed below (*tala*) it is called 'tala'. Besides pure and transparent qualities of the mirror are symbolically observed in Lord Balabhadra Himself, who is, therefore designated as '*Talanka*'. In this way His car is named as '*Taladhwaja*'. The outline of mirror is perpetually found in the banner of the car. The car of goddess *'subhadra'* is called both *"Devadalana"* and *"Padmadhwaja"*. Goddess Lakshmi who is identified with *Subhadra* is again called *Padma* (the goddess on the lotus). *Subhadra* represents wealth, prosperity and grace (Sree). Hence there is the lotus profile in the banner of her car and it is called *'Padmadhwaja'* too. On the eve of the car festival, the cars are virtually worshipped and the wind and other deities are admirably invoked. It is believed that such deities descend into the cars and protect the cars for nine days. Hence the three cars are considered as divine during this time. The tradition is, all categories of people ought not to ascend these. In *Puranas* various rules and directions of ascending the cars have been mentioned. It is said that the protection of the cars for full nine days is much more important than all sorts of worship and meditation before the deities therein. It is enjoined to safeguard and protect the attires, decorations, the weapons, the *Parsva Devatas* placed in the cars when these move.

When the hilarious people drag the cars with the help of ropes, they are advised not to drag these speedily either out of excitement and fun or out of exhibiting their strength indicating lack of respect for the cars. To drag the cars in high speed is unconventional, which is discouraged. As the hymn says :-

[The car ought to be
Dragged very slowly
And the Holy wheels
Shall move slowly.
And with sounds.
Of universal love.]
Sanch Sanch ratho neyo
rath snehatu cakrna
(Surya Purana)

In this way the Gods descend into the cars and gradually seat themselves in the cars in supreme comfort. Hence the Gods get rest and poise if the cars move in a slow, sober manner. If the cars move otherwise, there might be some harm and it is believed that if by chance, some part of a car is damaged, it leads to disaster for the country and humanity.

It attracts people from different parts of India, nay from the world. Hundreds of foreigners too flock to Puri on this occasion.

After a particular kind of *bhog* is offered to the deities, they are brought to the Chariots one by one. The Chariots are kept ready on the day before the *Ratha-Yatra* ceremony and they are placed in front of the *Singhadwar* (the lion's gate) facing North. They are placed in a row, the car of Balabhadra being in the first position, after which come the cars of Subhadra and Jagannatha. Just before the carrying of the deities from the temple to the Chariots they are adorned with flower crowns and their mode of exit from the temple is known as *Pahandi*.

Jagannath's car "*Nandighosa*" stands 45 feet high and is supported on 16 wheels each with a diameter of 7 feet high and is beautifully painted in yellow. "*Taladhwaja*" is the name of Balabhara's car which is 44 feet high and is blue in colour while Subhadra's car known as "*Darpadalana*" or '*Deviratha*" is 43 feet high and dark-red. The colour of the covering cloth of the Rathas is prescribed according to the colour of the dresses the deities generally wear. Jagannatha is conceived by some as Krisna who wears *Pitambara* or yellow cloth. Balabhadra is '*Nilambar*' clothed in blue whereas Subhadra is conceived as Sakti, the red-robed mother-goddess. So the colour is scarlet. Inside these cars are installed the deities decorated in golden garments.

The cars do not start immediately after the installation of the three deities unless the Raja of Puri, the descendant of the builder of the Jagannatha Temple comes in a palanquin, pays homage to the deities and sweeps the platform of each car one by one . This process is called as "*chera panhara*" (sweeping of the floor of the chariot).

Then comes the most auspicious moment. Thousands of people seize the huge ropes and begin to pull the cars. The cars grind forward slowly along the Bada-danda or the main road till their journey ends at *Gundicha Mandir*, at the end of the road. Balabhadra being the eldest, his car is drawn first. Then follows the car of Subhadra, Jagannath's car moves behind the two.

After the seventh day of their stay at the *Gundicha Mandir* which is the Lord's garden house, the deities make their return trip or "*Bahudayatra*". On the Ekadasi day the deities are ceremonially dressed which is called *Sunavesa*.

It is a widely known fact that great religious importance is always attributed to the construction as well as the final consecration of the *Rathas* or the Chariots. The construction of the *Rathas* begins with the *Vanajaga* ceremony on the day of *Aksaya Tritya* and the *Rathas* are made only of Sala wood supplied by the Raja of Dasapalla (Now of course, the Government of Orissa supplies the wood).

As has been said before, every religious rite of this sacred place, *Nilacala*, has some unique significance of its own. Indeed, every ritualistic performance breathes nobility and sanctity and always takes place according to the religious scriptures.

The construction of the *Rathas* from the *Aksaya Tritya* day, the christening of the cars, the different bases of the cars, perhaps every thing bears some deep religious and philosophic signficance.

The *Aksaya Tritya* day heralds the commencement of *satyayuga* and as it conjures up a sacred idea because of its association with *satyayuga,* that may perhaps well explain the reason why the construction of the Rathas starts on that day.

The conception of the body as a Ratha is found in the *Upanisad*.

"*Atmanam rathinam viddhi sariram rathameva tu*"

The Vedas, the Tantras and Puranas - all speak about the infinite nature of the Supreme Being. The Srimad *Bhagawat*, while giving an account of the 24 incarnations of the Lord, mentions His first incarnation as *jiva-svarupa*. This *jiva-svarupa* nature is but the first *apurvavatara* of that Eternal Being.

The structure of the Ratha has been taken as the gross body of this material world, while the Paramataman or the Supreme Being, in the *caturvyuhc* manifestation of *Vasudeva*, *Sankarsana*, *Pradyumna* and *Aniruddha*, is believed to ascend the Rathas. This opinion is held by many scholars. Again, it is believed that the creation of this material world starts at the end of *Mahapralaya* or the great universal cataclysm. So the *Aksaya Tritya* day, because of its association with *satyayuga*, is the most suitable day for the beginning of the construction of the Rathas or the outer bodies of all beings. The importance of *Aksaya Tritiya* as the most auspicious day for sowing medicinal seeds has also been widely acclaimed in the scriptures.

All people, irrespective of caste, creed and religion can of course get maximum facility as to the seeing, touching and worshipping of the Lords placed on Rathas. This is possible because the evil of untouchability is conspicuously absent here.

The worship of the deities on the Rathas (cars) during the *Gundicha* and *Bahuda yatra* is associated with offering of non-cooked food stuffs like milk, ghee etc., while for the remaining seven days all the rituals are performed in the manner of those performed inside the Jagannatha temple, and cooked food-stuffs are offered as usual.

Now, if the reason for holding *Adhamatarana-Yatra* (the festival for the redemption of the ill-fated people) for a period of nine days is investigated, it will appear that the nine days correspond to the nine marks on each foot of the Lord which are nothing but the elementary and abstract properties or the creative manifestation of this material world.

The subject of the present discussion is, however, about the structure of the three Rathas (cars) of Sri Jagannath of *Purusottama-Kshetra*. The car of Sri Jagannatha has 16 wheels indicating 16 kalas or divine principles of the Lord.

The supreme being, in order to assume His *Jiva-svarupa* nature, created this living world with the help of five subtle elements and eleven perceptive organs. These five subtle elements and eleven organs eventually led to signify 16 *kalas* or principles of God. These 16 emanations, permeated by *maya*, found expression in creating *avataras* or incarnations which God desired to create.

As has been said above, the name of the Ratha is *Nandighosa*. The charioteer is known as *Matali*. The four horses are known as *Sankhika, Rocika, Mocika, Jwalini*. The Kalas are 16 in number. There are 16 Aras or axles. The presiding Risi of the chariot is *Pandu*. The car of Subhadra is termed as *Devi Ratha* or *Devidalana*. It has 12 whels representing the twelve months. The Charioteers is known as *Devadatta*. The Horses are *Prajna*, *Anujna*, *Ghora* and *Aghora*. The Kalas are twelve in number. It has 12 axles or *Aras*. The presiding Risi is *Yajnabalka*. Balabhadra's car is called *Taladhwaja*. It is supported on 14 wheels, which indicate the life-time of Brahma involving caturdasa-manvantara. Balabhadra is the Lord of this gross material world, and has, therefore, a huge body. He is thus *Virata*. The Charioteer is known as *Taladhwaja*. The horses are *Rig, Yajur, Sama, Atharva*. There are 14 kalas or wheels representing the fourteen worlds. The *Aras* are 14 in number. The presiding *Risi* is *Angira*.

On the 11th day of the bright fortnight of the month of *Asadha*, the *Sayana Utsava* or sleeping ceremony is performed. Previous to that day the '*Adhivasa*' rites are performed. At night the representative images (small golden images) *Laksminarayana*, *Anantavasudeva* and *Bhubaneswari* representing Jagannatha, Balabhadra and Subhadra respectively are brought to the well-decorated sleeping chamber and placed on the cots. They are all four-armed with usual attributes. They are invoked with the prayer. 'Oh Lord, do please sleep for four months for the welfare of the universe. Then they are laid on their respective cots.

On the day the sun begins to move to the Equinox a festival is observed which is called *Daksinayana yatra.*

A popular festival known as *Jhulana Yatra* is held in the precincts of the temple of Lord Jagannatha. On the Muktimandapa platform, which is *elaborately* decorated, the *Jhulana Yatra* is held from *Dasami* upto the *Purnima* day in the month of *Sravana. Madanmohan* is placed in a beautiful ornamented swinging chariot. The festival is also held in the different Mathas (Monasteries).

On the *Haribasara* day or the 11th of bright fortnight of the month of *Bhadrapada*, the *'Parsvaparibartana'* (turning of sides) festival is performed. On this day at evening, after the usual rituals, the God is requested to change the side.

Again on the 11th day of bright fortnight of the month of *Kartika* the gods are awakened from divine slumber. This festival is called "*Probadhana yatra*" or rising ceremony.

On the 6th day of the bright fortnight of *Margasira* the deities are dressed in winter garments. This festival is called *'Pravarana Utsava'*.

On the full moon day of month of Pausa, a Yatra called *Pusyabhiseka* is performed. During this festival the same rites such as *Adhivasa* etc. are performed as in *Snana Yatra.* Pots filled with perfumed water are taken from *Bhogamandapa* to the *Ratnavedi.* This *Abhiseka* is performed for the representative deities like Ram, Sita and Laksmana. That is why this festival is also called *Ramabhiseka.*

Then the *Uttarayan Yatra* is performed on the *Makara Sankranti* day when the sun moves towards the southern equinox. The next important yatra is the *Dola Yatra.* The *Arcaberas* or the representative deities are taken out to *Dola*

Vedi which was introduced during the reign of Narasimha Deva, the grand son of Ramachandra Deva, who was popularly known as Abhinava Indradyumna. That is according to *Vasantostsab kavya* of Haladhara Mishra. The book is still unpublished. Another yatra, called '*Damanaka*' is also observed when *Damanaka* plant is offered to the images. This is observed in the month of Chaitra.

The last of the annual festivals which lasts for 21 days is called *Chandan Yatra*. The entire road from the shrine of Jagannatha upto the Narendra tank along with houses on both sides is decorated. At some places big toranas are erected where the images take casual rest and receive offerings. The images of *Madanmohan*, Goddess *Lakshmi* and *Saraswati* are taken in palanquin by the sevakas to the *Narendra Sarovara*. These images are followed by different deities from different shrines. After reaching the Narendra tank, the images are placed in different well decorated boats and they are rowed for a long time by the Sevakas. During this rowing ceremony *devadasis* (the temple dancers) dance and sing in the boat. Generally the colours of the boats are white and red. The peculiarity of this ceremony is that *Madanmohan* with *Lakshmi* and *Saraswati* rides on the white coloured boat whereas *Ramakrisna* with *Panca Siva* rides the red boat. All the deities on the boat take trips in the tank for several times. Some of the festivals observed in the Jagannatha temple excepting *Pravarana Utsava* are also performed in other Vaisnava temples of South India which follow the *Vaikhanasa* and *Pancaratra* Agamas.

The Goddess *Laksmi* has been housed in a separate shrine in the precincts of the Jagannath Temple at Puri. From the traditional mythological point of view, she is regarded as the Mother of the Universe and the possessor of the wealth of all the three worlds. But according to common belief, as recorded in legend, her nature and behaviour are like those of an Oriya housewife. She herself cooks and serves, it is said, her husband, her brother-in-law and sisters-in-law like an Oriya house-wife. Therefore, the image of Lakshmi is never carried close to the throne of the Lord because there stands Lord Balabhadra, elder brother of Jagannatha. Lakshmi is not only an ideal, devoted wife but she is also lovely and touchy. Sometimes she behaves like a sensitive Oriya housewife with her husband for lack of mental understanding. This sensitiveness and touchiness by Goddess Lakshmi is best manifested on two occasions : first, on the "*Hera Panchami*" day (fifth day) on the journey to *Gundicha* temple and second, onthe return journey of the Lord Jagannatha. This letter occasion is usually known as the festival of "Opening the door".

The Lord Jagannatha launches his car festival accompanied by his brother and sister, Subhadra. Laksmi is deprived of this pleasant privilege. Thus, on the Hera (beholding) Panchami (fifth day) this aggrieved and lovely wife, starts secretly for the Gundicha temple in a fighting and angry mood. In her impotent anger, she breaks up one of the several wheels of Lord Jagannatha's car and comes away as surreptitiously as she had gone.

This fine psychological insight into a woman's mind also reveals one of the typical features of Oriya culture and the Oriya woman's place in it. A woman has a rightful share in her husband's happiness. If the husband neglects her and forces upon her a separation not in accord with her wishes, her natural reaction (in spite of her noble birth and breeding) would be jealousy and anger. Besides, such a separation does not augur well for either of them. Thus, Lakshmi is depicted as '*Adhira Nayika*' the aggrieved heroine.

Nine days after, when Lord Jagannatha returns home, Lakshmi shuts the door on Him on the ground of her undeserved deprivation. The king of Puri, however, tries to patch up the misunderstanding by arranging a meeting of reunion between them known as *Laksmi Narayan Bhet*. An elephant is sent to fetch her from the temple which she promptly declines. However, when the offer is renewed, she comes in a palanquin to meet her Lord. But her feelings are hardly assuaged, and she nurses her neglect and humiliation. Thus, when the Lord appeals to Laksmi to open the door, the Goddess replies, "You are the Lord of all the three worlds, why do you come here ? Take back your sister with you, for left alone she may feel the pangs of separation." The Lord tells her, "I had with me my elder brother, Balabhadra. How could you accompany me ?" And then to pacify her the Lord promises her valuable gifts. But Laksmi says she does not deserve all those for she comes of a poor family. In the end, the insistent appeals of the Lord make Laksmi open the door and take him in.

Every year, on the occasion of the return journey, this ceremony is observed. '*Devadasis*' represent Laksmi, whereas '*Daitas*' represent Jagannatha. In the musical exchange of words, *slokas* in Sanskrit are recited and the dialogue continues in the presence of the countless devotees.

Another interpretation as to why Lasmi could not accompany the Lord during the car festival to Gundicha mandir is given by the *Gaudiya Vaisnavas* or the followers of Caitanya. According to them, the Gundicha Mandir is regarded as Vrndavan, while Lord Jagannatha is regarded by them as Lord Krisna himself, and this Car Festival is taken as His journey to Vrndavana. Vrndavana is exclusively the abode of *Gopis*. None else can take part in the Divine sports of the Lord with the Gopis, let alone Laksmi. According to *Srimad Bhagavata* (X. 16.32 and X.47.60), Laksmi once practised severe penance to take part in the lovely sports of *Rasa Lila*. But as she was the Queen of the Lord of *Vaikuntha* and the Goddess of *Aiswarya*, she was not allowed. Thus Vrndavan is the abode of unmixed *Madhurya* or unalloyed, pure love.

There is an interesting conversation between Caitanya and Swarupa Damodar Goswami narrated in Caitanya Caritamrta (Madhyalila, Ch. XIV) regarding *Laksmi*, the aggrieved consort of Lord Jagannatha and her intriguing behaviour as she goes to Gundicha mandir in a warlike fighting mood rather than nurse her pangs of separation as a *Manini-Nayika*.

Of the twelve festivals held in connection with Lord Jagannatha this occasion is both important and interesting. This is an episode which brings the Gods down to men. They become human beings, whom they themselves created, creatures infused with the same sentiments and same sensitiveness. Thus the Gods assume the garb of human beings and human beings assume the role of the Gods.

The Myth goes further. Once Lord Balabhadra became displeased with Laksmi when she accepted the offer of worship from an untouchable lady. But Laksmi had extracted a promise from Lord Jagannatha at the time of marriage, the promise to permit her the right to be worshipped by all on Thursdays. On this ground she left the temple. Her anger caused the disappearance of the property of the Lords. Her servants made the temple empty of its precious possessions. Even the precious beds of the Lords were exchanged for ordinary cots. Jagannatha and Balabhadra were reduced to street beggars. Even begging could not fill their bellies. They starved, Balabhadra realised his folly, accepted food from the hands of Laksmi who had become untouchable in the process. The difference between the high and the low was abolished and Laksmi returned to the temple. The formidable barriers of casteism were thus overcome in the temple of the Lord.

Besides, another festival known as *"Rukmini Harana"* is traditionally observed in the temple premises. One of the *Sevakas* (temple servants) appears as *Sisupala* (rival of the lord) and consequent upon the mythical battle between them, he is forcibly dragged by the deity *Madanmohan* who represents Lord Jagannatha. In an interesting manner Sisupala's pigtail being tied up in the palanquin of the lord, provides fun and enthusiasm to the devotees around.

"The Cult of Jagannath" by K.C. Mishra published by Firma K.L. Mukhopadhyay, Calcutta - 1971, pp. 128-139

Annexure XIII

"Memories of Bengal Civilian" narrated by John Beams

"We returned to Balaswar in the first week of the 1870. New Year compared with the crowded massive city of Cuttack we felt Puri town being a small place. The pilgrims who come talking to Puri from their native places were the only busy crowd that we noticed in Puri town. The Orissa Trunk Road which formed a part of Calcutta-Madras Great Imperial highway appeared to be the backbone of the whole of Balaswar district. The Balaswar sector of Orissa Trunk Road length is of 120 miles. It has been constructed in such a way that from a distance it appears to be a massive and strong dam. During festivities at Puri particularly Dol Jatra, Basanti Uchhaba and Rath Jatra there were streams of pilgrims of different parts of the country proceeding to Puri along this road. The poor pilgrims come walking and the rice people come by bullock cart and palanquin to reach their destination, that is, Puri to witness the festivals and offer prayer to Lord Jagannath. The police staff used to station at various places all along the route to give protection to the pilgrims against the attack of Dacoits. However many pilgrims being fatigued by walking meet death enroute to Puri and many others come back carrying epidemic with them. Generally women pilgrims suffer most in the pilgrimage. The Panda pilgrim guides play a greater role in attracting the pilgrims to visit Puri in large number. Particularly the women more allured to visit Puri during festivities. It is a common sight to see the Pandas having strong physique leading groups of Bengali ladies with sweat soaked clothes on in their body and a palm leaf woven baskets packed with their clothes carried on their head including the Pandas baggage trailing behind the Pandas.

Annexure XIV

A narrative of breakout of Cholera in 1899 as seen by Nilakantha Das who was then a student of Puri Zilla High School

"The unhygienic condition that prevailed at Puri, and the insanitary condition in which the pilgrims had to stay at Puri in lodging and other houses are largely responsible for the breakout of cholera during festivities particular Car festival. Pandit Nilakantha Das who was a student at that time of Puri Zilla School has given an account of what he saw in Puri in the year 1899 in respect of breakout of Cholera. This is what he has narrated regarding breakout of Cholera at Puri in 1899. Virulence of the cholera that broke out in 1899 was unprecedented and thousands of people were the victims of this breakout. The dead bodies in thousands were lying on the grand road. When they were asking for some water to drink they met death and the Municipality in their Vehicles carrying dead bodies dumped them in a pit which was dug in the seashore. The officers in charge of picking up the dead bodies from the ground threw these victims whether they were dead or alive. Many people have seen people who were in the dying stage or at the point of death and thrown into the pit got out of the pit alive sometime later. In every house in the city there were cases of death. The epidemic spread from village to village in the rural areas. The transport service whether it is bullock cart or any other conveyance on the Jagannath road was disrupted. Our school remained closed for a fortnight and a relative of mine who was in the hostel took me the Jagannath Road to my village. It was raining and my relative held the Umbrella upon my head so that I could walking close to him by his side. I saw many dead bodies lying on the road and my relative was trying to keep the umbrella in such a way that many of the dead bodies were out of site. But the number of dead bodies which were lying on the road was so great that it was difficult for my relative to keep them out of my sight. At Hata damodarpur we got down to the passage through paddy field. From Puri upto this village covering a distance of about unites the number of dead bodies that I counted was 39. There were also many dead bodies lying by the sides of the road and I have not counted them. Putrefied smell was there throughout. As one place I saw the Jackals were busy in making a dead body into pieces. I recall the bloodless white flesh which the Jackals were in agony dragging in their teeth to make them into pieces.

This is what the pilgrims were suffering from in their pilgrimage to Puri.*

* Puri Jatri, Jatri Gumastha, and Jatri Kala Pratha by Anantaram Kar Kaundenya, Shri Mandir, July 1997, Pp 46-47

Annexure XV
The Pilgrims

"Pilgrimage to reputed holy places have ever been so popular in India. But no pilgrimage was ever so extensively practised and so generally famed as that of pilgrimage to Juggernaut. By what fortuitous circumstances that idol became so celebrated, it is difficult to imagine."[1]

"This national reverence for holy places has been for ages concentrated on the city of Puri. On these inhospitable sands, Hindu religion and Hindu superstition have stood at bay for 18 centuries against the world. Here is the national temple whither the people flock to worship from every province of India.".[1a]

Groeme in his Report on the Temple gives an account of the pilgrims resorting to the temple of Jagannath. "The collection from the pilgrims coming from the north began at a place called Khunta on the border of Mohurbunj country, and continued up to Autura Nullah at the entrance of Poorshuttum."

"Pilgrims coming from the south-ward were subject to the same restrictions as those from the north-ward and paid their respective taxes at the stations situated near the principal one at Autura Nullah.".

"It is usual to examine whether the pilgrims were Lal Jatrees who could pay the fixed rate. They were named and numbered and delivered over to respectable Pundahs or their agents to whom the list was entrusted. On their arrival at Autura

Nullah, they were again counted. All pilgrims of an inferior rank passed the ghaut after being numbered."

The poorest classes were detained at each station about half a day and after getting their clothes well examined if nothing was found, they were allowed to go to Autura Nullah, except at the time of different Jattras.

The ordeal of the destitute pilgrims was not over. "At the time of near approach of several Jattras, they were prevented from passing, until the very day of the Dool Jattra, and until the Ruth, at the time of the Ruth Jattra, should have reached the Goondicha Mundup."[2]

The Snan and the Rath Jatra attracted a large number of pilgrims from Bengal and upcountry. Most of the pilgrims came to Puri during the last two or three days before important festivals and were detained at Atharanulla for checking.[3]

"For about 50,000 to 200,000 persons, the major part being Desees and Punjkosees, gather at Autura Nullah, which entirely impede collection to the great loss of Government".

"The Punjkosees suddenly arrive in a large body on the day and a day before the holy day, mixing with the pilgrims liable to pay the duty, and with other description of pilgrims exempted from the payment of the tax, all of whom crowd themselves in such an immense number in and about Autura Nullah."[4]

In 1813, the Car festival took place on the 30th June. Pilgrims of all descriptions, Desees, Kangals and Bhurrungs crowded at and in the vicinity of the Autharanulla ghat, "mostly from the 28th to 30th ultimo, so much so on the last day."

The Collector of the tax proceeded to the spot and ordered the Daroga to open the gate, "having reason to suppose that as there were and in the environments upwards of one lack pilgrims waiting, there was not the least possibility of collecting the tax even if they were inclined, either from the Bhurrungs or Desees."

As soon as the gate was opened, there was a great rush in which thirty-six persons, eighteen men and eighteen women, were trampled to death.

Busby wrote that when the gate was opened, "the pilgrims in their eagerness to prostrate before the idol, trampled on one another, and were not restrained even by the cries and groans of the sufferers, one man falling and then some followed. Had I not been present on an elephant and forced my way round to close the gate and the current of the crowd. I fear instead of thirty-six one hundred would have been added to the number."

Busby's explanation was that "the above evil annually prevailed from the time of the Marhattas to the present, as no method could be adopted to prevent it." He pointed out that the pilgrims would not be checked even by military force during the Asnan and Ruth Jattras, as they did not value their lives when lost at Juggernath.[5]

Trower forwarded Busby's letter to Richardson, the Settlement Commissioner. He remarked : "Mr. Busby is greatly mistaken in supposing that a life thus lost is a subject of rejoicing to the relatives of the sufferers. I never before heard that an involuntary death on entering the town even before the sufferer had obtained the sight of the idol entitled him to a set in the paradise. That the relatives of the sufferers do not express joy, I can positively affirm, for I never witnessed sorrow more acute than was witnessed on the occasion."

Trower proposed that sepoys be employed to control the crowd. "What activity, zeal and humanity can make will be heartily applied to prevent the loss of lives." The Collector suggested alterations to the existing barriers and a medical establishment at Puri for the treatment of sick pilgrims. "It appears that such an establishment was supported for the above purpose by the Marhatta Government and humanity certainly pleads for such a provision."[6]

Richardson in his letter to the Governor General in Council dated 8 January 1814, described the loss of 36 human lives as 'shocking to humanity'. But he agreed with Busby that it would be impossible to prevent the pilgrims from entering the town during the festivals "in spite of the most penal ordinance and the strictest prohibition."

He further observed "It cannot be reasonably expected that the religious devotees, periodically raised to a degree of frenzy by religious enthusiasm will pay regard to the rules and ordinances of Government, when they value not their lives on such occasions, when no orders or threats are sufficient to restrain them. In contrary they deem it a blessing ensuing them future happiness."

As large number of pilgrims crossed the Atharanulla ghat during the last two or three days before important festivals there was a great rush of darsan in the temple. "During the Jattras, the pilgrims were with greatest difficulty prevented from breaking (in a body) the barriers to which should they by chance succeed, their next step would be to repeat the same violence at the gate of the Pagoda from forcing which it would be impossible to prevent, without really endangering persons".[7]

The number of pilgrims was very great if the Car festival was held early, or if the year was considered auspicious. In 1806/07, 113,266 persons attended the Car festival. The British Government hoped that the Pilgrim tax would be an additional source of income after meeting the expenses of the temple. The Board of Commissioners reported that the annual collection from the Pilgrim Tax fetched two to three lakhs of rupees during the Maratha rule.

But the number of pilgrims did not come up to expectation in the first three years after the imposition of the Pilgrim tax. The average annual collection from January 1806 to 30 April 1808 was only Rs. 76,891.

The construction of new Jagannath road from Jaleswar to Puri attract the pilgrims began in 1812. It was completed in 1825. The total expenditure for the construction of the road was Rs. 8,19,158-11 excluding Maharaja Sukhamoy Roy's donation of Rs. 150,000. In 1804, the Court of Directors intimated that the Pilgrim tax should not be treated as a source of revenue.[8] Consequently, the surplus proceeds of the Pilgrim tax were spent towards the construction of the new road and for amenities of the pilgrims.

In 1812, a well was constructed at Atharanulla for the convenience of the pilgrims at a cost of Rs. 6809. The Government sanctioned construction of two rest sheds for the pilgrims at Puri in 1827 (O.S.A. 24 April 1827).

In 1827, Sarais (Pilgrim shelters) were erected at Balasore, Akhuapada, Basta, Bhadrak and at Rajghat near Jaleswar from the donation of a Hindu zamindar of Bengal.[9]

Shady trees were planted on roadside to afford rest to the pilgrims. The zamindars were asked to plant such trees where the road passed through their estates.

These amenities encouraged the pilgrims to visit Puri during the festivals in large numbers. "A Pundah said that before the Company took care of the idol's establishment, the idol had not the glory, he now say. The people said 'There is no road, no shelter; there are robbers abroad, and how can they go so far ?' Thus saying, they stayed at home. But now the thieves are taken, good roads are made, sheltering places built. The people have no excuse and therefore they come."[10]

Number of Pilgrims in the first quarter of 29th Century

(i) Table I- In the first three days in 1806.[11]

Date	No. of Pilgrims	Free	Kangal	Byragee	Bhurrang	Lal Jatree
22.1	96	96	70	26	x	x
23.1	125	120	99	21	5	x
24.1	226	221	207	14	3	2

(ii) Table II - 22nd January to 30th April 1806 at Atharanulla.[12]

Number	Free	Kangal	Byragee	Desee
48720	26841	19140	3124	4577

During this period 7097 pilgrims passed through Lokanath ghat.

(iii) Table III - 22nd January 1806 to 30th April 1814.[13]

Average number of pilgrims	90,273
Average number of admission by Atharanulla	75,712
Average of admission by Lokanath ghat	14,561
Average of Lal Jatrees	2,185
Average of Bhurrung Jatrees	23,565
Average of Khyratee Pilgrims	64,523

(iv) Between 1817/18 to 1821/22.[14]

	Tax-payers	Exempted person	Total
1817-18	35,941	39,720	75,661
1818-19	36,241	4,870	41,111
1819-20	92,874	39,000	1,31,874
1820-21	21,946	11,500	33,446
1821-22	35,160	17,000	52,160

Section One
Classification of Pilgrims

There were checkposts at the Atharanulla and Lokanath ghats (bridges) to regulate the admission of pilgrims in to the holy city of Puri. There were two Darogas, one at each ghat, getting a salary of Rs. 40 per month. They were assisted by Potdars or Accountants.

The Butwa or Pilgrim canvasser handed over the pilgrims whom he brought to his Pratihari at the Atharanulla ghat. The

Pratihari reported their arrival to the Daroga. "After making many difficulties, he agrees that he has so many Lall, so many Bhurrungs and so many Kangal jatrees and receives a Shoomaree not signed. This he shows to the Potdar, pays the money and gets it signed by him; and on returning to the Daroga he also signs it."

"The Pilgrims are then passed and they come to the Sudder Katcherry where the Shoomaree (Certificate) is lodged and a Rowanna (permit) with the tax Collector's signature is given in exchange. The Rowanna is the passport for admission in to the Pagoda (I have ordered the Dewul Purchas to admit no person without one) and after making dursan i.e., seeing the god as often as they wish, they present a petition at the Sudder Katchery, stating that they wish to return and receive a Khalas Chithee' (Certificate of release) by which they are allowed to leave the town."[15]

I believe that the Purharees refuse to procure the Khalas Chithee until they had taken everything they possess from the pilgrims. Such is their power."[16]

The pilgrims were provided with a form mentioning the names of pilgrims, places of residence, caste, class, and lastly, the amount paid by them.

The form contained the following particulars :

A.........the inhabitant of .... in the district of ....is entitled to perform the customary ceremonies under the charge of ....during..........days, from the ....day of the month of.............until the.........of the month of ....; and for that period you will afford the holders free access to the temple of Juggernath; at the expiration of which you will return the license at the office of the Collector of Pilgrim tax.

There was a form permitting the extension of the duration of stay at Puri. In case of Lal Jatrees, there was another form, mentioning the names of attendants, amount of tax paid respectively and the periods of visit to the temple.

1. Lal Jatree

Affluent persons from the north paid Rs. Ten at Atharanulla and Rs. Six at Lokanath ghat. They had also to ay Rs. Two as fee for the Pundas and Pratiharis.[17] The pilgrims were given red tickets and were consequently known as Lal Jatrees.[18]

A Lal Jatree was allowed to stay at Puri for 30 days. The Regulation IV of 1809 laid down that "in case a pilgrim of first class may be desirous of visiting the Temple with his family and attendants, not exceeding twenty persons, they will be admitted to remain in the temple so long as the master does, provided they at the first instance pay the prescribed fee, either as Bhurrang or Nim Laal, but they will not be allowed to enter the Temple for a longer period of time than they may respectively be entitled to".

With the previous sanction of the Collector, a Lal Jatree was allowed to enter the Temple with Chauris in day time and with Masals at night.[19] He was to be attended by a Punda or Pratihari during his visit to the Temple, but was allowed to enter the Temple without being escorted by a priest, on further payment of Rs. Ten.

2. Nim Lal Jatree

The Regulation IV of 1809 provided for a pilgrim of second class. Those coming from the north were required to pay Rs. five, while the pilgrims from the south passing through Lokanath ghat paid Rs. three.[20]

As the Collector of Pilgrim tax pointed out : "Bhurrang Jatrees paying Rs. 2-6 are allowed access to the Temple for four days, and after that period, if they choose to pay Rs. two again, they were allowed access for a further limit of four days : while a Nim Lal Jatree pays five rupees and is allowed for seven days only, whereby he loses the privilege of one days' darsan besides the loss of a rupee.[21]

3. *Bhurrang Jatree*

Those pilgrims who paid Rs. two as tax and annas six as fee, were called Bhurrang or Bhuranga. They paid the same amount at either ghat.

Hunter pointed out the loophone in the classification of pilgrims. "The pilgrim who states his means at twelve rupees is assessed agreeably to the present rate of Rs. 2-6 including (the Pundah's) fee, which leaves the balance at Rs. 9-10, to be expanded in the Temple; while one possessing thirteen rupees were assessed the full amount."[22]

4. *Pancha Tirthee*

The low caste people were despised, but not their money. They visited 'Pancha Tirtha'* in and about the town under the charge of 'Bata Peada' (Chowkidar). After visiting the Tirthas on payment of Rs. four, they were given a 'Punjtirthee' certificate. On the production of this certificate at the Kutchery of the Collector of Pilgrim Tax, a 'Panchatirthee' was given a pass which entitled him to perform the customary ceremonies "without the gates of the temple within 16 days (Report of Groeme).

Persons of the following professions were not allowed to enter the temple.

1. Ghooski - Private Woman
2. Kushee - Prostitute
3. Sooree - Liquid seller
4. Pano - Basket maker
5. Tiar - A class of fisherman
6. Hadee - Scavenger
7. Kahar or Bauri - Palki bearer
8. Chamar - Shoe maker
9. Raj Bunshee - A class of boatman
10. Machua - Fisherman
11. Yogee - Weaver
12. Bagdee - Bengali low caste
13. Majur - Labourer who carried basket on head.
14. Dhobee - Washerman

15. Chandal - Bengali low caste
16. Tantric Sadhus like Aghorepanthi

The list was not exhaustive. Some more low castes, such as, the bird-catcher, the snake-charmer were also excluded from the Temple.[23]

From the crowd of pilgrims, specially after the abolition of the Pilgrim tax, it was difficult to distinguish a well-dressed woman or man as prostitute or liquor-seller. It is said that even a European managed to enter the Temple.[24]

Groeme wrote that it was not difficult for well to do Punjtirthees to get into the Temple after palming the hands of the temple priests.

Low caste men from Nepal and the Mug country sought admission into the Temple. "Their caste prevented their entering the interior of the Temple, but they entertain hopes that their liberality to the Pundahs will gain that admission."[25]

The Punjtirthees abstained from entering the temple due to the complex of lowliness which they imbued from the centuries of caste Hindu oppression. Thus only the lowest and most impure castes did not enter the temple.

5. *Special type of pilgrims*

There were two special types of pilgrims, prostrating and water carrying. When Dr. Buchanon visited Puri in 1806 he noticed a devotee "laying himself down at every step measuring the road to Juggernaut by the length of his body as a penance or merit to please his god."

Rev. Lacey asked a pilgrim "How far you have arrived by in that manner by constant prostrations" ? "750 miles". "How long have you been on the road" ? "About eight months". The Gungajalees carried water of the Ganga to be poured on the image of Lokanath before darsan of Jagannath.

6. V.I.P. Pilgrims

There are references to V.I.P. pilgrims also. As intimated by Mr. Secretary Edmonstone, the Board of Commissioners wrote to Groeme : "you will conform to the desire of His Excellency the Governor General in Council in regard to your manifesting every degree of attention towards Juggat Seth on his arrival at Cuttack and that you will facilitate his progress towards Juggernath.[26]

Pakenham, Commissioner, was informed : "Gossain Damodarjee Maharaj of Sri Nath Dwar of Mewar being about to leave the Presidency, in which he has met with a highly favourable reception from the Governor General, is in progress to Juggernath. You will manifest towards him every degree of civility and attention, suitable to the respectability of his character and the high estimation in which he is held by a large class of our Hindoo subjects.[27] The Governor General exempted him and his one hundred followers from the payment of the Pilgrim tax.

Similarly, the Maharaj of Vizinagaram and his attendants (O.S.A. 14 December 1827) : the zamindar of Bobbili (O.S.A. 24 June 1826) : the Chief of Gheroulee in Bundelkhand (O.S.A. 30 April 1827) : Nirmal Giri Goswami and his followers (O.S.A. 20 November 1827) : and Seth Bishan Chand (O.S.A. 27 June 1827) were exempted from the payment of the Pilgrim tax.

Busby, Collector of the tax[28], was informed that His Lordship in Council had been "pleased to a grant a remission of duties on pilgrims at Juggernauth in favour of Seetaram Banerjee, an officer of His Highness the Rajah of Nagpore". The letter added "should the followers of Banerjee be arrived, you are to intimate in terms not to calculate offence that it is a standing order of Government that all arms are to be given in to the charge of guards at Pooree, but they will be returned to himself and his followers on quitting the town.[29]

Section - Two
Khyratee (Exempted) Pilgrims

Groeme in his Report gave a list of persons who were exempted from payment of the Pilgrim tax. "Among exempted were the principal Suthoos whose business it was to induce the Hindoos from all parts of the country to perform pilgrimage to Jugunath and for this they were not only exempted but were permitted to bring pilgrims. Some one and some two who were likewise exonerated from paying the tax. Besides this, Government allowed all Suthoos without distinction, four annas two pies for every pilgrim brought by them exceeding eleven."

"Pantooreeas (Patta daurias) are likewise exempt from duties from the circumstance of their bringing with them at their own expense silken ropes by which the idol is hoisted into the Ruth. Several pensioners in lieu of receiving cash are allowed to bring some one, some two, pilgrims who instead of paying the established duty at the Auturanullah pay it to the pensioner."

"Why the professional musicians and singers were exempted from duties. I am unable to learn; but the sick who had no hope of recovery and were poor withal, were exonerated on religious consideration." The Government servants who were "continually going forwards and backwards" were also exempted.

A large number of pilgrims were exempted on religious grounds.[30] "Dundee Sunnaisees and their attendants were supposed to be wholly devoted to the deity and had no concern with worldly affairs besides the veneration paid to them by all ranks of Hindoos-which was the main reason of their exemption from duties."

The list of exempted persons, given by Groeme, contained more names. "The Mutdharis and their attendants are likewise exempt as they have charity lands in Bengal and elsewhere. As they reside at Poorshuttum it is necessary to go themselves or send their servants occasionally to collect rents; therefore as these people were supposed to be employed in the service of Jugunath, they were exempted from the duties."

"There are twelve principal Jattras to each of which a Brahmin on the part of certain Tributary Rajas is admitted free of duty - for what reason I cannot learn. Beoparis with articles of trade and inhabitants of Poorshuttum are likewise exempt from the payment of duties."

The Regulation IV of 1806 exempted the 'Gungajallees' and the "persons resorting to the town of Juggernath for trade."[31]

Section 17 of Regulation IV of 1806 allowed the 'Desees' (the persons residing in between the Baitarani and the Ganjam or Rishikulya rivers) to visit the temple without paying the Pilgrim tax.[32] This exemption was found to be 'detrimental to public revenue and was restricted by Regulation XI of 1810.

During the Rath and The Dol festivals, the exemption was confined to the persons who were called (Punjkosees) (Pancha Koshi) - living between Pipli in the north and Manikpatna in the south-within 5 Kos or 10 miles from Puri.

To relieve congestion, they also were required to pay a tax varying from four annas to one rupee during the Rath and the Dol festivals, unless they arrived at least 3 days before the commencement of those festivals. At all other times, the exemption hitherto granted to the Desee pilgrims continued.[33]

The Gungajalees poured water of the Ganga on the image of Lokanath and then visited the temple of Jagannath. The Regulation of 1809 modified "the existing rules respecting persons exempted from the payment of the tax, as frauds have been committed by persons professing themselves to be the carriers of the water of the Ganges."

Under the modified rules, a person professing to be a Gungajalee was allowed to pass the Atharanulla ghat under the charge of a Punda, who was to see him pour water on the image of Lokanath before his admission into the Jagannath temple to perform religious ceremonies.

The following classes of persons were fully or partly exempted from the tax.

(i) The Sepoys in the services of the Company, producing certificates from their commanding officers.

(ii) The servants of the European Officers on duty at Jagannath.

(iii) The Amlas of the Puri Collectorate or of the Police establishment. "On paying on the first day of January every year the tax payable by Bhurrangs, they shall receive from the Collector's office a Mafee (exemption) Chithi bearing his seal and signature, which shall entitle them free access to the temple for the whole year."

(iv) Bonafide residents of Puri. They were exempted from the tax on payment of rupees twenty-five to the Collector which entitled them to free access to the Temple throughout the year.

The British government, like the Maratha Government, exempted the destitutes, called 'Kangals'. According to section 9 of Regulation IV of 1806 pilgrims in a state of poverty were required to sign a form. It was stated in the Regulation. "Persons likewise in actual state of poverty, shall be exempted from the payment of the established tax on declaring that they cannot contribute the tax of Rs. two, and that they have not in their immediate possession more money then is absolutely necessary to defray their expenses for their return from the pilgrimage. The Kangals were allowed to stay at Puri for three days only, so that the place might not be congested with destitutes during important festivals.

Busyby, the Collector of the Pilgrim tax after Hunter, found flaws in the provisions relating to the Kangals. He pointed out that great many pilgrims pretended to be Kangals "to evade tax and who on examination found to be well clothed with various gold and silver ornament."

In his opinion, the Bhurrung Jatrees were tempted to pass as Kangals. "The Bhurrang pays Rupees two and has access to the temple for four days : when a Kangal pays nothing and has access for three days, which makes one more day of dursan for a Bhurrang. In consequence, many pilgrims that can afford to pass as Bhurrangs call themselves Kangals and pass accordingly after waiting two or three days at the ghaut."[34]

Toynbee has vividly described the lot of the Kangals; "At the principal jatras of Ruth, Dol, Asnan, those who claimed exemption as Kangals were detained outside the barrier until the principal day of each festival. The consequence of the restriction can be imagined. Huddled together in crowds, without proper food or shelter from the weather, in a place surrounded by jheels and noxious vegetation, thousands have fallen victims to disease endangered by exposure and privation. Of those who escaped the pernicious consequences of their detention, numbers perished in the rush which always ensued when the barriers were at last opened to them."[35]

Section Three
Pilgrim Tax in the First Quarter of the 19th Century

The collection of the pilgrim tax began on the 23rd January 1806. On the 22nd January, ninety-six pilgrims entered Puri without making any payment. On the 23rd January the tax was realized from five Bhurrang pilgrims paying Sicca Rs. two each.

Table 1
23 January - 30 April 1806

23 - 31 January		Rs.	1,229
February		Rs.	46,880
March		Rs.	12,980
April		Rs.	11,599
	Sicca	Rs.	72,688
Expenditure -			
Establishment		Rs.	26,300-14
Collector's salary		Rs.	1,035
Collector's Commission		Rs.	1,089
	Total Sicca	Rs.	28,424-14[36]

Table 2
22 January 1806 - 30 April 1807

Pilgrim Tax		Rs.	1,90,211-6
Other receipts		Rs	15,397-9
Sicca		Rs.	2,05,608-15
Collection charges	Sicca	Rs.	20,309
Contingency charges	Sicca	Rs.	12,279
Temple charges	Sicca	Rs.	36,378-7[37]

Table 3
18/12/13

Receipts from the Temple land	Rs.	15,102
Receipts from the sale of Bhog	Rs.	5,364
Pilgrim tax	Rs.	51,024
	Rs.	71,490[38]

Expenditure on a well	Rs.	6,804
Temple charges	Rs.	30,660
	Rs.	37,464

Table 4
Pilgrim tax in Sicca Rupees

1805/1806	72,684
1806/07	1,17,527 - 6
1807/08	40,500
1808/09	38,436 -8
1809/10	44,891-12
1810/11	70,499 -6
1811/12	93,240 -4
1812/13	51,024-10
1813/14	87,084-12
1814/15	2,08,037-12
1815/16	53,652-10
1816/17	60,255 -8
1817/18	93,434-10
1818/19	80,708 -2
1819/20	2,63,724 -3
1820/21	58,811 4
1821/22	1,00,013 -5
1822/23	2,30,063 -14[39]
1823/24	1,65,779
1824/25	73,968-10
	Rs. 18,02,741-15

Pies are omitted. The financial year began from the 30th April.

Table 6
Total collections and charges from 1806 to 1825.[40]

(i)	***Collections***	***Sicca Rs.***
	Proceeds from Dhaja Binding	5,118- 7
	Sale of elephants received as gifts	2,336- 4
	Rosoom and fines on the priests	27,854- 7
	Sale of holy food	77-607-10
	Fixed assignment of pergunah Kodhar	77,509- 1
	Revenue of 27 Hazari Mahals	2,05,905- 4
	Total	21,99,073-1
(ii)	***Charges***	
	Establishment and Commission of the Collector	3,23,848 -4
	Hospital	16,443 -5
	Saraee	434 -8
	Jagannath Road	8,19,158-11
	Miscellaneous charges	2,47,980-15
		Rs. 14,07,864-15

"In 1825, the tax collected and the amount realized are largest than ever had been known since this Province became a portion of the territory of our Government".

In one day, the sum of Rs. 28,000 was collected from the tax office though the number of pilgrims was only 7,000. The pilgrims who arrived previously to the Snan Jatra were allowed to pay double the tax which entitled them to remain until the Ruth Jatra 'without molestation'.[41]

Section Four
Pilgrim Mortality in the First Quarter of the 19th Century

The two most important festivals of the Jagannath temple are the Snan Jatra and the Rath Jatra. The Snan Jatra or the festival of sacred bath is held during the month of Jyestha on the full moon day. After the festival, the deities are kept away from public view for fifteen days. The first ceremonial appearance of the deities is called 'Nava Yauban' which attracts a large number of pilgrims.

The Rath Jatra is observed on the second day of full moon in the month of Ashada. Jagannath with his brother and sister leave the Temple on that day. They are placed on chariots and taken to the 'Gundicha' temple in a mile long procession. The deities come back to the temple after a week's sojourn in the Gundicha temple. This appearance of Jagannath in public gives thousands of pilgrims, irrespective of caste, the opportunity of beholding him. Moreover, the pilgrims cherish the belief that the darsan of Jagannath, Balarama and Subhadra on their chariots will spare them from the misery of re-birth.

Pilgrims who come to Puri during the Snan Jatra are tempted to stay for a few more days to witness the 'Nava Yauban and the Car festival. The festival generally takes place in the first week of July, when coastal Orissa is generally in the grip of monsoon.

There was 'a very heavy and unprecedented fall of rain' in 1821 which damaged the Jagannath road (Letter of C. Broughton, Superintendent, Jagannath road). The intermittent rainfall in 1825 caused cholera epidemic.

The journey to Puri was hazardous. Pilgrims coming from the north crossed unbridged rivers swollen with flood water. They trudged their way for several hundreds of miles under scorching heat or heavy rainfall. As they could not get sufficient food on their way, they depended mainly on parched rice.

In the first quarter of the 19th century, there were no shelter for them on the Jagannath road before they reached Cuttack. They could not get medical assistance in cases of illness. Nevertheless the people suffered willingly because they believed that the merit of pilgrimage would increase in proportion to the hardship they endured on the way. The darsan of Jagannath was a spiritual yearning which drew the faithful to the sands of Puri.

At last they reached Puri with "feet bound in rags plastered with dirt and blood." With the end of the grim determination which sustained them during their journeys many pilgrims physically broke down and died, "being lulled to their last sleep by the roar of the eternal ocean" (Hunter).

Captain Phipps who attended the Car festival in 1822 gave a vivid description of their suffering; "The aged, the sick the weak are persuaded to attempt the pilgrimage as a remedy for all evils. The number of women and children are also very great. The pilgrims leave their families and occupations to travel immense distance with the delusive hope of obtaining eternal bliss. Their means of subsistence on the road is scanty and their light clothing and little bodily strength are ill calculated to encounter the clemency of weather."

"Their difficulty is more severely felt as they approach the temple till they find scarcely enough left to pay tax to Government and to satisfy rapacious Brahmuns. The pilgrim on leaving Juggernaut has still a long journey before him and his means of support are often almost if not quite exhausted. The work of death then becomes rapid and the route of the pilgrims may be traced by the bones left by jackals and vultures."

The country near the Temple seems suddenly to have been visited by pestilence and famine. Dead bodies are seen in every direction. Parriar dogs, jackals and vultures are observed watching the last moments of the dying pilgrim and not unfrequently hastening his fate."[42]

Feeble and sinking for want of nourishing food and way-worn with heat and fatigues of journey, without means of subsistence the poor pilgrims were decimated by epidemic during their return journey.[43]

The Maratha Government, and the British Government in the first quarter of the 19th Century concerned themselves only with the collection of tax from the pilgrims resorting to Puri. They were indifferent to the miserable condition of the pilgrims.

The epidemic in 1825

The mortality among the pilgrims in the year 1825 was appalling due to the outbreak of cholera in epidemic form. Thomas Pakenham, Collector of Cuttack informed the Commissioner that there was a very large gathering of the pilgrims that year at Puri, even before the Snan Jatra.

The crowd was controlled by erection of barrier at the entrance of the temple "on the day of nobojauban when not only the pilgrims but every resident in and about Pooree hurries to make dursan". But at the time of the Rath Jatra, "mortality to a very lamentable extent" took place, as cholera broke out just before the festival. "The ravages committed by this dreadful disease are really most melancholy."

Pakenham in his letter explained the cause of the high mortality. "Up to the period of the setting of the rains the heat was unusually oppressive. Many of the pilgrims were carried forward by their anxiety to reach Jugunnath and urged to exert themselves when taken ill by the fear of being deserted by their fellow travellers until their strength completely failed.

"Exposed to the intense that during the day and to the damp at night, worn out by the fatigues of a long journey and subsisting principally upon food (parched rice) which is unwholesome, there must exist a great predisposition to disease, which their exhausted strength is unable to resist and consequently the cases are generally fatal."

The pilgrims left Puri in great numbers (estimated between twenty and thirty thousand) on the 19th July and continued to move off for several days. The rains set in Puri on the 20th July, and for three days, there was heavy downpour.

Cholera, which was raging at Puri, soon overtook the pilgrims during their return journey. Pakenham wrote that the greater part of the pilgrims must have been unable to procure shelter in the villages where they stopped at the end of their day's journey."[44]

The desire to reach their homes and the same dread of being left behind by their relatives when attacked by illness hurried them forward on their return - as fast as the desire to pay their devotion had carried them down - in such weather as prevailed; the greater part of those who were at last compelled from sheer exhaustion to halt, never moved from the spot where they fell."

Those sick pilgrims who were 'within reach of assistance' were removed to the hospitals at Cuttack and Puri.[45]

Pakenham suggested "erection of Seraees at convenient distances for the accommodation of the pilgrims and travellers generally", and temporary sheds during the important festivals, "to afford comfortable shelters from the sun and the rains."

He made the recommendation "in the fullest conviction of its being the anxious desire of Government to prevent the recurrence of such misery, as the residents of this District have witnessed in the present season."[46]

The Bengal Government considered Pakenham's proposal of providing accommodation "with a view of alleviating the suffering of the pilgrims" to be "judicious". At the same time the Government pointed out that the available money should be carefully spent, "considering the extent of accommodation required, so as to do the greatest possible good."

The letter from the Government concluded with the remarks ; "If the residents of the District, and specially the holders of endowments would be particularly induced to take an active part in affording relief to the pilgrims, benefits might be expected to result beyond what can be anticipated from the best exertions of the officers of Government."

"Indeed, if the pilgrims themselves abandon their sick relations and friends to perish on the road side, the utmost efforts of Government must prove a very partial remedy for this evil. It is nonetheless however to do what humanity requires."[47]

The Missionaries described the mortality in 1825 with zest. Rev. Lacey wrote : "The mortality did not much appear before the 16th (July). On the 19th it was exceedingly bad, for the day before, the rain began to fall and more came on the 19th and 20th and for the next three days it fell in torrents. At this time, the scene has reached its height. In every street corner and open space - in fact wherever you turn your eyes - the dead and dying meet your sight. On the evening of the 19th I counted upwards of sixty dead and dying, from the temple down to the bottom end of hospital (about half a mile) leaving out the sick that had not much life. At a corner opposite the hospital on a spot of ground I counted ten dead and five sick."[48]

---

1 Orissa and its Evangelization, Rey Sutton, p. 59

1a Orissa-Hunter, p. 83

2 Groeme's report

3 "From the place where I now stand, I have a view of a host of people like an army encamped at the outer gate of the town of Juggernaut, while a guard of soldiers is posted to prevent them from entering the town until they have paid the tax."

Christian Researches - Rev. C. Buchanon, P 37

4 Busby, Collector of Pilgrim tax to Trower, 30 October, 1813.

5 Busby to Trower : 15 July 1813, J.T.C. Pt 1

"The greater the number of deaths, the greater are the honour and satisfaction of Jugunnath, in their opinion - all dying within the sacred precincts of the Kshettra are supposed to secure immortality."

J.B. Mactier, Collector, Puri to Commissioner : 25 January 1859.

7 Hunter to Board of Revenue : 10 June 1806, J.T.C. Pt 1

8 Court of Directors to Governor General, Revenue letters to Bengal, 1813-15 Vol. III p. 191.

9 A sketch of the History of Orissa (1803-28) Toynbee p. 83-84.

10 'Calcutta Literary Gazette' August 1820.

11 Hunter to board of Revenue : 1 February 1806, Papers relative to E.I. Co. affairs : National Library.

12 G. Webb, Collector, Cuttack to Board of Revenue : 7 March 1806, J.T.C. Pt 1.

13 Trower to Richardson, Settlement Commissioner : 26 March 1816, J.T.C. Pt 1.

14 An account of Orissa - Stirling p. 83.

15 Collector of Pilgrim tax to Board of Revenue : 27 March, 1806. Bengal Revenue Consultations : Parliamentary papers National Library.

There were three Persian knowing Mohurrirs one at each gate of the temple to check the Rowannas.

16 Collector of Pilgrim tax to Board of Revenue : 15 March 1806, J.T.C. Pt 1.

17 Hunter to Board of Revenue : 25 March 1806, J.T.C. Pt 1.

18 Hunter to Board of Revenue : 16 June 1806, J.T.C. Pt 1.

19 Chauri - 'Chamara'. In 1846, Lecey, a Missionary, described it as 'Blue cow tail'. 'Masal' is lighted torch.

20 Nim Lal ticket did not attract the pilgrims. "The class denominated as Nim Laal is very unproductive. Indeed that seldom pilgrims enter the town under that class." Trower, Collector to Richardson : 18 March 1814, J.T.C. Pt 1.

21 Busby, Collector of Pilgrim tax to Trower 30 October 1813, J.T.C. Pt 1.

22 Hunter to Board of Revenue, 26 July 1806, J.T.C. Pt 1.

* Swarga Dwar, Sweta Ganga tank, Markandeya tank, Indradumnya and Chakratirtha.

23 "Vasu, the Fowler, would now be driven out from the doors of the temple dedicated to his god." Orissa Vol. 1 : Hunter, p. 356.

24 "We have read somewhere of one solitary case in which a major Carter managed to enter along with the pilgrims the famous shrine of Juggernauth."

'An account of Juggernauth' - Col. Phipps. Asiatic Journal : March 1824.

25 Facquier, Collector to Buller, Commissioner : 28 September 1808 Bengal Revenue Consultations : National Library.

26 The Board of Commissioners to Groeme : 12 January 1805 O.S.A. Vol. 1804 - 1805.

27 A Stirling, Fort William to Pakenham, Commissioner : 11 November 1825 O.S.A. Vol. 1825.

28 Though officially Busby was Assistant to the Collector of Pilgrim tax who was also the Collector of land revenue, Cuttack up to June1828, he was generally called in the Records at the Collector of the tax on the pilgrims. (O.S.A. 1828, No. 313).

29 Trower to Busby : 9 January 1817 O.S.A. Vol. April 1814 - December 1818

30 Hunter, Collector of Pilgrim tax, observed that many of the pilgrims who might have paid the tax evaded it by taking up the dress of mendicants. He calculated that the loss of the Government for such evasion amounted to about Rs. 30,000 annually.

Hunter to Board of Revenue : 28 December 1806 J.T.C. Pt. 1.

31 Groeme's Report

Hunter, the Collector of Pilgrim tax, objected to this concession to the trades.

"Any pilgrim may declare that he does not intend to visit the Temple, or he may procure a few cheap articles and pass free as trader. Having once crossed the Ghaut, a ticket will be easily borrowed under the rules at present without any real loss to the proprietor of the ticket."

Hunter to Board of Revenue : 29 December 1806 J.T.C. Pt. 1

Subsequently, the Beoparis or merchants were excluded from admission to Puri for 12 days from the beginning of the *Car festival*.

Pilgrim tax in India - Rev. Peggs P. 10

32 "It being the holy land of Juggernath according to the Shelokes or sacred records of the Hindoos." Webb to Board of Revenue : 7 March 1808 J.T.C. Pt. 1.

33 Ramachandra Modi made an application complaining that he was harassed at the Atharanulla ghát for the payment of Pilgrim tax. In his petition he stated that he remained at Puri for 12 years and that he had to go frequently to Cuttack as he owned a shop there. He added that he paid usual taxes at the time of Ruthjatra and Dolijatra. He prayed that he and his family might be exempted from payment of taxes at Atharanulla (Petition in Persian dated 1825 A.D. in O.S.A.).

34 Busby, Collector of tax to W. Trower, Collector : 30 October 1813 J.T.C. Pt 1

35 A sketch of the History of Orissa - Toynbee p. 60

36 Board of Revenue to Offg. Governor General : 30 May 1806 Bengal Revenue Consultation : National Library.

37 G. Webb, Collector to Board of Revenue : 7 March 1808 J.T.C. Pt. 1.

38 Statement of accounts of the temple of Juggernath Accountant General's office :

13 March 1813 J.T.C. Pt. 1.

39 "The cause of the decrease in 1820/21 is that the number of pilgrims resorting to Juggernath was very small owing to the lateness of the season at which the principal festivals took place. In 1822/23 the Snan and Ruth fell in comparatively early dates and in consequence the concourse of the pilgrims was unusually large."

Commissioner to Secretary, Territorial Deptt. : 11 November 1824 J.T.C. Pt 2.

40 Office of the Accountant General : 6 October 1825 No. 742 were given by the former government and are continued to 4 Sannaisees, 45 Brahmins and 5 Bishnoos (Vaishnavas)".

Hunter to Board of Revenue : 16 June 1806

41 Collector, Puri to Commissioner : 21 July 1825 O.S.A. Acc No. 25.

	Pilgrim tax
1825/26	Sicca Rs. 2,71,022 - 14
1826/27	Sicca Rs. 68,826 - 4

Office of the Accountant General : 15 March 1828 J.T.C. Pt 2

42 The Missionary Register, 1824 p. 578

43 (i) "At this place, Bhudruck, there are more than a hundred skulls. The dogs, jackals and vultures seen to live here on human prey. Whatever I turn my eyes, I meet death in some shape or other."

Buchanon's Christian Researches, p. 93

(ii) "The road to Juggernath for about fifty miles is strewn with human bones - This however cannot exact surprise when J.T.C. Pt 2

It is considered that about a million of pilgrims resort hither annually from the remotest part of India, some for fulfilment of vows to expiate anything but moral transgressions, other from the delusive idea that to behold the fane and its idols, is the attainment of a high degree of perfection, and many aged persons are impressed with the belief that death in the sight of Juggernath is a passport to supreme felicity."

Memoir of wars in India (1818) Major Thorn p. 261.

(iii) "At Cuttack and at Juggernaut, I have seen numbers of dying and dead pilgrims; and one morning near the Temple I counted between twenty and thirty skulls. At one place on the last stage to Juggernaut, I counted thirty seven bodies or skeletons, Where the Suttee has slain its hundreds, the pilgrimage (to Juggernaut) has slain its tens of thousands."

India's cries to British humanity (1830) - Peggs p. 124.

44 Pakenham wrote that at Puri there was a large building called 'Dhurumsala' in which the well-off people took shelter. From Puri to Cuttack, there were several 'Bazars' - "which afforded accommodation for a moderate number of pilgrims". But beyond Cuttack, there were no shelters for the pilgrims at that time.

45 There was no hospital for the pilgrims at Cuttack till 1823 Pakenham suggested

the establishment of a native hospital at Cuttack, "which might be the means of saving the lives of many jatrees travelling during the rainy season, who could not reach Pooree". (Pakenham to Blunt, Commissioner, 28 July 1823 : O.S.A.).

46 Pakenham to Commissioner Blunt : 21 July 1825 O.S.A. Vol. October 1824 June 1826.

47 Secretary, Territorial Department to Commissioner : 25 August 1825, O.S.A. October 1824 - June 1826.

48 'Reflection on the incidents which occurred this year at the Rath Jattra of Juggernath in Orissa' Friend of India' October 1825.

Peggs, 'the Cuttack Missionary' referred to this article and did not miss the opportunity of vilifying Jagannath. "There is a most harrowing account of the miseries suffered by poor creatures who crowded to Juggernaut to attend the Satanic festival of Rath jattra. It is humiliating to read such things. These are degrading to us as men, degrading to our character as Christian masters of the Country".
India's cries to British humanity p. 169

It was indeed degrading to the Christian masters of the country who realized tax from the pilgrims and remained indifferent regarding their fate.

Extract from 'History of the Jagannath Temple in the 19th Century' by Prabhat Mukherjee, Published by Firma KLM Private Limited

Annexure XVI

Visit of David B. Smith to Jagannath Temple, Puri

A narrative of the visit of David B. Smith, M.D. Sanitary Commissioner for Bengal to the temple Jagannath on the occasion of the Car festival of 1868 is given below.

Dr. Smith left Calcutta on 11th June 1868 and reached Puri at midnight of the 23rd June 1868. The following account gives the route, Dr. Smith followed during his journey to Puri from Calcutta. Dr. Smith left Calcutta on 11th June for False Point in Steamer. He reached False point at 3 p.m. on the 18th June. Before day break on the 19th June he left False point by one of the ship boats and reached the mouth of the river Mahanadi which was immensely flooded. He took a small green boat at the mouth of the river on the way he passed the Rice gola at Karanssa at 9 a.m. and Bakoot at 2 p.m. Beyond Bakoot he crossed the river and travelled southward. He reached the village of Burhaie at 6 p.m. The entire area from Bakoot to Burhaie was under flood water.

He left Burhaie at day light of the 20th June and reached Toldunda at 10 a.m. In the afternoon he left Toldunda and went to Chandpur where he slept in the boat. At Chandpur he parted with the boatman who had brought him from False Point. He left Chandpur at noon of the 21st June and reached Jeypore at 3.30 p.m. and Maulpore at midnight. He reached Fakirpore at 7 a.m. and got into Cuttack at 10 O' Clock of the 22nd June. He left Cuttack that night and reached Puri at midnight of the 23rd June. From 23rd June to 2nd July he was at Puri what he saw at Puri during this period of a little over a week is reproduced below, from this narrative which is given in the report on "Pilgrimage to Juggernaut in 1868".

Midnight scene around the temple of Juggernauth

I had been anxious to get to this celebrated place before dark; but this I found to be impossible. My first view of the city was by starlight. As I passed up its principal street-the "Burra Dund" - which is nearly a mile long and very broad, I observed, chiefly at the far end of it, many thousands of pilgrims lying on the ground, sleeping quietly; there was no noise; here and there a small wick lamp was burning, which had been it by one of a party of individuals lying huddled together, a little apart from the rest of the slumbering crowd. The scene was peculiarly impressive. Those numberless men and women, enjoying much-needed repose, had come together from every point of the compass, many of them from every very distant places, - all actuated by the one burning desire to reach Juggernauth. Here at last they had accomplished their desire, and wearied with the accumulated fatigue of many marches, they lay in perfect stillness on the bare ground, Not a sound was to be heard; the stars yielded faint light, and before me I saw, as if in dreamland, an army of religious enthusiasts, who, in the fervour of a fanatical creed, had completed a pilgrimage which to the Hindoo mind, is the surest viaticum to a happier state of being.

Arrived just to see the idols brought out of the temple

Passing quietly through this crowd, I soon saw, looming in the darkness, those great idol-cars and that temple regarding which so much has, at different times been written. In consequence of detention during the trip from Calcutta, I had arrived just too late to see the famous idol taken out of the temple and deposited in its car. But this did not much matter, as in every single respect but this I could still make myself familiar with all the circumstances attending the great Ruth Jatra or Annual Car festival.

General allusions to Orissa

Orissa has been described by one who lived in it for many years in the following words; - "It is to India what Jerusalem was to the whole land of Israel. It is the holy land of the Hindoos. As the Israelites went up to worship at Mount Zion, so do the inhabitants of the various provinces of India go on pilgrimage to the great temple of Juggernauth." (Sutton's "Orissa and its Evangelization, "Preface, P).

A Hindoo sage, Bharadwaja Muni, describing this country to his pupils, said:" Of all the regions of the earth, Bharata K'hand" (i.e. Hindoo India)" is the most distinguished, and of all the countries of Bharata K'hand, Utkal" (i.e. ancient Orissa)" boasts the highest renown. Its whole extent is one uninterrupted Tirt'h (place of pilgrimage). Its happy inhabitants live secure of a reception into the world of spirits, and those who even visit it, and bathe in its sacred rivers, obtain remission of their sins, though they may weigh like mountains, (Vide stirling's very able Article on Orissa, in Vol. XV of the Asistic Researches, P-166).

Sir Archibald Alison, in his "History of Europe" (Vol. XI, P. 100), writes of Orissa as "this rich and highly important province, alink lying on the sea-coast between the Presidencies of Bengal and Madras."

Situation of Pooree

Pooree, or Puri, is in the southern part of Orissa, in latitude 19.49 north, and longitude 85.54 east, distant about 300 miles from Calcutta and 49 miles from Cuttack.

General allusions to Puri Juggernauth (Jagannath)

Laurie alludes to Juggernauth as a venerable fane of Hindoo reverence - "He states that pilgrimage thither one of the most important acts of observance enjoyed to a Hindoo in the ritual of his religion" (Vide "Orissa and the temple of Jagannath, "by William F. B. Laurie, Lieutenant, Madras-Army).

Sutton alludes to the Car Festival of Juggernath as "the general meeting of the Hindoos of all India" (Op. Cit., P. 56).

Characteristics of Pooree, as believed in by pilgrims

The very ground around Pooree for ten miles is to the Hindoo mind of such sanctity as to absolve from the deepest sin all who proceed thither. The priests of Juggernauth speak of its as "the city of heaven upon earth". They say that "the fruit of the trees there is as the fruit of the tree of life; "that" the tanks contain the waters of immortalize "that" to bathe in them is far more meritorious than to bathe in all the sacred rivers of India; "that" the people are all holy; that the goddess of fortune resides there;" that "pilgrims may actually eat of food cooked with her own hands; "that" the gods of heaven over and anon send showers of beautiful scented flowers upon the city; "that" all the celestial deistic would delight to become incarnate there "that" the very dust of the city is pure gold;" and that the great idol is so mighty and gracious that he pardons the sins of those who may have killed a million Brahmuns (Vide "Sketch of the Orissa Mission" P. 13).

The reality

In this report I have endeavoured to show that, in reality, the said city of Pooree is anything but a heaven upon earth, in a sanitary point of view, its tanks, I am afraid, contain the waters of death and not those of immortality; the scents appreciable in the streets are other than those of fragrant flowers.

The sanctity of Juggernauth

It is to this place Pooree and to this temple and idol of Juggernauth that. for seven centuries, Hindoos have thronged, weary, footsore, feverish, yet ever patient under fatigue, toil, and hardship, to get that sight of their god which they believe obliterates the transgressions of a whole life. Their belief being what it is, we can scarcely wonder at that invincible enthusiasm which urges them on to a place so sacred.

It was in this place that I found myself at midnight. Before me, placed across the road, were the three curious cars of Juggernauth, Bulbudhra, and Subudhra; behind them in dim outline, the famed temple of Juggernauth, holiest shrine of the Vaishnavas; and all around lay tranquilly that multitude of pilgrims who had come to pay homage to a painted idol which they believe to be "Lord of all the World."* The stillness of night heightened the sense of mystery, which gather round so many human beings congregated from far-distant homes for purpose of deep-felt devotion.

Abuse is often heaped on the pilgrims

The pilgrims before me, and such as they, have incurred abundant abuse in the pages of many writers who have discussed their acts. Their moral blindness, their wickedness, their very degradation have but too frequently been made the subject to uncharitable declamation.

This is much to be regretted; a spirit of religious bravery brings them to Juggernauth, and perhaps it would be better if we did not disdain such pitiable beings. I would plead, even to the Government, the cause of extended charity and benevolence towards poor creatures who, being ignorant, distressed and uncared for, I have (and this not seldom) heard spoken of in terms of heartless abuse.

The pilgrim is worthy to pity

It will appear, in the course of this Report, that I have a particular object in pointing to the sad state of the poor Jatree, in whose behalf the Government has evinced a certain amount of solicitude, but for whom, I trust, yet much more may be done. Very deplorable are the misfortune of the pilgrims in Orissa, and it

---

* The Editor of the Calcutta Review, in a foot-note, p-205, Vol. X; 1848 (Article" Puri and the Temple of Jagannath"), gives the etymology of the word thus; - Jagad (in composition Jagan) world, and Nath, lord-"Lord of the world."

seems to me very necessary that this class of people should be regarded, not with aversion and harshness, but with feelings of sympathy and genuine human kindliness. Even with protection, assistance, and commiseration, the fate of the Indian pilgrim is by no means a happy one, as I shall presently show.

Reach the staging bungalow at Pooree

Leaving the temple and the scenes that surround it, I found my way to the staging Bungalow, where I remained the night.

Courtesy of Mr. H.C.B.C. Raban, the Magistrate of Pooree

The following day I communicated with Mr. Raban, the Magistrate and Collector of Pooree, informing him with what object I had visited the place, under the orders of the Government of Bengal. He invited me to stay with him expressing his desire to enter into the spirit of my enquiry, and offering me every assistance in his power.

Assistance most readily afforded by him.

I accepted Mr. Raban's offer of hospitality, and was his guest during the period of my stay at Pooree, which extended over ten days. I can not refrain from bringing to the notice of the Government that Mr. Raban afforded me valuable official assistance, that he placed me in such a position that I could personally make full enquiries, on all sides, regarding the state of Pooree and the circumstances of pilgrimage to it even directly from the Pandahs of the temple and the Mohunts of the native monasteries (Mut'hs). He also accompanied me daily into the filthiest purlieus of the place, where I found (almost to my surprise) that a sense of duty had often led him before then. For great part of all the information I now possess regarding Juggernauth and its votaries, I am indebted to Mr. Raban, who himself takes a deep interest in all that relates to the possible mitigation of the abundant evils attending the annual pilgrimage through Orissa.

Return to the scene of the idol cars

During the day we discussed the subject that engaged my thoughts, into which he was always ready to enter with avidity; in the afternoon. We proceeded towards the town, to observe the assembled or owes, to see the cars being dragged along, and to watch the general progress of the festival. I again found myself on the same ground where I had made observations the night before. The scene was now very different. The same masses of people were there, the same cars, the same surroundings. But it was now the hour when the sun was blazing before it set, and everything was astir. The spirit of religious fervour was up and awake; there was no mistaking it, the cars bearing the idols were to advance; tens of thousands of pilgrims were aware of the fact, and had their attention fixed in one direction. The priests were assembled on the cars; musicians also were there on the surroundings platforms, with various instruments, from which they evoked wild and discordant sound. The preparations were gradually completed; and at last the animal was given that the god to be dragged along by that thought of enraptured beings, who at once either shouted along with joy, or silent cast themselves on their knees and bowed their foreheads to the dust, in solemn acknowledgement of the idol's supremacy. Each car is pulled forward by two coir hawsers or cables, of great length, on both sides of which are placed those who drag. These functionaries are called "Kalabetiahs", they are assisted in their efforts by the crowd.

The excitement at its height

One car advance at a time, and creaking, slowly progress along a deep rut. As advance is made, the excitement heightens: the people yell with delight; the priests ("Dytahs" or charioteers) advance up the projecting planks, which are fixed in front of the cars, with long canes in their hands, which they wield with excited (and sometimes, it is said, with obscene, ithio-phallio) gestures. The musicians raise demoniacal sounds from conchs, tom-toms, bugles, bells, cymbals, tambourines, and gongs. The strect resounds with deafening turmoil; yet clear above all is heard that shrill utterance of frenzy "Jye Jagannath", "Jye Jagannath" (victory to our god Jagannath; victory to Juggernauth) and the wailing of women calling aloud, "Hululu;" Hululu."

Allusions to former human sacrifice

It was in moments of maddening excitement, such as I now describe, that, in former years, devotees were inflamed with a desire to die beneath the wheels of that great car, casting themselves down before it as it advanced, and being crushed beneath its weight. It is a happy thought that such human sacrifice is no longer tolerated by the Government; and indeed, each bar has now a strong netting, hung at some distance in front of it, to prevent the possibility of a human being passing beneath the wheels. There are still living, however, those who have witnessed such appalling and ghastly sights, the description of which are amongst the records which must for ever blacken the annals of this celebrated shrine. Laurie, writing in 1850, observes:- "It is perhaps useless to state that human sacrifice under the wheels of the car has long been abolished", But Sutton, whose work was published in the same year, informs us that devotees were still at that time occasionally crushed beneath the car.

I am inclined to think that Sutton does not here speak from personal knowledge of the facts; because Stirling, so far back as 1825, thus writes: - "During four years that I have witnessed the ceremony, three cases only of this revolting species of immolation have occurred, one of which, I may observe, is doubtful, and should probably be ascribed to accident; in the other two cases the victims had long been suffering from some excruciating complaints, and chose this mode of ridding themselves of the burthen of life, in preference to other modes of suicide so prevalent with the lower orders under similar circumstance" (p. 324).

At Juggernauth, as in the worship of Egypt and Phoenicia, human blood used to flow freely, and the mutilated corpses of those who accepted a fate so terrible were ruthlessly trampled finder foot by the crowd, all believing that the dead were glorified by the very sanctity of the ground on which they fell.*

Such sacrifice no longer occurs

Now, I believe, no such thing happens, overtly, in any part of India, the Government having humanely opposed and prohibited murderous rites of all kinds. If suttee, infanticide, ghaut murders or sanguinary offerings to Shiva or Kali ever occur (which doubtless is sometimes still the case), they are performed clandestinely by those who are perfectly aware of the illegality of such atrocious practices. Although, however, the immolation of human beings beneath the car of Juggernauth no longer occurs, there are numberous general circumstances connected with the place, the mode and the season of pilgrimage, which prover very destructive to life. I shall revert to a special consideration of this subject.

The great temple stands in the centre of Pooree within an enclosure measuring 620 feet by 600 feet, and surrounded by a stone wall 20 feet high. On each side the enclosure is an entrance; the most celebrated of which is the gate on the east side; opening into the Dando; it is flanked by colossal figures of lions, and thence called "Singh Dawar," or Lion-gate. In front of this gate, in the centre of the road, stands a beautiful fluted column of black basalf, about 40 feet high. Most strange to say, it is of Grecian architecture, and was brought to its present site some years ago, from the Black Pagoda at Konarok. A small figure of Honuman is placed at the top. Within the sacred area more than 50 temples dedicated to the principal deities of the Hindoo Pantheon, but the most conspicuous building is a lofty stone tower, 200 feet high and 42 feet square, called the Boro Dewal, or Great Temple; within it is a large platform, made of marble called the Ratnosinghason, or "Throne of Jewels," on which the images of Jogonnath, his brother and sister continually

---

* References, tracing the similarities existing between the worship of the ancient Egyptians and the people of Hindoostan, are to be found in Laurie, Op. Cit. P-46, in Heeren's "Historical Researches, "Vol. III, Chap. 1; and in Volney's Ruin of Empires (Les Ruines"), pp. 245, 259, 260-61, 274, 277, 280, 297, 356, 360, 378 and 390.

stand. Two large pyramidal buildings, called the Mukhsala and Bhog Mondop, with a small of one between them called the jogomohan, complete the temple. In the Bog Mondob is daily placed the sacred food intended for pilgrims; in the Jogomohan, "the delight of the world, the dancing girls amuse the idol and his priests. The roof and sides of the temple are ornamented with various sculptures representing elephants, griffins, and other hugo monsters. On the inside of the temple wall also are many figures of the grossest kind; indeed, all the temples of Orissa, great and small, are distinguished above all the other temples of Hindoostan for the obscenity sculptured on them. No European, however high the rank, can enter into the temple-area; the place would polluted say the priests, by his very touch."

The temple establishment

The establishment of the temple is thus described by the same author (Op. Cit., P-393) :

"The establishment connected with the temple of Jogonnath is immense: it includes thirty-six different kinds of offices, some of which are subdivided into several more: about 640 persons are required to fill up all the appointments, of whom a few may be mentioned. There is the Khatsaj mecap who takes Jogonnath his bed, the pasupalok who wakes him, and the much prokhyalok poriari who gives him water and a tooth-pick to wash his face and mouth; there is the painter to paint his eyes, an officer to give him rice, and another to give him pan; other is a dhua to wash his linen, the changra to count his robes, the chhattarua to carry his umbrella, and the khuntia to tell him the hours of worship. Besides all these there are 400 families of suars or cooks, and 120 dancing girls. The priests number in all about 3,000, who also have different grades of employment, and many of whom are exceedingly rich. Two classes may be specifically named, the Purharies, who perform the internal service of the temple, and present the pilgrims to the idol; and the Pandas or pilgrim hunters, who are employed by the former to entice worshippers to Pooree: by the pilgrims all the priests are called Pandas indiscriminately."

Annexure XVII
Puri Pilgrim Study : Area of Origin and Some Socio-Economic Characteristics of the Pilgrims

• *Prafulla Chakrabarti* • *K.C. Malhotra* • *Ila Pal*

The Indian Hindu Institution of pilgrimage to holy places (*tirtha-yatra*) is an ancient and continuing religious tradition. The numerous sacred places found in various parts of Indian attract millions of pilgrims. This circulatory mechanism of Hinduism, in the past two decades, has received considerable attention. Bharati (1963, 1970) has provided a cogent and well-documented survey of the nature and growth of pilgrimage in India. Diehl (1956) systematically analysed the nature and motives of pilgrimage. Cohn and Marriott (1958) analytically examined these places as 'networks' and 'centers' in traditional India.

Sopher's (1968) 'Pilgrim Circulation in Gujarat' based on field data is indeed outstanding. Sopher's finding that above-average pilgrim activity is associated with high service castes reinforces use of caste groups in understanding socio-economic problems in India.

More recently Bharadwaj (1973) in his study 'Hindu Places of Pilgrimage in India' examined the institution of pilgrimage in its historical and social context. Based on both historical and extensive field data Bharadwaj provides excellent materials with respect to pilgrim fields, caste composition and hierarchical status of 12 sacred places in Himachal Pradesh, Himalayan district of Uttar Pradesh and Madhya Pradesh. Besides these a few more descriptive studies on the subject are also available (Bhowmic 1960, Chowdhury 1974, Jha 1974).

Surveying published literatures four noteworthy points emerge: (1) considerable work is now available on the nature and growth of pilgrimage: (2) Limited studies are available on pilgrim circulation; (3) very little is documented about the socio-economic profile of the pilgrims; and (4) despite the presence of several major places of pilgrimage in Eastern India, very few systematic studies have been made on the pilgrims attending to such places (Sinha 1972, Chakrabarti 1976).

The purpose of this paper is, therefore, two fold:

1) to examine the pilgrim field at Puri in order to ascertain its pervasive influence.

2) to examine socio-economic profile of the Puri pilgrims in terms of their caste affiliation, family type and educational status.

The present study is based on a survey of 1240 adult pilgrims at Puri in Orissa - the famous Vaishnavite *tirtha* of the 15th century. As the sample frame was not available and the pilgrim population is highly floating it was not possible to select the sample randomly in the true sense of the term. Instead, the selection was made as follows : out of the inflow or outflow of the pilgrims into the temple or at the different lodging houses where they were sheltered we had contacted the individuals and interviewed them. The selection therefore is not strictly purposive. It is "pseudorandom" if one may like to use the term. The theory of simple random sampling can be used approximately for inference purpose in this case also. The survey was conducted on two occasions: at the time of maximum assembledge of pilgrims: June-July (Ratha Yatra), and when the assembledge is considerably thin: (March-April) in 1976 covering a total period of six weeks. Semi-structured questionnaires were administered to collect pilgrims' purpose of visit, area of origin, demographic, socio-economic and other particulars.

1. *The area of origin of pilgrims*

For each of the 1240 sampled pilgrims information regarding their place of origin (village/town) together with district and state were collected. The State-wise distribution of the pilgrims is shown in the table. 1. In figure 1, however, we have shown the origin of pilgrims by districts. From table 1 and figure 1 the following salient points emerge :

1) The sampled pilgrims came from 15 Indian States. Over half of the pilgrims (54.75%) were from West Bengal. Other States contributing appreciable proportion of pilgrims are : Orissa (18.71%), Bihar (9.19%) and Madhya Pradesh (6.77%). These four States thus account for nearly 90% of the pilgrims and form a contiguous region. The remaining 11 States contribute only 10% of the sampled pilgrims.

2) In all the States, except Andhra Pradesh and Tamilnadu which accounts for only 1.37%, languages belonging to Indo-Aryan family are spoken.

3) Broadly speaking its appears that as the distance from Puri increases the proportion of pilgrim decreases.

2. *Rural/Urban affiliation of the pilgrims*

From table 1 it is evident that there is a slight preponderance of rural-based pilgrims (56.61%) although marked variations can be noticed in between States with regard to it. For instance, the proportion of rural/urban pilgrims is roughly of the same order in West Bengal, Uttar Pradesh and Maharashtra, the rural component is appreciably higher in Orissa, Bihar, Madhya Pradesh, Andhra Pradesh and Tamilnadu, whereas the urban pilgrims notably exceed in Rajasthan, Delhi, Haryana, Assam, Punjab, Himachal Pradesh, and Gujarat. It is noteworthy that as one moves away from Puri the rural component of pilgrims decreases considerably.

3. *Caste composition of the pilgrims*

The sampled pilgrims were ascertained for their caste affiliation. The numerous castes of the pilgrims were later grouped into three categories on the basis of their ritual hierarchical position. The first category *uchcha-varna* Hindu ('High') castes includes the Brahmins, Baidya, Chatri, Kayastha etc. The second category *jal-chal* Hindu castes ('Middle') comprise of a score of castes from whose members of an orthodox Brahmin may accept water. The third category *jal-achal* castes ('Low') includes castes from whom the orthodox Brahmin will not usually accept water. 5.48% of the pilgrims, however could not be classified into any of the three categories.

The distribution of the pilgrims, each State considered separately, into caste categories is shown in table 2. A great deal of inter-State variation is noticed in caste composition of the pilgrims. It is noteworthy that the bulk of the pilgrims of each State belong either to 'high' or 'middle' or both these castes, though the proportion of 'high' and 'middle', between different States, varies considerably. Thus while 'high' castes account for 11.11%, the 'middle' castes constitute 77.78% of the pilgrims from the State of Maharashtra. Conversely, while 29.41% of the pilgrims from Delhi belong to 'high' castes, 70.59% come from 'middle' castes. The pooled State-wise distribution, however, reveals that 'high' and 'middle' castes occur in more or less similar proportions being 36.54% and 35.48%, respectively. These two caste categories together thus account for more than 72% of the pilgrims. The 'lower' castes are distributed between States quite unevenly. Of the 15 States pilgrims belonging to 'lower' caste are represented only from 7 States and their range of variation is 3.51% in Bihar to 29.74% in Orissa; the series average being 22.5%. With respect to the 'low' castes there are two more noteworthy features. Firstly, the highest number of pilgrims belonging to this category come from

Orissa (the exception being Andhra Pradesh and Tamilnadu- the high proportion may be due to small sample size), and secondly, except for Maharashtra, all the States contributing to 'low' caste pilgrims have common boundaries with Orissa where the temple of Lord Jagannath is situated. It is thus evident that as the distance from Puri increase the proportion of 'low' castes decreases. Is this observation a function of mere distance or is due to something else ? We shall say more about it in the concluding part of this paper.

4. *Educational status of the pilgrim*

The pilgrims were questioned for their educational status and the responses were entered into five-category classification: (1) Illiterate, (2) Upto IV standard, (3) standard V to X, (4) matric and intermediate, and (5) B.A. and above.

The distribution of the sampled 1240 pilgrims, separately for each State, into different categories of educational status are presented in table 3. When the pooled sample is considered it is noticed that only 12.42% of the pilgrims are illiterate, while 87.58% had some formal education. Further breakdown of the later category indicates that 22.34% had received education upto IV standard, 29.43% between V and X standard, while 35.80% had studied metric and beyond. Thus, the bulk of the pilgrims represented in the sample were educated.

A further examination of the distribution of illiterates reveals interesting pattern. There are eight States which constitute the total illiterate pilgrim population. Out of these, four States - West Bengal, Bihar, Madhya Pradesh and Orissa - are contiguous and Orissa shares borders with the remaining three. Except for Andhra Pradesh and Tamilnadu the other States from where only literate pilgrims came do not share borders with Orissa. Interestingly enough, it is noticed that as the distance from Puri increases the proportion of pilgrims with higher educational attainments increases. A relationship thus appears to exist between the pilgrims source of origin and educational status.

Family types of the pilgrims

For each of the pilgrims data were collected pertaining to household size, and the relationship between the head and the household members. Based on this information the pilgrims were classified into 6 types of families - (1) single, (2) conjugal, (3) nuclear, (4) lineally extended, (5) fully extended, and (6) complex.

The distribution of sampled pilgrims, separately for each State, into various family structures is given in table 4. For the pooled series it is noticed that single member and conjugal family structures are represented by only 1.37% and 2.34% of the pilgrims, respectively. Over 96% of the pilgrims thus have either nuclear or joint families, but in reality it is found that about 70% of the pilgrims, however, have joint families. There are marked differences between States with respect to proportion of different types of families. From this analysis there is a strong suggestion that family type does influence pilgrim participations, and that above-average pilgrim activity is strongly associated with joint families.

Table : 1

Area of origin of Puri Pilgrims (N =1240) :
Pilgrims classified by States

Name of State	Area of origin of Pilgrims			Number of districts	Av. No. of pilgrim/ district
	Urban	Rural	Total		
1	2	3	4	5	6
West Bengal	50.96	49.94	54.76	15	45.2
Orissa	27.59	72.41	18.71	12	19.3
Bihar	25.44	74.56	9.19	23	5.0
Madhya Pradesh	22.62	77.38	6.77	13	6.5
Uttar Pradesh	46.15	53.85	3.14	14	2.8
Rajasthan	63.16	36.84	1.53	5	3.8
Andhra Pradesh & Tamilnadu	17.65	82.35	1.37	4	4.2
Delhi	100.00	0.00	1.37	1	17.0
Haryana	80.00	20.00	0.81	2	5.0
Maharashtra	44.44	55.56	0.72	5	1.8
Assam	100.00	0.00	0.72	3	2.6
Punjab & Himachal Pradesh	75.00	25.00	0.64	3	2.6
Gujarat	100.00	0.00	0.24	1	3.0
Total	***43.39***	***56.61***	***100.00***	***101***	***12.2***

Sri Mandira of Puri.

Gundicha Mandira of Puri.

Sakhi Gopinath, Sakhi Gopal Temple.

Charkratirtha Temple of Puri

Cars on the Stand.

Gajapati King of Puri of the way of perform "Chera Pahanra" on the cars

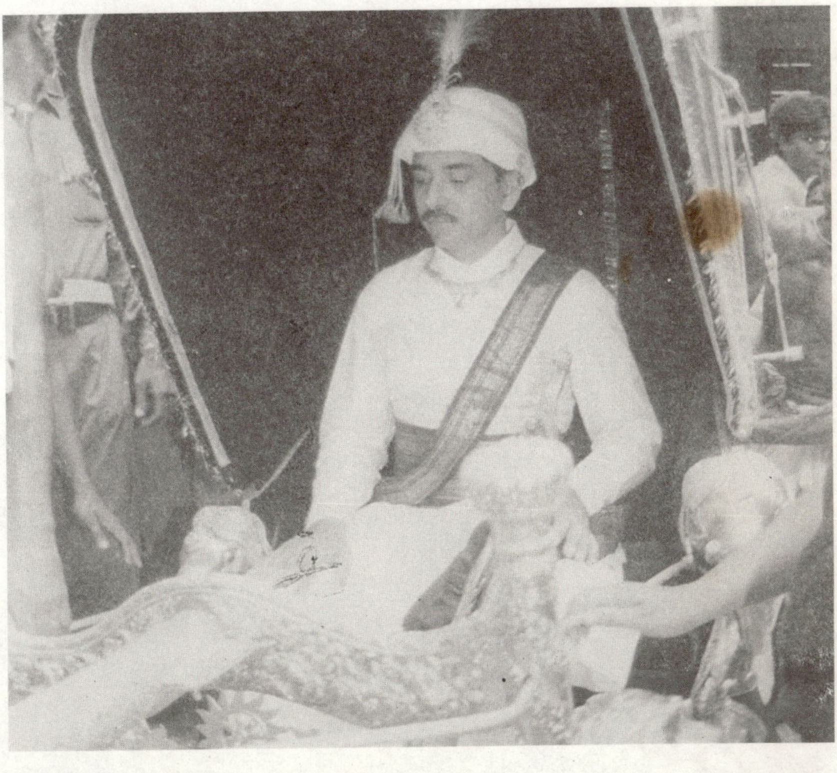

Meeting of the Luxminarayan.

Narendra Puskarini.

Barahi temple in the Balisahi.

Adaitya Brahma Ashram.

Mahaprasad (consecrated food) of Shri Jagannath.

Bagala Inn (Dharmasala).

Potter making pots for Mahaprasad.

Pilgrim preparing their food at the bus stand.

Tourist Bun low (Pantha Niwas).

Puri Railway Station.

Table : 2

Caste composition of the pilgrims arranged State-wise

Name of State	Caste-categories of Puri pilgrims				Total
	Uchha-varna Hindu	Jal-chal Hindu	Jal-achal Hindu	Unclassi-fied	
1	2	3	4	5	6
West Bengal	36.78	31.81	27.39	4.42	679
Orissa	30.60	29.74	29.74	9.91	232
Bihar	44.74	47.37	3.51	4.39	114
Madhya Pradesh	29.76	46.43	14.29	9.52	84
Uttar Pradesh	58.97	35.90	0.00	5.13	39
Rajasthan	73.68	26.32	0.00	0.00	19
Andhra Pradesh & Tamilnadu	11.76	47.06	41.18	0.00	17
Delhi	29.41	70.59	0.00	0.00	17
Haryana	60.00	40.00	0.00	0.00	10
Maharashtra	11.11	77.78	11.11	0.00	9
Assam	55.56	44.44	0.00	0.00	9
Punjab & Himachal Pradesh	0.00	100.00	0.00	0.00	8
Gujarat	100.00	0.00	0.00	0.00	3
Total	***36.54***	***35.48***	***22.50***	***5.48***	***1240***

Table : 3

Educational level of the pilgrims, arranged State-wise

Name of State	Educational level of Pilgrims					Total
	Illiterate	Upto IV	V-X	Matric-IA	BA+	
1	2	3	4	5	6	7
West Bengal	9.28	21.65	30.49	15.46	23.12	679
Orissa	6.90	28.02	29.31	20.26	15.52	232
Bihar	15.80	22.81	42.98	9.65	8.77	114
Madhya Pradesh	33.33	17.46	10.32	1.59	3.97	84
Uttar Pradesh	20.51	28.20	38.46	7.69	5.13	39
Rajasthan	15.80	21.05	10.53	42.10	10.53	19
Andhra Pradesh & Tamilnadu	—	—	11.76	88.24	—	17
Delhi	—	—	—	64.70	35.30	17
Haryana	30.00	—	20.00	50.C0	—	10
Maharashtra	11.11	—	44.44	44.45	—	9
Assam	—	22.22	—	77.78	—	9
Punjab & Himachal Pradesh	—	—	—	75.00	25.00	8
Gujarat	—	—	100.00	—	—	3
Total	***12.42***	***22.34***	***29.43***	***18.06***	***17.74***	***1240***

Table : 4

State-wise distribution of the pilgrims in family types

Name of State	Family types of Pilgrims						Total
	Single	Conjugal	Nuclear	Lineally extended	Fully extended	Complex	
1	2	3	4	5	6	7	
West Bengal	1.18	2.65	25.33	48.31	16.05	6.48	679
Orissa	—	0.86	34.05	56.03	7.33	1.72	232
Bihar	2.63	1.75	13.16	73.68	7.02	1.75	114
Madhya Pradesh	1.19	3.57	25.00	39.29	22.62	8.33	84
Uttar Pradesh	10.26	—	2.56	56.41	23.08	7.69	39
Rajasthan	—	—	42.10	31.58	26.31	—	19
Andhra Pradesh & Tamilnadu	—	—	70.59	29.14	—	—	17
Delhi	—	—	35.29	64.70	—	—	17
Haryana	10.00	—	30.00	60.00	—	—	10
Maharashtra	—	22.22	11.11	33.33	33.34	—	9
Assam	—	—	55.55	44.45	—	—	9
Punjab & Himachal Pradesh	—	25.00	—	75.00	—	—	8
Gujarat	—	—	—	—	100.00	—	3
Total	***1.37***	***2.34***	***26.05***	***51.14***	***13.90***	***4.84***	***1240***

Glossary

Abakas .... Morning rituals
Akhada .... Recreational centre/club house
Amala .... Clerk
Amalu Bhog .... A type of offering
Ananda Bazar .... The place where the consecrated foods are sold
Arati Thali........................ A plate with necessary waving of lamps
Arsa tirthas .... One kind of pilgrim centre
Asura tirthas .... One kind of pilgrim centre
Atharanalla ghat .... A bridge with eighteen opening
Avatar .... Reincarnation
Bada danda .... Grand Road
Badasinghara .... Last offering at night
Baisi Pahacha .... Twenty-two steps
Bajemahal......................... A part of territory having land of Jagannath
Batpeadas .... A class of Peon
Batua .... Assistants of the Pandas who go out to bring pilgrims
Beharan dwar.................... The door of the place where the functionaries are seated
Beharan Mandap .... A platform used for sitting by the officials/ functionaries of the temple
Bethia .... Labourers
Bhanga .... Narcotic
Bhurrung Jatrees .... A class of Pilgrims
Bidyapati .... Minister of Indradyumna

Bindu Sagar .... A sacred tank at Bhubaneswar

Biswabasu....................... A sabar who was worshiping Lord Jagannath.

Chakrabula Ekadasi .... A particular day in the calendar of ritual list

Chamar .... Whisk

Chandanlagi .... Offering of sandal wood paste

Chardhama .... Four pilgrim centres

Chhapan Bhog................ Fifty six types of food offerings

Chitrapati......................... Painting

Chulas .... Oven in kitchen room

Daiva tirthas.................... One category of pilgrim centre

Dakhina .... Fees or gift given to a priest for his ritual performance

Dantapura........................ A name for Puri

Darshan .... Seeing

Deepa .... Lamps

Desees .... Local pilgrim

Deswari........................... Country side

Devadasis........................ Female sebakas of the deities. Mainly they perform singing and dancing before the deities to invoke slumber.

Dhama............................ A holy place

Ekharajat mahal .... A territory having land of the temple

Ghats.............................. A fixed place

Gotra .... Clan

Gundicha ghar .... A temple of Gundicha where the three deities spend nine days during car festival

Handi kudia .... Earthen vessels

Indradyumna................... King

Jagaghar .... The place used by youths in different wards for gymnastic and other ritual purposes

Jagir .... Service land

Jamnika Khetra .... Puri

Jatri Gumasta .... Assistants of Panda who take care of the Pilgrims

Jatri Panda...................... Pandas in charge of pilgrims

Kaliadalana Ekadasi......... A particular day in the calendar of ritual observances

Kalpa .... A special name for a holy object
Kangal .... A class of pilgrim (destitute)
Kapila Sanhita .... A sacred text
Khalasi .... A worker of ship
Khei .... Share of consecrated food paid to functionaries towards their services perform
Khiri .... A type of sweet preparation from rice.
Khuntia Mekapa .... A class of ritual functionaries
Kotha Khanja .... Royal gift for share
Laal Jatrees .... A class of pilgrims
Lakshmi Bhandar .... Store room
Lakshyabati .... Lamps of one lakhs in number
Lokanath Ghat .... A place of Lokanath temple
Madeli .... Expert drummers
Madhyanna Dhup .... Mid-day offerings
Mahajatri .... Noble journey
Mahaparikrama .... Entourage for visiting pilgrim centre
Mahaprasad .... Consecrated food
Mahaprasad Sebasadan .... Place where consecrated foods are available
Malikana .... A share
Mandap .... Pavilion
Manusa tirthas .... One kind of pilgrim centre
Marfatdars .... In charge officer
Markeanda .... A saint
Martya Baikuntha .... Heaven upon earth
Masal .... Torch
Mathas .... Monastry
Maths .... Monasteries
Matsya Purana .... Sacred text
Meghanada Pacheri .... Outer compound wall
Mokshya .... Free from re-birth
Mongal Arati .... Morning waving of lamp
Mukti Mandap .... Pavilion of Brahmin Pundits
Nadia Kirtan .... Music of the type of Nadia a place where Chaitanya used to live
Nakakana .... Nose and ear
Nazir .... Gift

Nilachala........................... The abode of Vishnu
Niladri Bihar .... Lord Jagannath
Nilamadhaba .... A name of deity installed at Nilachal (abode of Vishnu)
Nilamani .... Blue emerald
Nim Laal........................... A class of pilgrims
Nirmalya .... Dried cooked rice grains which are most sacred items
Nirvana .... Dying
Nities .... Daily sacred performance
Padukakunda .... A receipted where the sacred water is kept
Pana Sankranti .... A particular day in which sweet water is offered
Pandas .... Ritual functionaries
Paniki Mahal .... A territory having landed property of the deities
Paniky .... Cutting instrument
Parichas .... A class of ritual functionaries
Patala .... Underground
Patitapaban .... Lord Jagannath
Peethas............................. A sacred place
Pindika .... A place used for keeping gifts from pilgrims
Pratiharis .... A class of ritual functionaries
Pujari................................ Priest
Puranas .... Sacred text
Raktabahu .... An invader during Mughal time
Ramitota........................... An orchard
Ratna Bhandara .... Store room
Rohini kunda .... A sacred place in the temple compound
Rosha .... Place where consecrated food are prepared
Sadhi bandha.................... Tying a piece of silken cloth on head as a grant of certain rituals to perform
Sadhus .... Saints
Sahi.................................. Wards
Sahi Naik .... Head of a ward
Sakal Dhup .... Morning offerings
Sandhya Dhup .... Evening offerings
Sandya Arati .... Waving of lamp in the evening

Sankha Kshetra .... A name for Puri pilgrim centre
Sankirtan .... A type of offering in which cymbals are played
Sankirtan .... Music using drums and cymbals while uttering the name of Hari
Sanyasis .... Saints
Saptapuris .... Seven pilgrim centres
Saragharas .... Store room
Sarva Dharma Samanwaya Dhama .... Congregation of all sects
Satabakara .... Seven rooms
Sataisa Hazari Mahal........ An estate of lands belonging to Lord Jagannath
Seba puja .... Rituals
Shri Kshetra..................... A name for Puri pilgrim centre
Sinhasan .... The throne on which the deities are installed
Slokes.............................. A sanskrit hymn
Snan Vedi .... Bathing platform
Suar sebakas .... A class of ritual functionaries who charge of cooking food
Suba................................ A define territory
Subadar .... The chief of the territory
Swargadwara .... Gateway to heaven
Tantrik .... Occult performances
Tirtha .... Pilgrimage
Tirthasthana..................... A holy place for pilgrimage
Tirthayatra .... Pilgrimage
Tirthayatri .... A person going on pilgrimage
Upadhi............................. A kind of offering given by pilgrims
Vanajaga ceremony.......... A kind of ritual performance
Yajnya .... A kind of sacred worship
Yama .... The God in charge of death
Zamindar .... Landlord

Reference Literature

Religious Life in Orissa : "A Study of the Interrelation of Cults" 2000 by Niranjan Satapathy, published by R.N. Bhattacharya, Antiquarian Booksellers, 6 M.M. Feeder Road, P.O. Ariadaha, First Edition - 2000, Calcutta - 700 057, India.

History of the Jagannath Temple in the 19th Century - 1977 by Prabhat Mukherjee, Published by Firma KLM Private Limited, 257B, Bipin Bihari Ganguly Street, Calcutta - 700012, India.

Orissa, The garden of superstition and Idolatory : including an account of British connection with the Temple of Jagannath : to which are added, Lighter Literary Recreations of a Critic Abroad. - 2000 by William F.B. Laurie, Lieut, Madras Artillery, Author of "The French in India", ETC., Published by R.B. Bhattacharya, Antiquarian Booksellers, 6 M.M. Feeder Road, P.O. Ariadaha, 2000, Calcutta - 700 057, India.

Bihar and Orissa District Gazetteers PURI, 1926 by L.S.S.O' Malley, I.C.S. Patna Superintendent, Government Printing Press, Bihar and Orissa.

Cultural Tradition in Puri : Structure and organisation of a Pilgrim Centre - 1977 by Dr. Nityananda Patnaik,

Published by the Registrar, Indian Institute of Advanced Study, Simla 171005.

A History of Orissa by W.W. Hunter, Andrew Stirling John Beams, N.K. Sahu, Vol. 1 published at Susul Gupta (India) Ltd., Calcutta - 12.

Sacred Complex of Orissa (Study of three major aspects of the Sacred Complex), 2000, by Dr. Nityananda Patnaik, Published by Gyan Publishing House, 5, Ansari Road, Darya Ganj, New Delhi - 110002.

The Orissa Gazettee, No. 164, Cuttack, Wednesday, Sept 8, 1954, Report of the Special Officer under "The Puri Shri Jagannath Temple Act" (Act XIV of 1952).

Jagannatha in History and Religiuos Traditions of Orissa - 1982 by Dr. Gopinath Mahapatra, Published by Punthi Pustak - Calcutta.

Religion and Pilgrim Tax under the Company Raj by Nancy Gardner Cassels.

The Cult of Jagannath -1971 by K.C. Mishra, Published by Firma K.L. Mukhopadhaya - Calcutta.

The Cult of Jagannath and the Regional Tradition of Orissa 1978 by Annchaarlott Eschmann, Hermann Kulke, Gaya Charan Tripathi, Published by Manohar Publications, 2 Ansari Road, Darya Ganj, New Delhi - 2

Origin of Jagannath Deity - 1991 by Jitamitra Prasad Singh Deo, published by Gyan Publishing House, New Delhi.

Shri Jagannath Cult of Orissa by Maharaja Shri A.P. Singh Deo of Saraikella.

Temple of Jagannath Puri 1999 by Robert Dunbar, published by Shudhi Publication, FK-30, Shastri Nagar, Delhi.

The Cult and Culture of Lord Jagannath - 1984 by Daitari Panda, Sarat Ch. Panigrahi, Published by

Rashtrabhasha Samavaya Prakasana, Cuttack, Orissa.

History of Lord Jagannath Temple by Dr. Arjun Joshi P. 146.

Lord Jagananth His Temple, Cult and Festivals - 1994, by Himanshu S. Patnaik, Published by Aryan Books International 437B/4B, Pooja Apartments, 4 Ansari Road, Darya Ganj, New Delhi - 110002 (India).

Puri Paintings (The Chitrakara and his work) 1982, by J.P. Das, published by Arnold - Heinemann Publishers (India) Pvt. Ltd. AB/9, Safdarjang Enclave, New Delhi - 110029.

Sacred Sites, Sacred Places, Edited by David L. Carmichael, Jane Hubert, Brian Reeves and Audhild Schanche, First published 1994, by Routledge, 11 New Felter Lane, London EC 4P 4EE.

Somavamsi Rule in Orissa - 1983 by Bina Kumari Sarma, Punthi Pustak, 34, Mohan Bagan Lane, Calcutta - 4.

Medieval Orissa and Cult of Jagannath - 1005 by Baba Mishra, Published by Navrang, RB-7, Inderpuri, New Delhi - 110012.

Puri Jatri, Jatri Gumastha, and ***Jatri Kala Pratha*** by Anantaram Kar Kaundenya, Shri Mandir, July 1997 pp. 46-47

Niladri Mahadaya, written by Dr. Brajakishore Swain of Sadgrantha Niketana (2000) Jagannath Process, Cuttack.

Utkal Khanda of Shri Purusottama Mahatma (1st Part) published by Shri Chaitanya Ch. das.

Puri Pilgrim Study : Area of Origin and some socio-economic characteristics of the Pilgrims by Prafulla Chakrabarti, K.C. Malhotra and Ila Pal, Indian Statistical Institute, Calcutta

Index